The Letter E

The Letter E

Claire Audibert

Published by Nightstand Press

PO Box 356
Katoomba, NSW, 2780

www.nightstandpress.com.au

First Edition © Claire Audibert, 2022

A catalogue record for this book is available from the National Library of Australia.

Title:	The Letter E
Author:	Audibert, Claire
Subject:	Memoir, Epilepsy
ISBN:	978-0-6452762-9-9 (paperback)
	978-0-6452769-1-6 (epub)
	978-0-6452769-0-9 (mobi)
Cover Design:	Emma Bennetts
Cover Photo:	Paq Photography

Author's note

The stories in this book reflect the author's recollection of events. Where possible, the people mentioned have been contacted prior to publication for their permission to use their names and likeness in the narrative. Some names and identifying characteristics have been changed to protect the privacy of those depicted. Dialogue has been re-created from memory.

Dedication

To Eliott and Oscar, thank you for choosing me to be your mum, I love you more than you will ever know.

To Ced, thank you for being with me on this journey, for making me laugh every day, especially in the worst situations, and for loving us so fiercely. We're lucky to have you.

And to all the families like ours, who are managing one day at a time, you are not alone.

Introduction

'E' stands for epilepsy, electroencephalogram and emergency room. But for us, most importantly, it stands for Eliott, and for energy, enthusiasm and encouragement. Being a French-speaking family, it also stands for *espoir* (hope).

When we found out we were going to become parents, we were living in Sydney, having moved to Australia six years earlier. Cedric and I are French; we worked together in Paris and started dating shortly after. At the time, he was offered a two-year contract to work in Australia, and we both jumped at the opportunity to move abroad.

The first couple of years 'down under' were an emotional roller-coaster. I found it difficult to be away from my family and friends. And although I found a job that I really enjoyed, it was challenging.

After the initial few months of settling in, we finally made new friends and started to explore this country we were now calling 'home'. When Cedric's two-year work contract was extended, we were happy to stay on. And before we knew it, we'd built a new life here.

When Cedric's contract came to an end, he took on a new role in a different company, and we committed to staying in Australia for a few more years.

During our early years in Australia, we travelled extensively, trying to get to know our new home. Tasmania, in particular, stole my heart. It was during our second trip there that Cedric proposed, and we married one year later in France.

By the time we celebrated our first wedding anniversary, I was eight months pregnant. We were so excited to have a little French–Australian baby who would grow up playing outdoors, learning to surf and going to Nippers, but who would go to the French school so he could learn both languages and learn about his origins. In our heads, it simply couldn't get any better.

It was a healthy pregnancy. I was very active, and we continued to travel. I stopped work a few weeks before the due date, and when the contractions started just days before the baby was due, everything was ready. We had a nursery set up, the car seat was installed, the hospital bag was packed, and we couldn't wait for the baby's arrival.

After three days of pre-labour at home and another eighteen hours of labour in hospital, I could finally hold our baby boy in my arms. However, I was losing a lot of blood. Cedric took the baby so the doctors could work on stopping the blood loss. I witnessed the fear on Cedric's face as he watched me lying on the bed while the doctors swiftly stitched me up.

As they were finishing the paperwork and doing their handover, one of the doctors approached me, put her hand on my arm and said, 'You're going to be fine. There's nothing to worry about.' She gave us a reassuring smile. 'But you've lost a lot of blood, so we're going to have to run a few tests and check whether you need a transfusion. Have a cuddle with the baby, rest while the midwife is doing all the newborn checks, and then we'll take you up to the intensive care unit where we can assess the next steps.'

I sighed as I looked around the room. I felt utterly exhausted — the expression 'hit by a bus' had never rang truer. I looked over to where Cedric and the midwife were measuring our precious little baby, and it was surreal to think that he was in my tummy only a few minutes before. 'Can I hold him? How is he doing?' I asked, propping myself up on the bed.

'Hey, darling, don't move,' Cedric replied. 'He's doing great. I think we're almost done?' His tone was interrogative as he addressed the last comment towards the midwife.

The midwife smiled, gave the baby another rub to feel his fontanel, and then wrapped him in a hospital blanket. It was one of the blue, yellow, and pink blankets all my friends had in the pictures of their newborns — like a rite of passage for all babies born in a New South Wales hospital: 'Welcome to the world, baby, here is your blanket'. And my dear baby had been welcomed to the club.

The midwife handed the baby to Cedric, who walked over and in turn handed him to me.

'Have you decided on a name yet?' the midwife asked.

Cedric and I gave each other a quick look, checking that neither of us had suddenly changed our minds. We had agreed on the name months ago — both in love with it.

Cedric smiled at me, and then looked at the midwife. 'We have. This is baby Eliott.' He then began packing our things so I could be moved to the intensive care unit (ICU).

I was now holding Eliott, wondering if I should feed him.

Suddenly, his whole body became stiff. 'Ced, did you notice the baby doing something weird?' I asked.

The midwife promptly stopped what she was doing to come to me, followed by Cedric. 'I noticed a movement too when I was doing the newborn tests,' she said. 'But I thought it might have been a one-off.'

Cedric chimed in, 'Oh, he did this in my arms as well when the doctors were with you. What is it?'

The midwife seemed a little concerned. 'It may be sleep apnoea. Are you okay if I take him under observation for a couple of hours?'

'Is it serious? What is it?' we both asked.

'I don't know, but all his vitals and his newborn checks are good, so I'm just going to observe him for an hour or two until they're ready to transfer you to the ICU. Why don't you get some rest?'

A quick rest sounded appealing.

So, the midwife took Eliott, and both Cedric and I fell asleep within seconds.

When she returned, rolling Eliott in the little hospital

plastic bassinet, she smiled at us, saying all was fine. No more movements. She congratulated us again and made me promise to look after myself.

Arriving in the ICU, I was told that my results were good, I didn't need a blood transfusion but a lot of rest, iron supplements, and a healthy diet to replenish my depleted iron levels.

I felt so taken care of. After making sure Eliott was asleep in his little bassinet by my bedside, and Cedric was also asleep in the armchair, I went off to sleep feeling grateful for the safe delivery of my baby boy.

Chapter One

The first 18 hours
(9-10 June 2015)

Day 1

Eliott

I have arrived! I have a quick cuddle with Mum — I recognise her voice — then I get passed to Dad, whose voice I also recognise, and we have our first cuddle. I like finally meeting him, but he isn't really looking at me, he's looking over at Mum. He's talking to me, though, in a soft voice, while other people seem to be busy around us.

We're skin to skin, and I am tired. It feels nice, so I fall asleep. However, I wake up briefly, as something is bothering me; my whole body stiffens, and it feels a bit strange. It only lasts a few seconds, and no one seems to notice, so I go back to sleep.

Finally, all the people leave the room, and I get to have a proper snuggle with Mum. It feels so wonderful to look at her and smell her. I have a bit of milk, and I immediately know that the three of us are going to get along well.

But then my body suddenly feels weird again — it tightens and makes it hard for me to move. I hear Mum and Dad ask if it's normal. A lady then takes me to another room so she can watch me. I manage to sleep and don't do the thing again, so I get to go back to Mum and Dad. So many adventures for my first day out!

Eliott

Dad sleeps on an armchair while Mum and I each sleep in a bed. I hear Dad get up and give Mum a kiss.

'Hey, hon, how are you feeling?' he whispers. He looks sleepy. 'Do you mind if I go home and have a shower? I'll come back in a few hours.'

'Of course. I'm okay, it just feels like I've been hit by a train,' she says. 'He seems to be okay too, doesn't he? He hasn't done the sleep apnoea thing again. You go and have a shower, and I'll give you a call when he wakes.'

I feel a gentle touch on my feet and hear Dad's footsteps as he leaves the room.

Shortly after, I wake up crying because I feel my body stiffening. Mum takes me in her arms to see if I am hungry, but I'm so tired I fall back to sleep.

I'm hungry when I next wake up. We're not alone in the room this time; a nurse is asking Mum how she feels. They both smile at me.

'Hello, gorgeous, it's good to see you awake. Are you ready for a quick feed?' The nurse puts me on Mum's lap and helps Mum make sure I'm in the right position and opening my mouth well. It's lovely to drink some milk, but I can't drink as much as I'd like, as my body does that thing again.

This time, everyone seems a bit scared, and Mum asks if it is normal for newborns to do this.

A doctor arrives quickly to run some tests and says it's probably nothing. They put a little monitor on my foot to check my heartbeat and oxygen levels. Then they put me back in bed so I can sleep.

But an hour later, it happens again!

Maman

Oh, my gorgeous little baby, he's just so precious.

He's still having weird episodes of stiffening, though,

and we have no idea what these could be. However, the paediatrician and the nurses have been reassuring.

Until now.

They're sending him to the newborn intensive care unit (NICU) for observation, to see if it's sleep apnoea or something else.

The nurses in the ICU said that I should be able to go to the postnatal ward later today. I'm still weak, which I know is normal after such a long labour, especially after losing so much blood, but I'm glad to hear that I can leave the ICU.

I'm looking forward to being on the postnatal ward with Eliott. Ced can even stay with us, and our friends have told us that you get to attend classes to help with breastfeeding, bathing, and other newborn care.

I'm quite stressed about all this — reading the books about having a newborn isn't the same as having one. So, it will be good to get some support and build our confidence before we go home.

I'm sure that by now Ced has made it home and found the package I prepared for him — in anticipation for when he'd first go home after the birth. There's a little wooden toy car and a coffee mug I ordered online. The mug has a red label with white text that reads: *Keep Calm, you're Eliott's Daddy.* Good thing we didn't decide to change the name at the last minute!

I'm sitting on the bed, and Eliott is back in his bassinet while the nurses are on the phone with NICU. I'm waiting for them to come and get him ready. My phone chimes; it's a picture of Ced smiling and holding the little toy car. He has messaged: *Thank you, darling. I love it. How's our little man doing?*

I try to sit more comfortably and wince as I move. I type back: *I'm glad you like the little gifts. He's doing well, but he did those movements again where he goes red and gets stiff, so they're going to take him under observation. No need to worry. The nurses are going to help me take a shower and then will take me down. Why don't you head there, and I'll meet you downstairs? They call it the nursery, on level one.*

When the nurses walk back in, the paediatrician is with them. Smiling, the paediatrician says, 'Okay, we're going to take little Eliott here down to the nursery so they can have a look at him. It's most likely nothing, but we want to make sure.'

Everyone is so lovely here, it's very reassuring to see that they're going to check him, even if there is nothing to worry about. And from what they're all saying, it looks like he won't stay in the nursery for very long.

I give baby Eliott a big kiss, and they take him away. I then have a much-needed shower, which feels amazing!

Another nurse comes in and confirms that I can go down to the postnatal ward, but I want to see Eliott first.

All the staff have taken such good care of me, it's wonderful to hear that my results are good. The birth was difficult, but my body is recovering well.

I pack everything and am ready to leave the ICU and be wheeled downstairs to see my new baby.

Chapter two
What the h*** is happening?
(10-25 June 2015)

Day 2 (continued)

Eliott

When we arrive at the nursey, there are noises, bright lights, and a few people who want to see me. I'm not sure why I'm here; I don't know any of the faces or the voices. I sleep for a while and wake up when Dad picks me up, then Mum arrives — I get hungry as soon as I see her. It's not that easy learning to feed. Mum needs to find the right position and hold me the best way, and I have to learn how to open my mouth and drink. I drink a little, but very quickly, my body does the thing again ... and again.

Maman

Everyone said not to worry, but no one is talking when I arrive down in the newborn intensive care unit. I've been trying to breastfeed, but I'm tired and weak. I can't hold Eliott very well, and he had the weird movements again. *How can it be sleep apnoea — wouldn't he have to be asleep?*

After the second episode in a row, the nurse informs us that the doctors are moving Eliott to 'level three' — it's a higher level of surveillance, where one nurse will look after only two babies. He'll be monitored more closely, and they'll give him some medication to prevent the episodes.

One of the nurses asks if we have milk to give Eliott. He's been in the nursery for a couple of hours now, and given he hasn't been able to feed, he will need to have formula.

Wait, what? Why is that? He's moving to level three, needs medication, and now he needs formula?

I thought breastmilk was preferred. Shouldn't he be getting my colostrum — the first milk? And if I don't feed him, what happens to my milk supply and my ability to feed him in the future? Doesn't the milk go away if you don't feed your baby?

So many thoughts are crossing my mind, I feel overwhelmed. He's not even a day old ...

Two doctors then come to us almost at the same time.

They suspect Eliott might be experiencing neonatal seizures. It happens sometimes and isn't anything to be worried about, but they need to give him some anti-epileptic drugs. They're recommending a loading dose of Phenobarbitone — one of the most common anti-epileptic drugs. And they'll run some tests to check what might be happening, in case it's an infection. It could be something he contracted during birth.

The first doctor asks a lot of questions, about the birth, about Ced's and my health. Do we have any history of seizures in the family?

No. We don't.

The doctor tells us that they'll do blood tests and put him on a constant EEG (electroencephalogram). This involves electrodes being placed on Eliott's head, so they can study his brain activity. It won't hurt him, but he'll also need a lumbar puncture to rule out serious infections and a gastric tube to be fed.

By this stage, there is just too much information for me to absorb. When Ced asks the other doctor why they want to give him formula first, she looks a little embarrassed and says, 'The nurses mentioned you didn't want to give Eliott formula.'

'Well,' I start to reply, holding the wheelchair for support, as I feel faint, 'we just don't get it. If he's here just under observation and for some tests, I thought my milk was best? Shouldn't I be giving him my milk?'

'But you haven't, have you? He hasn't been able to take it, and he needs milk,' the doctor responds.

Oh, that's a bit harsh — I've been trying to give him milk.

Ced, clearly understanding how desperate I am and knowing that breastfeeding is important to me, asks, 'But he doesn't need to have the formula straightaway, does he? Why can't Claire give her milk to him?'

I even suggest, 'I can come back and feed him whenever he needs. I want him to have my milk. Everyone says it's important. And what happens if I don't give it to him now, I won't have any milk?'

It must finally hit the doctor that we want to understand why they don't think that 'breast is best'.

She then proceeds to explain that Eliott will be sleeping a lot and have wires attached to him running the tests overnight. And seeing as he needs to get more milk into him than most newborns at this stage, the best way to do that is via a feeding tube.

She then concludes, 'But you can express, and we can give that to him first and top it up with formula. Does that make sense?'

I'm sobbing at this stage, as I realise that this is no longer a 'don't worry about it, it's probably nothing' scenario. This is not what I had in mind for my first twenty-four hours as a mum. But what she said does makes sense. 'Yes,' I respond. 'And the feeding tube isn't going to hurt him?'

'No, it won't. And it will mean he can rest as much as he needs to.'

Shortly after, we kiss Eliott and tell him what's going on. I don't want him to think that we're just leaving him. Then we go down to the lobby and get everything sorted for our stay.

We're told that they've managed to find us a room where Cedric can stay, so I won't have to be on my own.

Ced wheels me back into the lift and up to the postnatal ward. I have been here once to visit a friend, and it's nothing like I imagined my time would be.

How can I be here without a baby?

I feel so out of place; I feel like an impostor. Our suitcases are in the room, and once we've settled in and seen the midwife, we go back down to see Eliott.

Eliott

I've been moved again. The lady who is looking after me is lovely, and very gentle. When Mum and Dad come back, I can hear them talking with her. She shows them how my feeding tube is going to work. A new doctor will visit us tomorrow and explain everything to them. Mum and Dad tell me it's very late now, and they give me lots of kisses before they leave.

Maman

It's close to 10pm when we get back to our room. It's been a huge first day. They've loaded Eliott with the drug that will hopefully sort everything out. They want him to have an MRI tomorrow to rule out any potential bleeding from the birth.

We call our friends, Charlotte and George, to let them know of Eliott's birth and that, unfortunately, it's not going well. George is French too, and both his parents are paediatricians practising in France. Shortly after we hang up, Ced phones George's father. He goes through how Eliott is presenting, the birth, and then explains all the tests that the doctors are running.

We have no medical experience and have such limited experience of what the Australian medical system is like, let alone the paediatric system. We trust George's father to help us understand everything more and tell us if the Australian team is covering the same things they would in France. He reassures us that they would have done the exact same things. He also thinks it might be an infection, and the fact that he's responding well to everything else, besides experiencing these movements, is a good sign.

Just like every doctor, midwife, and nurse has said today, 'Without the seizures, he would be a perfectly normal little newborn'. The scores given to all newborns after one minute and five minutes of life to assess things such as activity, skin colour, pulse rate etc. were excellent, and all the test results are coming back negative. He's also been able to look at us and even feed a little. It means that there is nothing obvious pointing to a major issue. So, we go to sleep feeling a tad better and more hopeful.

However, I'm awoken later by a nightmare. I often have vivid nightmares, so that's not unusual. I usually calm down as soon as I wake up, realising that it's all a dream. But it's different this time — I dream that I have just given birth, and the baby is sick, so they take him away, and I must go back to the ward on my own. A mother without her baby ...

I wake with a loud gasp, and as I sit in the strange bed, in the darkness of the room with my body aching, I realise that for the first time in my life, my nightmare is not a nightmare. I'm living it. I start to cry so much that I wake Ced up. 'Can you take me to him? Please?' I realise how desperate I sound.

'Of course, just let me get dressed. Don't move, I'll help you get in the wheelchair, and we'll go.'

When we arrive, the nurse is sitting by Eliott's side. He's sleeping peacefully. She smiles at us, and when she notices my puffy eyes, she asks if I'm okay. I try to smile and then ask how Eliott is.

'He's doing really well,' she replies. 'He's been sleeping since you left and hasn't had any seizures.'

I'm so relieved.

We go back to our room about an hour later, feeling unsure as to what the next day will bring. But somehow, we manage to get more sleep.

13

Maman

We go back early in the morning, wash our hands in the large sink on the way in, and head to the level three section of the nursery. The nurse is about to finish her shift. She tells us that Eliott had a good sleep. He didn't wake after we saw him and hasn't had any further seizures.

We each sit on a side of Eliott's bassinet and look at all the machines: the EEG electrodes stuck on his little head to monitor his brain; the foot monitor to check his oxygen levels; the IV with the antibiotics flowing through the cannula into his tiny wrist; the feeding tube, and all the cables across his legs and chest to check his heart rate.

I see the nurse heading towards us with a doctor.

'Hi, I'm Todd, the paediatric consultant looking after Eliott,' he says with his hand outstretched towards Ced. Todd then turns to me, smiling brightly, and shakes my hand. 'I'd like to run through what we've been doing and the next steps.' He pulls out an extra chair to sit down.

It's a relief to have someone explain this nightmare and help guide us. Todd runs through the tests, the reasons for the lumbar puncture and for the feeding tube. He's heard we came back during the night and is concerned. When he asks if there was a specific reason for us to visit Eliott then, we explain that I had a nightmare and wanted to see Eliott.

His smile disappears for a minute. 'Oh,' he says, 'I'm sorry. Of course, I understand. You can come and see Eliott whenever you need. It's good for you all. And you'll be able to do skin to skin when he leaves level three again. Just make sure you're getting some sleep and rest too.'

Todd thinks the MRI will give us more answers. Eliott should be able to leave the nursery tomorrow. This morning he will have a more precise EEG, and Todd is also getting the neurologist to come and see us later in the day.

So far, all the tests have come back negative, and this is good news. However, I'm having trouble understanding why that is, as it's the second time we've been told this, and I don't get why they still need to 'treat' him.

Todd is clearly used to talking to new parents. He takes a breath and continues, 'I know it might not make sense. But the first tests are for serious conditions, to rule out the worst-case scenarios. So, the fact that we haven't found anything is good. It means it's none of those serious conditions. The MRI tomorrow should give us more answers.'

Eliott sleeps a lot, which we're told is normal, because of the medication — it's a good sign that he wakes up every three hours for his feeds.

During the day, one of the nurses shows us how to take care of Eliott, change his nappy, clean his face and umbilical cord, etc. And I manage to call my mum to give her some information. She'd booked her flights to arrive early July, a couple of weeks after the due date. Our initial plan was to spend a few weeks together as a new family of three before she would come and help us.

Today, after giving her an update of Eliott's condition, she offers to change her flights and come early. We're still hoping that despite the challenges of the first days, we'll be able to go home soon, so I decline, but thank her for offering.

In the afternoon, we see Todd walking towards us with a few people. Ced gets up as they approach, and I try to do the same, but due to my lack of strength, I sit back down in the wheelchair. My legs can't support me after another long day in NICU.

Todd smiles and introduces his colleague. 'This is Dr T. He's the neurologist who's been looking at Eliott's file, and we thought it'd be good for you to discuss it with him and ask any questions you may have.'

The new doctor thanks Todd and turns towards us. 'Call me Henry. I'm sorry that you had to come here and that the first few days have been so tough, but your son is responding to treatment. He's been doing well since being on the medication, and the MRI tomorrow should help us understand what was causing the seizures. But at this stage, we shouldn't worry. Neonatal seizures are more common than you think. All his tests are normal. If he's doing well tomorrow and the tests are good, we can discharge you.'

When he touches Eliott's forehead before examining him again, he gently rubs his head as if to say hi. He and his team then leave, and we're left feeling hopeful. Eliott is responding well to treatment, his tests are normal, nothing is pointing to a serious condition. We're already talking about being discharged. What a rollercoaster of emotions the past few days have been.

When Todd and his team come to talk to us again, they find us energised and ready to think about the next step: going home!

However, even if Henry clears us and discharges us from neurology, they need to see Eliott feeding independently first. Discharge requirements are different for the two specialties. They can't let us leave without Eliott feeding properly. So, we have a new plan: focus on feeding so we can go as soon as Henry clears us.

We give Eliott a kiss and go upstairs to the ward. The midwives explain how important it is for me to see them so they can check that I'm recovering well, but we've been spending all our time in the nursery, I haven't had a chance to even be in the room. The priority has been staying by Eliott's side and being there in case the doctors need to talk to us. I promise to make time and see the midwives tomorrow so they can check that I'm doing well.

I wake up halfway through the night again, and we go to see Eliott, but he is fast asleep. We find ourselves daydreaming about taking him home in the next few days.

Day 4

Eliott

Mum and Dad come to see me and tell me today we're going somewhere else to get more tests done. They give me a little toy that their friends bought for me — a white, soft, fluffy bunny, which is going to stay with me today. Dad looks a bit upset and asks if he can push my bassinet across the hospital. The nurse agrees, and off we go!

Mum and Dad explain that I'm going to have a very important test that might help understand why I keep doing funny movements. Mum and the nurse give me some milk in my tube so I can sleep during the test — only the nurse is allowed to stay with me when she rolls my little bassinet into the room with a noisy machine.

She puts her whole hand softly on my head, just like she's been doing when I'm upset, and it makes me feel better. We enter the dark room, and I start to feel sleepy. When I wake up, everyone says I've been a good boy. The afternoon is quiet. Mum and Dad stay next to me.

Maman

When we're ready to go to the MRI department for Eliott's scan, Ced wants to push Eliott's bassinet, and I realise that he probably just needs to be active and help.

On the way to the MRI department, we pass the café where lots of new parents are enjoying coffee and a snack, with their newborn babies sleeping in the little plastic bassinet next to them. I notice Ced trying to avoid looking at them — I know he's thinking exactly what I am: *Why does OUR son have to have an MRI?*

We can't go with Eliott into the procedure room, so while the nurse is in there with him, we go for a walk. I'm still in the wheelchair, so Ced pushes me outside for some fresh air.

When they finish the test, everyone says Eliott slept for most of the time. Now we just have to wait for the results.

So, we bunker down to spend yet another afternoon by Eliott's side. He's still hooked up to all the machines, and as the medication starts wearing off, we're hopeful that he will have enough strength to breastfeed.

But early afternoon, we get a message that we must go back up to the postnatal ward, as the maternity ward administration person needs to talk to us about the room.

After giving Eliott a kiss and telling him once again that we'll be back shortly, Ced wheels me away.

I'm wondering if they want to see me about not making an appointment to see the midwife, the physio, or the lactation consultant, but I just haven't been able to.

We get to the room, and a midwife tells us that the 'admin person' will be with us shortly.

When the admin person arrives, she says, 'I look after the room allocations here, and unfortunately, we have a bit of an issue. We need the room for someone else, someone like you who's coming down after being in the ICU. She needs a single room so her husband can stay with her. You've been here three days, so we need to discharge you.'

Ced gets up and comes around the bed to sit next to me. 'But how can you discharge us? She's still in a wheelchair and no one has been able to see her?'

'Yes, but we've tried, and she was never in her room.'

I feel invisible — they're talking about me like I'm not here, but more importantly, it feels like we're getting kicked out without getting proper care. 'But our baby is in the nursery. I have to be with him,' I manage to say.

'I know this is difficult. We can move you to a shared room, so you have more time to see someone, but you must make sure you're here so the doctor can discharge you,' she replies, her flat tone unchanged.

Ced is adamant, 'We're not leaving the hospital before a physio and a doctor have seen her. She's lost a litre and a half of blood!'

'I can't move to a shared room,' I plead. 'It's hard enough hearing all the other babies through the walls overnight; I can't be in the same room as someone who has their baby with them. My baby isn't with me. I can't.'

'I get that,' the admin person says, more gently. 'We're going to put you in a room with someone whose baby is also

18

down in the nursery. And we'll make sure you see the physio and the doctor.'

As soon as she leaves, I burst into tears. I just want to have Eliott next to me. I want him to be with us. I want to be one of the new mums who send text messages to everyone that reads: *We're tired, but it's all going very well. He's gorgeous, and we couldn't be happier.* I've received so many of these messages from my friends, and I never expected mine could be any different.

Minutes after the admin person has left, there's a knock on the door. 'I'm the physio. You wanted to see me?'

Wow, they really want us out.

We chat for a few minutes. She examines me and gives me some recommendations and advice and informs me that the doctor will see me in the new room once I've settled in.

Ced wheels me into the new room on the other side of the ward, and immediately I see a little clear bassinet. I turn to Ced and feel the despair in my voice when I say, crying, 'There's another baby. I can't, just take me home. Take Eliott and me home, please.'

Ced kisses me and goes to talk to the admin person, again.

Unfortunately, they just messed up the room. So, I'm moved once again; my room, when I get there, has another mother without her baby. By then, it's been over an hour since we left Eliott, and I'm desperate to see him. I don't want to miss an opportunity to try breastfeeding him — it's the only thing preventing us from going home at this stage.

I gather all my strength and tell Ced I need to start walking, no more wheelchair. I'm slow, need support, and I sit as soon as we get to the nursery, but I'm happy I can move again. I need to focus on making sure we're ready to go home as soon as Eliott can feed.

Eliott

In the evening, Henry and his team come back. He's kind, gentle, and asks me how I am before talking to anyone else

— including Mum and Dad. Plus, he wears colourful pants. I can't see very well yet, but I like the colours.

Henry explains that the tests from this morning were good. He says that another doctor will review one minor thing to confirm, but everything seems to be fine. He wants to talk to his team, but at this stage, he's not worried.

Mum gives me lots of cuddles and kisses. Henry and Dad continue talking, and Henry says he would like us to stay in the nursery over the weekend, just in case. I need to feed before I leave, anyway. Because I'm doing so well, he agrees with Todd that I can go back to level two. I say goodbye to the nurse, who has been looking after me, and I'm handed over to a new person. Everyone seems so happy.

I haven't been given new medication, so I find it easier to open my eyes, and I even have my first breastfeed tonight. What a good day! I can't wait to go home!

Day 5

Eliott

Mum and Dad are coming to see me early so I can feed. The new nurse is giving Mum lots of tips. Breastfeeding is still tricky, but Mum looks happy, and it's nice not having all the wires on me like I did on level three. I can be in her arms, and I like that. But during one of the morning feeds, my body starts doing the thing again ... and again ... and again.

The doctors say they must give me more medication. Mum cries a lot. What they're giving me is making me sleepy again, and I spend the day sleeping in Dad's arms.

Day 6

Maman

When we arrive at the NICU in the morning, we're told that Eliott had another seizure overnight. He's managing to feed a little today, but as most of the seizures seem to happen while breastfeeding, probably due to the stimulation, we've decided to stop. It's too stressful, and knowing that these seizures might be triggered by overstimulation when I feed him makes me nervous.

This time, the seizures don't seem to be controlled by the one drug. They can't give him another loading dose, which will make him sleep again for three days, so they're having to introduce a few new anti-epileptic drugs.

Henry spends a lot of time with us today. He says he's waiting for a second review on the MRI results — that minor concern he had on the MRI yesterday could be a brain malformation, which means Eliott would need surgery. The hope is that he could make a full recovery because newborns' brains can compensate and learn to work differently.

We've entered such a complex world.

It's hard to understand how there could be so much uncertainty about whether Eliott has a brain malformation, but Henry explains that only the newborns with health concerns get an MRI, so things may appear on the MRI that could be completely normal. A baby with no concern could have the exact same thing, it would just be undetected because it's not causing issues.

After the seizures yesterday, and again this morning, we've decided that I will stop breastfeeding, but I'd like to keep giving him my milk. It's good for him, and I feel like this is the only thing within my control that I can do to help while he's in hospital.

Ced and I have even learnt to read what the hospital monitors are indicating; we watch his heart rate and oxygen levels, hoping they don't drop, and thankfully they don't, which is reassuring (even if we don't know what the seizures can do to his brain, at least we know there's oxygen flowing). Every seizure is harder than the last, taking us further away from going home with Eliott.

One of the nurses tells me that I need to start pumping

my milk if I want to keep feeding Eliott. It would be easy to just give up, but I listen intently as the nurse shows me how to use the breast pump. She gives me some labels to put on the bottles of expressed milk, which I then put in a little basket with Eliott's name and place in a fridge. Once more, there's a whole new process to learn — my new normal.

I don't feel comfortable expressing in the big room with everyone around, so the nurse suggests that I use the expressing room, but I miss Eliott. I don't express much the first time, and I can't help thinking that it would be better if I was next to him.

I'm being discharged from hospital today — the admin person told us again that she needed the space, so I had to go. When it's time to go home, I can't hide my tears. I don't want to leave my baby; I don't want to go home without him.

Before we leave, I explain to Eliott that I can no longer sleep at the hospital, and that we won't be able to visit him during the night. He's so tiny, and we know he can't understand everything that's happening to him, but we're convinced he still understands a lot. At the very least, he might understand the fear and stress in our voice, so we're trying not to cry in front of him and to be reassuring when we speak to him.

I walk away and burst into tears. I don't want to go, not like this. I can't go without Eliott.

These have been the hardest days of my life. I was coming to terms with the fact that our introduction to parenthood was different from most people, that I wouldn't have these first few days on the postnatal ward with Eliott by my side and thinking that it didn't matter, as long as we could go home. It was just a bump in the road.

But now, that seems so insignificant. I naively thought my biggest problem was a bumpy start. Now it's looking more serious. We're trying hard to not show how lost we are, but it is impossible to process everything. We give Eliott a kiss, then Ced takes my hand and leads me out of the NICU

— I walk out on autopilot.

Arriving home, without my pregnant belly and without Eliott, is even harder than I imagined. I briefly think about mums with stillborn babies and how they carry on after such a trauma. I feel so weak.

I want to go into Eliott's room and look at everything we dreamed of — I want to relive that moment when we left for the hospital to give birth, and try and capture that joyful feeling that our life as parents was about to start.

But Ced sees me walking towards the room and catches up to me. He grabs my hand and softly moves ahead of me and closes the door. 'Come and sit down for a minute. I'll cook you some dinner, and then if you want, you can spend some time in his room. But we're not getting sad about this; he will come home and be in his room,' he says firmly.

I nod and give him a half-smile.

I sleep a dreamless sleep that night. The alarm clock wakes me at 4am so I can express milk. My friend Sophie has lent me her electric pump, but it takes forty-five minutes to get what I could get in ten minutes with the hospital pumps. I'm exhausted. Ced tells me we'll find a way to get the same pump so I can get more rest.

The alarm clock goes off again at 6am, and we quickly get ready to be back at the hospital for the 7am feed. Even if I'm not breastfeeding anymore, we want to be there and give him his bottle as much as possible.

Day 7

Eliott

Today doesn't feel good; my body does the thing a lot — Mum and Dad say I've done it eight times. They put me on my side each time and talk to me quietly, which makes me feel calm, but I hear Mum crying.

'Eliott, my baby,' she says, and tells me it's okay.

I can't stop what's happening to me — my body stiffens,

my head turns to the side, I feel myself getting red, and sometimes I'm so stiff that I stop breathing for a few seconds.

Maman

We arrive at the NICU for the 7am feed. I'm starting to get more confident with the breast pump, so I express next to Eliott in the big room, rather than in the privacy of the expressing room.

The doctors do their rounds at around 8am and discuss Eliott's progress and provide us with any updates; they also answer a few of our questions. Shortly after, Ced leaves for work. He's lucky to have two weeks of paid parental leave, but we made the decision that he wouldn't use them just yet. The idea was to spend time with Eliott together as we settled into our new life as a family. But with Eliott in the NICU, Ced's going back to work to save his leave.

Eliott has yet another EEG in the morning and has a seizure while they're doing it. It's hard to watch his body stiffen again. My heart sinks. However, the EEG operator points out that having a seizure recorded will help the doctor assess what is happening to Eliott, and I guess that's right.

Ced returns after lunch, just before Henry and his team arrive. We're sitting next to Eliott, as per usual, watching over him in his bassinet as he sleeps.

Henry suggests that we go to a separate room for our discussion. I put my hand on Eliott's belly and tell him we'll be back soon. I look at the nurse and ask her to keep an eye on him.

When we get to that windowless room just next to the NICU entrance, Henry points us towards an old-looking sofa to sit down, and I can't help but think of all the parents who have probably sat on this sofa and cried their hearts out hoping their babies would leave the NICU and come home.

'How are you doing today? Ced, did I hear you went into work?' He gives us a faint smile.

'I did. I want to save my leave for when Eliott comes home,' Ced replies.

'That's a good idea. Okay, I wanted to have a chat with you about next steps. With the MRI coming back normal, and little Eliott having new seizures, I would like to increase the medication doses to get the seizures under control — this might make him sleepy again. And then we'll run more tests. We'll need more blood, and another lumbar puncture,' Henry says, pausing to seemingly gauge our reaction.

'Do we really need one? Can't you use what you took last time?' Ced asks.

'We don't have enough, and at this stage, we really need to understand what's wrong. The EEG he had this morning isn't good, as it shows the seizure that Eliott had at the beginning, but most importantly that there's some residual activity after. There's a possibility that it could be a B6 deficiency. It's a very rare condition, but the good news is that he would only need to take some B6 vitamins.'

'And that's it? When would we know if that's the case?' It's the first time since we sat down that I've been able to get words out of my mouth.

'Unfortunately, the results are going to take about six weeks to come back, but we'll collect the urine that we need for the test and start giving him the vitamins immediately — if it is a B6 deficiency, then we should see an improvement quickly,' Henry says, seeming hopeful.

Could it be this simple?

We have only known Henry for a few days, but we trust him. The chat turns into a two-hour meeting. He takes the time to answer all our questions. We ask him for studies and articles we can read, to inform ourselves. But he gently suggests that we don't spend too much of our time reading research, since we don't yet know what the cause of the seizures is. He promises to send us information and documentation on what Eliott has, as soon as they know. He emphasises that they have no idea what it could be just yet.

After the discussion with Henry, we go back to see Eliott

and talk to him while he sleeps. Six weeks to wait for the results of the B6 test feels like a lifetime. Eliott isn't even a week old, and so much has happened — it feels like ten years have passed, not just a few days.

I feel mentally and physically shattered. We've felt so many feelings, spent so much time looking for answers on Google, sat with so many different specialists and spent a lot of energy trying to understand all the medical concepts. And to top it off, my body has been through the strain of labour, delivery, and then a considerable loss of blood. That's not to mention the hormones, lack of sleep, and having to stay in the hospital chair by Eliott's side twelve hours a day.

To everyone else, a week can be such a short amount of time. But for us, it has been life changing; it feels like we have gone to Hell and not managed to find a way back yet.

How could this be happening to us?

We both feel lost, so Ced asks if we could get some psychological support. The doctors and nurses are trying to be reassuring and positive about Eliott's health, but every bone in my body is telling me that there is something seriously wrong. I pray for a quick fix, but I know that even if it does come, we are broken and need some help.

No one again mentions the chance of Eliott going home.

When we get home that night, we try to have dinner, but neither Ced nor I feel like eating. I just keep crying. We start discussing whether my mum should come earlier than planned — getting her help next week might make things easier.

We agree that I will call her in the morning. We keep trying to eat, me playing with my food and pushing it to the side. Ced looks at me, and then looks at the dinner he's prepared for us. I'm looking down at my food, but out of the corner of my eye I see him leave the table.

As he's walking back towards the kitchen, he suddenly falls to the ground. His legs give way, and he just crawls into a ball and starts crying. My husband, the father of my sick child, is in a foetus position on the floor, desperate for the pain to go away.

And I am scared. Scared like I've never been before, because there is nothing to control here; just like that, our life has been turned upside down, and we no longer know which way is up.

I rush to him and try to take him in my arms. 'Ced, I'm so sorry, I'm so sorry, my love. I'll ask Mum to come as soon as she can. We can't wait another week!'

But he can't stop crying, and I don't know what to do.

So, I call one of our best friends. 'Matt, I don't know what to do ...' I'm crying so hard I can hardly talk.

'Are you okay? Is it the baby? What happened?' He's clearly anxious.

We've told him how things have been progressing, but we haven't spoken to him in a few days, so he doesn't have the latest information.

'No, it's Ced. I don't know what to do.'

'Where are you?'

'We're at home. We were just trying to have dinner.'

'I'll be there in fifteen minutes. Are you going to be able to open the door when I arrive?'

'Yes, thank you.'

It's 8pm, and I'm vaguely conscious that Matt must be busy. I'm trying to save Ced, and I'm so grateful to know that help is on the way. 'Ced, Matt is coming,' I tell my husband.

When Matt arrives, Ced has semi-recovered and is sitting at the dinner table.

I open the door and Matt gives me a hug. 'How are you feeling, hon?'

I manage a nod and point to Ced, who's looking distressed.

'Come on, mate, let's go.' Matt's tone is decisive. 'Get your shorts and sports shoes on.'

Ced gets up and starts following him, and just before leaving, Matt turns around. 'Please call Sophie and ask her to come here,' he asks as he kisses me.

And then they leave.

I'm on autopilot. I call Sophie and ask her to come and stay with me. Like Matt, she knows what we're going through; she's been bringing us food and calling every day to check on Eliott since he was born. She's one of my closest friends, and I know she'll come if she can. She and her husband live with their daughter only minutes away, and as soon as she hears my voice, she says she's on her way.

Before she arrives, I have time for a quick call to Mum. She picks up with a cheerful tone, 'Hi, darling, how are you feeling? How is Eliott tonight?'

I just want a hug; I want my mummy. 'Mum, can you come?' My throat is tightening, and I can hear Mum taking a deep breath to calm herself on the other end. 'Please. We're not managing at all.' That's all I can say before bursting into tears.

Thankfully, Sophie arrives and talks to Mum for a few minutes, and then she keeps me company.

I get a text from Mum an hour later; she's changed her flight for the next day and packed her suitcase. It feels like a lifeline to know she'll be here soon.

Mum and I have an incredible relationship, and it's been hard being away from her, especially during the pregnancy and then for Eliott's arrival. We've been through difficult phases over the years — what mother-daughter relationship hasn't? But she's both the strongest and the most vulnerable person I know.

We were on our own for a while when I was a baby, and she was my hero growing up. She's always been an incredible mother and would do anything for my brother and me, and now for Eliott.

If there's one thing Mum has always modelled for me, it's the power that lies in 'being present' when it counts. She's always made sure I knew that if I needed her, really needed her, she would be there. She is one of those mothers who tells you that you can call her at any time of night, and she'll come and pick you up if you need her, no questions asked.

That doesn't mean she will handhold me through everything, but I know that if I need her, she will be there.

And she's always encouraged me to do the same for my close friends and family; they know that if anything happens, no matter where we are in the world, I will drive for hours in the middle of the night, board a thirty-hour flight, and do anything I can to be with them.

Throughout the years, knowing that I have a group of people around me, Mum being the first of them, on whom I can count on if things get tough, has always given me so much strength. It's easier to take on new challenges, and keep pushing just a little bit more when things are hard, knowing you have a strong safety net — someone who will catch you if you fall.

So, after Eliott's birth, and with everything that happened since, I've tried to keep going, because I knew Mum's arrival was only a few weeks away. I kept telling myself that we could manage on our own, that the doctors would find out what was wrong, and by the time Mum arrived, it would just be a bad memory. But tonight, it's all too much, and I need my safety net to kick in.

When Matt brings Ced back, Sophie is still with me. As they leave, Matt and Sophie look at us and ask if we're going to be okay.

'Yes, thank you. Thanks for dropping everything to look after us tonight,' I say.

Ced, however, looks shattered. I ask him, 'What did you guys do?'

'He made me go boxing for an hour, to get it all out. So, I'm going to bed.' He then hugs me before taking himself off to bed.

When I wake at 4am to express, Ced is sound asleep next to me and looks more relaxed. I express, but it still takes forty minutes to finish, and then I go back to bed.

The alarm goes off again an hour later, and we get ready for another tough day.

We are both silent in the car on the way to the hospital.

Eliott

Henry has decided that I need to change rooms, again. I am going back to level three where the one nurse can look after me — except, it isn't the same person, and the new nurse puts things all over my head. I'm so tired all the time that I sleep most of the day, not even waking for feeds.

From time to time, I feel Mum and Dad's hands on my belly and on my forehead, and they talk to me softly. I hear the noises, everyone chatting around me, but I'm so tired, it doesn't bother me.

Dad is going to work, but Mum stays; she sits next to me in one of the blue armchairs. She talks to me a lot, telling me that she and Dad love me very much, and I must keep fighting and be strong. She tells me that Mamie Veronique, my grandma, is coming soon.

It's been a quiet day, but tonight, I'm upset and cry a lot. Nothing calms me down; I don't even want the dummy that the nurses give me, and the gentle strokes Mum and Dad give me on my hands aren't enough.

One of the nurses tells Mum to put her little finger in my mouth, with her fingernail toward the bottom. I like that, so I start to suck a bit, like I would with a dummy. And suddenly, something amazing happens, Mum laughs. It's a nice sound; I heard it a lot when I was in her tummy, but I haven't heard it since. I love the sound of her laugh.

I am a week old.

Eliott

My body is doing the thing again. It's happening more often. I sleep most of the day, but when I do open my eyes, I notice that Mum and Dad look tired. Mum, especially, is looking sad, and she stares blankly across the room. Dad is talking to the doctors, who are worried about her. The social worker has asked for her to get some tests done, just like me! But she tells Dad she'll get them done later; she doesn't want to leave my side.

My body has only done the thing once today, and I heard the doctors say that they think the medication is starting to help. But I'm so tired. I manage to open my eyes twice, and Mum and Dad give me lots of smiles. I also drink a little from the bottle. In the afternoon, they give me a kiss and say they have to go somewhere, but they'll be back.

Maman

Today is a tough day. When we arrive, we're told that Eliott had multiple seizures overnight, and another one this morning. It feels like it's getting worse, and we're falling deeper into our nightmare.

Early afternoon, Ced must go to a different hospital on the other side of the city for his routine treatment. He has Crohn's disease and gets an injection every eight weeks. Seeing as I've spent so much time by Eliott's side, we've agreed I will go with Ced today, to clear my head. It's not really the best environment, going from one hospital to the other, but it's time together to chat without being in the NICU or too tired at home.

Before we leave, we have a brief chat with the doctors. We have so many questions, to which they have no answers. They make a note of our concerns and redirect us to talk to Henry and a geneticist. But they also try to reassure us and promise they'll be here to help us whenever we get discharged.

At this stage, it will likely consist of teaching us how to manage seizures, as we may need to consider going home with a baby that has ten seizures a day. I feel like the tiny bit of control we were holding on to is slipping away. Our life may become one of constant worry, always on the lookout for seizures and managing them as they come. A life dictated by the unpredictable.

These hours outside of the NICU are lovely. I go and get us coffees while Ced settles into his day bed at the hospital, and I stay with him for a little while. He's in the bed hooked to the IV, and I'm sitting next to him, my head resting on his legs. I can't even talk, but it's wonderful to be together.

I leave earlier than Ced so I can go back and express my milk while sitting next to Eliott. When Ced arrives an hour later, Eliott is asleep. It looks like he's having less seizures today, which is amazing, but he has slept most of the day. The medications make him drowsy. He is no longer taking antibiotics, but he has the three different anti-epileptic drugs, and the B6 vitamin.

I can't help but cry every time I think of this perfect little body already full of such potent medications. In the past few days, I've seen his little eyes open three or four times. My newborn has just spent the first week of his life in a drug-induced sleep. We have been online looking at what these anti-epileptic drugs are and do, and all the side effects make me anxious

In fact, I've been feeling quite dizzy for a few days. I know that I need to rest at some point, but how can I? Maybe if I push just a little harder, it will be okay? I know Eliott's asleep, but I can't leave his side.

The genetics team arrive later while I'm pondering how we're going to adjust to all this, and how I can make all these issues go away. They'd like to speak to us.

A middle-aged man steps forward, his name is Professor Daniel N. He speaks in a compassionate tone and tells us that we can call him by his first name, just like Henry did. He asks about us, the family, the pregnancy, the birth, even looks at Eliott's fingernails — but nothing concerns him.

I always feel sad when anyone asks about the pregnancy and the birth. Everything went well; I had such a healthy pregnancy. The birth went well too. It was a natural birth, and Eliott was doing great when he came out. I just thought everything was normal.

I've been asked about the pregnancy so many times already and have felt this twinge of guilt every time. *Could I have missed something?* I took pregnancy vitamins, gave up coffee, didn't drink one drop of alcohol, and gave up soft cheese. I keep thinking I did something wrong — surely there must be a logical explanation for this, but I can't figure out what it is.

No one can find anything obviously wrong with him.

And after all the questioning, people just keep reassuring me and telling me I have done nothing wrong. The fact that he's doing well outside of the seizures is still a very good sign.

Daniel then proceeds to talk about options for genetic testing. He asks if we know much about genetics.

Well, not really — learnings from our high school biology lessons have long been forgotten.

He gets a pamphlet with drawings of chromosomes and DNA and proceeds to walk us through what it means.

I vaguely recognise some of the concepts, but everything is a bit fuzzy. What I understand is that we may have to run a DNA test as a 'trio', which means that all three of us would get tested so we can see whether it's an inherited condition. That would also help us with family planning, in case we would like to have other children.

My head is spinning even more. For as long as I can remember, I've always wanted to have three kids. My brother and I get along so well, but I've always wished we had one more sibling. *Are they saying we may not be able to have other children? Is that what's at stake here if it's inherited? THIS could be our only experience of parenting?*

The team tries to explain that they just want to let us know all of the options to consider.

I, however, just feel overwhelmed.

Henry arrives shortly after to review today's EEG. He smiles and asks about our day, gives Eliott a little stroke on his foot, and starts reviewing the reading. Once he's read it, he turns to us, but his smile has vanished. 'I'm sorry, guys, but he has had quite a few seizures today again, maybe eight or ten.'

I start to cry, and Henry looks genuinely touched and sad. He obviously wants to find out what is happening. We trust him to help us find answers and a solution.

So, it's even more painful when he starts to speak again.

'I'm sorry, but I don't know what it is. I'm starting to get concerned.'

He's always been so positive. *How could this be happening? Please... someone wake me up.*

When we go home that night, I don't feel well. I feel weak, and shortly after arriving home I almost pass out. Ced is concerned. We know my iron levels have been low since the blood loss, but I've been taking the iron supplements — maybe that's not enough.

Ced cooks me a steak and puts me to bed. There's no arguing, I need to sleep. I'm only allowed out of bed to pump milk for Eliott. Thankfully, we've been able to rent a hospital-grade pump, so it now only takes me ten minutes to pump.

When Mum arrives later that night, I wake up just to say hi. She gives me a massive hug, but Ced has already briefed her on the earlier incident, so I go straight back to bed. Mum looks concerned but smiles at me and tells me it's going to be all right.

Ced has prepared Mum's room — we live in a two-bedroom apartment, and the sofa bed is still in the spare bedroom, which we converted into Eliott's room. We haven't had a chance to prepare anything for Mum's arrival. We were meant to have a few weeks to rearrange the apartment.

Mum says she's happy to stay in Eliott's room for now, and Ced has put a big white sheet on top of all Eliott's stuff. It's heartbreaking. Mum is fine with it and looking forward to meeting her first grandson.

Day 10

Maman

Today is Eliott's due date.

Ced is going to work this morning but has promised to come to the hospital mid-afternoon. He makes sure Mum understands that I need to get a blood test and a general check-up done. He's pretty upset about me being so unwell, and the fact that no one is looking after me, given I've officially been discharged from hospital.

I feel like Ced and Mum are talking about me and ignoring the fact that I'm sitting here, but I don't have the energy to complain about it.

I've briefed Mum about the NICU; how everyone is kind and gentle with Eliott, but the environment is noisy and stressful. I've also emphasised how Eliott is hooked to lots of cables and sleeps most of the time. She gives me her most reassuring smile, but I know this smile is her 'cover-up smile' to hide all the pain and the fears she's harbouring.

When we arrive at the NICU, and I look at Eliott, I start to cry — tears of happiness. His eyes are open. He hears my voice, and I can see his little eyes searching for mine.

Mum is behind me, and I know she's overwhelmed but trying not to show it. It's very emotional when she walks towards Eliott's bassinet and comes down to meet his eyes.

'Hi, Eliott, I'm Mamie. It's really nice to meet you. You look like you're doing great, baby.'

We then sit down.

I haven't properly seen his eyes for a good five days, and it's wonderful to see them. He's awake for twenty minutes before he falls asleep again.

Unfortunately, he has more seizures during the morning, and it feels increasingly difficult to cope with after such a victory.

Henry arrives mid-morning, and I introduce him to Mum. He has his team behind him again and is talking to a tall doctor; both look concerned.

'Claire, this is my colleague. I've asked him to come and review Eliott's file. We're just going to go through a few things. As I told you yesterday, I don't know what's going on, and I want to get someone else's opinion,' Henry explains.

I notice from the other doctor's attitude that he wants to be reassuring and help.

They review the past days' activity from the EEG, and then the tall doctor asks me the usual questions.

One of the interns then hands the folder full of Eliott's information over to this new doctor.

The doctor cocks his head to the side, and just as I am about to give up listening to their discussion, I hear, 'Have you tried Phenytoin?'

I haven't heard this name before. *Another drug?*

I see Henry's face light up. It clearly means something to him.

The doctor continues, 'Just in case it's a mutation of the KCNQ2 gene.'

Henry instructs the nurses to start straightaway. The doctor then leaves, and Henry stays to explain this new course of action.

Phenytoin is a medication that acts on a particular channel of the brain and is used for a very rare genetic disease. There are only 100 known cases in the world, but it's worth a try. Henry reassures us that some kids grow up completely fine, so it could be good news.

It's 11am when Eliott is given a 'loading dose' of Phenytoin, which is a large dose of the medicine to bring the levels in his blood up quickly, and Henry promises to be back at 5pm to check the results. If it works, Eliott shouldn't have any seizures by then.

More waiting.

Luckily, Mum keeps me company until Ced arrives.

In the afternoon, I head to the delivery ward for a full check-up with a midwife. It's emotional being back in the room, and I cry the whole time. Mum seems desperate, seeing me so upset.

The midwife, however, is amazing. She's very patient.

My blood pressure is low, iron levels are low, everything is low, but there's nothing too concerning. I need rest, and I need to make sure I eat as healthily as I can to ensure I replenish my energy levels — especially if I'm expressing my milk to feed him.

I explain our feeding situation. 'I'm about to catch up with my milk supply,' I say with a half-smile. Soon, Eliott will no longer need top-ups with formula. It is an accomplishment, but I feel bad that this makes me proud.

How has this become my life?

Before having Eliott, I anticipated going home with all the struggles and typical new parent challenges. I wasn't expecting to feel happy and proud about expressing so much that my baby wouldn't need formula top-ups while staying in the NICU.

The midwife seems to get it, and she gently recommends that I take a nap, but I want to go back to Eliott. So, she smartly suggests that I rest for just twenty minutes while she goes and checks on something. Eliott is sleeping, so I don't need to express for another hour at least.

When Mum and I go back, Eliott is still asleep, and I feel a little better.

Henry and his team return at 5pm, while Ced and I are talking about Eliott's tests. We're only allowed two people with Eliott in the NICU, so Mum is reading in the waiting room.

Henry is looking intently at the EEG, and then turns around and says with a huge grin, 'Not one seizure!'

This is amazing news!

We're going to have to wait and see a bit longer, but this is a great sign. After the last ten days, it is such a relief. It's five hours without a seizure!

On the way home, Ced asks me how I feel after having my check-ups. I feel better and am reassured that my blood test ruled out anything serious, such as a need for a transfusion. But, knowing Eliott hasn't had seizure all afternoon has had the best impact.

When we arrive home, Sophie brings over a box of food for us. She and other friends have been cooking and baking. They've also given us some mugs and tea, and a very cute pen and notepad, which I decide to start using to write about Eliott's sleep, feeds, and medications. I'm overwhelmed by such generosity and the time they took organising this to show us that they're here for us.

What a day!

Day 12

Eliott

My body feels good, and it isn't doing the thing anymore. I also have a new nurse who's funny and talks to me a lot, and she keeps telling me I need to get better. She says it not in the same soft tone as everyone does; it's as if she's giving me an order. I *must* get better.

Day 13

Eliott

It's bath day! I can now start wearing the clothes Mum brought from home. Mum and Dad were getting worried I hadn't been able to have a bath yet — my skin is starting to get dry. I'm not sure I am a fan of the bath though; I don't like being cold. It was much nicer when I was in my onesie and big blanket!

Maman

It's been three days without a seizure!

Every hour counts, and these past seventy-two hours have been amazing. So much has happened. Eliott doesn't have his constant EEG monitoring, and they've removed all the electrodes after forty-eight hours of no seizures. We can now cuddle him, and he can sleep in our arms. I feel like we're finally turning a corner.

I know that the coming few weeks are going to be incredibly challenging, but for the first time in a week, I see some light at the end of the tunnel — a week is a long time to go without hope.

Eliott's new nurse is great. She's straight to the point and has been the perfect balance between pushing us a bit and looking after the three of us. Yesterday, we chatted with her about breastfeeding and why we had to stop.

She noticed my disappointment when I gave her the rehearsed speech of wanting to take him home earlier, even if on the bottle, and suggested (ever so gently) we give it another go. Amazingly, Eliott fed well. It was an incredible feeling; he was awake, and it felt like such a victory.

In these three short days, we've also given him a bath and started dressing him in baby clothes. They're not the ones I'd reserved for the day he'd come home — dreaming of that moment — but he'll wear those soon.

For the time being, he's wearing the NICU ones, which are a lot more practical with buttons everywhere, so they fit even with all the cables. I also bought some baby body lotion for his skin, which was getting dry. It feels like such a mundane concern at this stage, but it's important to me, and it's one of the only things I can do to help.

He seems to be flourishing now, and the nurse even takes the cannula off his wrist. One less cable. Thanks to this, he can be transferred back to level two. Once again, we roll Eliott's little bassinet between the two levels. We're now one level closer to the exit.

Day 14

Maman

Mum and I spend the day with Eliott, and it's another good day! Eliott has only drunk from the bottle and the breast —

39

we haven't had to use the feeding tube. During the day, I breastfeed him, and at night, the nurses give him bottles of my expressed milk. He had a mini seizure this afternoon, but it was short, and Henry isn't worried. He says we will need to meet the nurse who specialises in epilepsy, to know what to do when we finally go home.

Later in the afternoon, Ced comes to pick us up and say hi to Eliott. His work has organised some food for us, and Ced suggests bringing the pre-packaged meals for my lunches, so I eat more nutritious food. I get emotional again that others would do something so kind for us.

After seeing the doctors, we head home for the day. That drive home feels long and strange, having to leave our baby behind. It's only a twenty-minute drive from the hospital to where we live, but it always feels so long — a weird journey from the hospital bubble back into the real world (which doesn't feel real anymore). Everything we're used to — the streets, the people, the smells, the colours of the sky, and even the ocean — is unchanged, but we've changed so much. We're so removed from what should feel familiar.

Day 15

Maman

When we arrive this morning, Eliott looks so different. There's something odd about him — he's asleep, with his little head turned to the side. He looks so peaceful. His skin is soft, his chubby cheeks round, and his little nose is turned up, like my sister-in-law's.

It takes me a few moments to realise ... they've removed the feeding tube! I can see his little face again! I take a picture and send it to Ced immediately.

Eliott has another EEG this morning — it's the third one, and he's not even two weeks old. Henry says there's still some seizure activity, but it's much better, and he agrees to let us go home tomorrow.

I feel like jumping with joy. I take Eliott in my arms and give him a massive cuddle. Now that he doesn't have too many cables, it feels extra special.

Even though we still need a final okay from Henry after he's reviewed the medication and given Eliott another blood test, it feels like a small price to pay to go home.

The nurses then spend time with us to teach us how to give Eliott all his medications. By now, Eliott has five different drugs, which need to be given at specific times of the day, in multiple doses — so, it's quite complex. But at least we'll all be home! After the discussion last week about going home and managing multiple seizures every day, it feels like a huge improvement.

Day 16

Maman

We have Henry's green light to go home!

We'll have to come back next Tuesday for more blood tests to get the levels of Phenytoin checked, and again the following week, but who cares? We're going home!

While Ced is at work this morning, I meet Elody, the nurse who specialises in epilepsy. She explains everything, especially what to do if Eliott has a seizure.

After lunch, the pharmacist is getting the medication ready. Some nurses are overseeing the preparation, organising the numerous follow-up appointments, talking everything through with me. The doctors are writing up all the notes. Everyone is busy!

Ced arrives mid-afternoon, ready to take us home.

Unfortunately, everything takes longer than expected, and the medication levels are too low, so around 4pm, the doctors tell us we'll have to wait until tomorrow.

We stay to feed Eliott at 7pm before we go home.

I now feel even worse than usual having to leave him. Knowing he should be with us and we're leaving him is unbearable. I even ask if I can stay in hospital with him just this one night, but we can't.

I have a bad feeling.

I remember how a few weeks ago, we thought he could come home with us. And then bad turned to worse and the uncontrollable seizures came back.

What if the same happens again?

I just want him to come home with us. I want him to sleep in his bassinet and wake up next to us for once. I fall asleep praying that he comes home with us tomorrow.

Day 17

Maman

We're home at last. What a feeling!

I'm overwhelmed by the logistical challenge ahead of us, but Mum and Ced are reassuring, and nothing beats knowing that Eliott is sleeping next to us. We've had to install a baby monitor with breathing pads, just in case he stops breathing in his sleep, and that's scary, but at least we're here together. Very quickly, the administering of the medication starts. When we leave, Eliott has four medications with doses to be given at different times of day.

At 8am: we must wake him up with vitamin B6 and an anti-epileptic drug called Topamax.

10am: Phenytoin.

12pm: Keppra.

6pm: he has Phenytoin again, as well as a dose of the B6 vitamin.

8pm: Topamax again.

12am: Keppra again.

2am: finally, he has his last dose of Phenytoin, and that's it until 8am ... when it all starts again!

Everyone sets their alarms. We even download an app to track everything. Administering the medication is more difficult than in hospital because we must wake him so he gets to swallow the medication — in hospital, he could sleep, as everything was given through the feeding tube.

However, we're happy that the four of us are at home together.

Ced will be at home with us for the next two weeks too, as he's finally taking his paternity leave.

Eliott is just over two weeks old.

Eliott

I said goodbye to everyone at the hospital today because I'm going home with Mum and Dad. Mum dressed me in some pyjamas she was saving for this special occasion — it was a gift from Mamie. Dad, Mum and Mamie are all laughing, and we're going quite fast to leave the hospital — like we're escaping from something.

There is some gentle music playing in the car, and I sleep for most of the way home. When I wake, we're walking up the stairs to our home. It's quiet here, which I'm not used to. I'm also still getting used to having the soft fabric of the pyjamas on my skin and nothing attached to me.

Mum and Dad give me a tour of the apartment. They show me their bedroom with the big bed, and we lie there for a few minutes, me in the middle and them touching my hands. And they show me my bedroom: the changing table with the soft pad; the stuffed animals and the toys; the little bassinet next to the wall.

Whenever I need a feed, we go to my bedroom. Mum has a chair set up next to a little blue table that has a lamp on it.

Tonight, I sleep in my bassinet in Mum and Dad's room, and when they take me in their bed for the night feed, it feels perfect. It's been a wonderful day, so good that I smile in my sleep — this is common for newborns, but it's a first for me.

Chapter three

Home sweet home ...
How are we ever going to manage?
(June-July 2015)

Day 20

Eliott

We've had some quiet days at home, but today we went out for a walk by the beach. Dad jokes about the fact that I'll become a surfer who enjoys baguettes. It's cold outside because it's winter, but I'm all rugged up. I can't see much lying down in the pram bassinet, but I enjoy being pushed around, and I take the opportunity to have another nap!

Day 22

Eliott

Today is my first day back in hospital; I'm going for a blood test. I fall asleep in the car and wake up when the nurse puts a little needle in my heel, then pinches it to draw some blood into a tube — but it doesn't hurt.

Mum gets a call and tells Dad and Mamie that the results are good. We just have to go back again next week. It's annoying doing all these tests, but the days at home are great. Everyone is pretty tired because I wake a lot to feed, and no one has recovered from the first few weeks in hospital.

Mum often looks sad, especially when they wake me to give me medication. So, I try to be a good boy and swallow the medicines without complaining — even the ones that don't taste good. The only time I really can't stop myself from crying is bath time. I don't like it one bit, and getting out of the bath is the worst — it's so cold!

Day 23

Maman

We've been home a few days, and it's been amazing. Well, it's been exhausting, but wonderful at the same time.

We still need to get a few tests done, to check the levels of Eliott's medication, so we go back to hospital regularly for blood tests, which is an added logistical challenge. However, I keep telling myself that it's better than staying in hospital.

The Phenytoin is tricky to manage in babies. Their digestive systems break it down quickly, and the doctors need to constantly adjust the dose. Eliott is on a very high dose, which could be dangerous in the long run, and the side effects are concerning, but between this and seizures, we don't really have a choice.

I've been reading about the side effects of the medication, as well as the testimonials from adults who are on it, and it's heartbreaking, as many suffer from low self-esteem, suicidal thoughts, memory loss, low muscle control. I am praying every day that Eliott outgrows the seizures and doesn't have to take it longer term. Henry said that was a real chance.

We must focus on the day to day and keep putting one foot in front of the other, but I can't help but think about the future. I hope for a full recovery, but I'm fearful that it will get worse.

This morning, a nurse is here for a home visit. She's friendly, but I quickly get the feeling that she doesn't get what we're going through. She questions why we didn't go to their local office, as they usually only do home visits for mums and babies who leave hospital a few hours after giving birth, not two and a half weeks after.

The truth is that I don't know anything. Someone called me and said I had to organise a midwife visit, and asked if I preferred going there or a home visit. We go back to hospital a lot, so a home visit simply seemed easier to manage.

I cry when she asks me to go through the whole story again, and then she proceeds with all the newborn checks. When she weighs Eliott, she says that he only put on 95 grams this week. 'He should be putting on a lot more weight, between 150 and 200 grams,' she says sternly. 'You have to feed him more,' she continues. 'How often do you feed?'

'I used to feed every three hours, and express after the feeds when in hospital, but he's been feeding every four hours since we got home. That's what the NICU doctors suggested we do.'

'Make sure you feed him every three hours,' she replies.

I feel like such a bad mum. It's all too much, having to wake every three hours, on top of all the medication — that's a lot. I'm exhausted, but I say 'yes' because obviously it's important he gets enough food. I'm also told that I need to pump again to get my supply up.

After that, the nurse asks whether we swaddle for sleeping — the answer is no, as Eliott doesn't like it. It's very common in Australia, but babies in France aren't swaddled, so it didn't seem like a worthwhile fight. By the end, we weren't even swaddling him in the NICU. I try to lighten the mood and tell her about the time I wore a pair of tight jeans when I was pregnant, and Eliott kicked so hard that whole day that I knew he wouldn't like swaddling!

Unfortunately, she doesn't find it funny. She says it's important to swaddle. It's good for babies, as it makes them feel safe and helps them sleep.

That's when I lose it and say, 'We're not going to swaddle him. This is not important, so let's leave it alone.' I use my firm tone, as firm as I can manage today, at least.

After everything we've been through, if he likes the sleeping bag and not the swaddle, he will sleep in the sleeping bag. She finally drops it and moves on.

I have one last question before she leaves. One thing that has been intriguing me: mothers groups. We don't have them in France, but my friends here have all said that they're great.

Am I meant to join one? How does it work? How do you get into one? Maybe that could help?

At least I could meet other mums, some may even have been through similar experiences, and we could talk.

The nurse gives me a pamphlet and says I can just go along; they run them every Tuesday morning, and they'll explain everything there.

The whole conversation with this nurse has been so average, but at least she's consistent ...

We'll have to figure it out ourselves.

Day 27

Eliott

We've had a quiet weekend at home, which feels good after all the appointments. We played a lot on my mat and with one of my toys that I really love. Mamie has named him 'Monsieur Renard', which means 'Mister Fox', and she makes him talk to me. Mum, Dad, and Mamie are taking lots of pictures of me. I slept and fed well, but it's tiring to wake every three hours — at least I go back to sleep easily, often even at Mum's breast!

Day 28

Eliott

This morning, we go back to the hospital to do another test. Dad takes me in his arms for this test; I like being in his arms.

He smells nice, has a reassuring voice, and I feel safe. I feel a pinch on my heel; I am used to the feeling, and usually it doesn't really hurt, but today, it really hurts. So, I start crying.

Dad tries to comfort me, and Mum turns around to cry — I know she hates it when someone hurts me, but the nurse explains that it's normal and all the babies cry. Mum and Dad are upset, but I finally go to sleep. We go back home and have a wonderful day, but every time anyone changes my nappy from then on, I cry a lot because my foot still hurts.

Day 29

Maman

Today is another busy day; it feels like it never stops. We have an appointment with Henry this afternoon, so we decide to try going to a mothers group this morning. Nothing in our parenting experience so far has felt normal, and everything has been so challenging. I feel so lost about the medication, the blood tests, the unknown, the seizures that may come back, but I also feel equally lost about being a mum: feeding, bathing, sleeping.

I'm hoping that joining a mothers group can help bring a bit of normality to the whole experience. Plus, the midwife said I could weigh Eliott there, and I've been feeding him every three hours again, so I'm hoping he's put on more weight.

Mum offers to come with me, and I'm grateful for the help and the company. It's a typical winter morning where the air is crisp, but it's sunny, and it's a pleasant walk alongside the beach to get to the church where the group is held.

On our way, we talk about the upcoming appointment with Henry. When we left the hospital, Henry hinted that if everything was going well, we could talk about stopping one of the medications.

The mothers group isn't what I was expecting, but it's good. We get there early and have a chat with one of the midwives facilitating the group. She's been briefed on our case and seems considerate of our situation. She invites me to ask questions and shows me where to put the pram so Eliott can sleep during the session.

There are about thirty mums there, and when the session starts, the midwives facilitate the discussions to help everyone talk about their successes and challenges over the past week. They start with an icebreaker — we go around the room sharing our baby's first and middle names and explaining why we chose them. There are the conventional responses, such as a name being passed on from generation to generation, and other less conventional ones, such as a middle name given after the city in which the baby was conceived!

Then it's my turn. I'm secretly hoping Eliott will wake up for a feed before I have to speak, but he's asleep in his pram.

'Hi everyone, my name is Claire. My baby here in the red pram is Eliott. We both fell in love with the name. His middle name is Hope. We've had a rough start, so we chose this name while we were still in hospital.' I don't feel like I can elaborate anymore, and thankfully, no one asks follow-up questions, so we move on to the next mum.

A lot of the mums talk about how their babies are hungry all the time, and I look at Eliott who sleeps most of the time because of the medication.

When the session is over, everyone rushes to the scales to weigh their babies. When it's our turn, I start undressing Eliott, because the babies must be weighed naked, which in this drafty church isn't ideal, and Eliott starts crying. I'm feeling a bit stressed, trying to be as quick as I can, but I'm not overly confident yet. When the weight flashes on the digital scale, it takes me a few seconds to mentally calculate the weight gain.

'So?' asks Mum.

I look again. *Wow, this must be what proud mums feel like! Two hundred and sixty grams in less than a week!*

When we arrive at the hospital in the afternoon, we're directed to the outpatient clinic. I feel lost because I don't know where to go or what documentation I need to show, but a part of me doesn't want this to become familiar at all. I don't want to get to know this clinic like I got used to the NICU.

Once I've given Eliott's name at reception, we're asked to weigh and measure him again. We undress him fully for the second time today, which I feel is not fair, given how cold it is.

When we go into the exam room, Daniel the geneticist welcomes us and gets straight to the point. We're going to confirm through genetic testing whether Eliott has a mutation of his KCNQ2 gene. The lab will need more blood, including from Ced and me, so Daniel starts walking us through all the paperwork.

First, we'll only do what's called a panel, which means that the geneticists are going to test the genes that are known to cause epilepsy. While Daniel is talking, Eliott starts to get agitated, opens his mouth and turns his head from side to side, letting me know how hungry he is. I put him at the breast, and he feeds for the rest of the consultation.

When Henry arrives, he's wearing one of his pairs of colourful trousers. I think they may be his own contribution to making the children's lives a bit more fun. And he confirms that we can stop administering Keppra.

Hooray!

He's happy to see that everything is going well and that Eliott has a good appetite.

When we tell him about the home visit from the nurse and how we've had to wake him every three hours, he's not impressed. He says we need rest, and so does Eliott. We can wake Eliott after five hours if we want, but not before. He then explains how we're going to start 'weaning' Eliott off the Keppra.

Wait, what? We don't stop tonight?

I get a little tense. I've never had to deal with this kind of medication before; it's a powerful drug and you can't just stop taking it. It means that Eliott will still have to take it for another six weeks while we decrease the doses. Ced and Mum reassure me that this is still good news.

Overall, it's been a great day.

In the evening, when we change Eliott, he cries. We don't really know what to think, but from hearing all my friends talking about some of their challenges as parents, it seems quite a normal experience — some babies just don't like to be changed. Poor Eliott has had to get naked in the cold to be weighed twice today, so maybe he's communicating that he doesn't like it. We will still have to go through all the normal challenges, the childhood sickness, the teething, the tantrums later on, on top of everything else. So maybe this is how it starts.

Day 30

Eliott

It's Dad's birthday, and I'm one day shy of my one-month birthday! Mum and Mamie wake me at 8am for my first dose of medicine for the day; they've left Dad to rest.

Today I've decided that I should tell them I've had enough of the bitter-tasting medication. I refuse it, cry and try to use my hands to keep it away from my face. I stick my tongue out to push away the medicine dummy.

Mum looks sad, but I don't know what else to do.

In the end, I do take the medicine, and Mum gives me a big cuddle, but then she goes to wake Dad. I'm not sure what happened, but they both then seem sad.

Maman

I have tasted Eliott's medications, and some have a bitter taste. I pray that we can stop them soon. Unfortunately, you can't just skip a dose without risking seizures.

Eliott usually takes the medication without fighting, but today, of all days, it's a battle. So, after the medication, Mum takes Eliott into the living room and I wake Ced.

'Everything okay?' He groans, half-asleep.

'Happy birthday, darling,' I say, before bursting into tears. I tell him how I feel — how it's hard to watch Eliott fighting the medication; how I wasn't expecting to keep giving him Keppra for another six weeks; how I don't want to be giving my baby four medications, seven times a day; how this is not what I thought it would be.

Ced is listening to me, tears in his eyes.

After five minutes, I finally manage to pull myself together a little. 'Sorry I had to wake you. I was feeling terrible. We'll go and bake your birthday cake.'

Ced is looking at me sternly. 'Don't worry about it. I don't want to celebrate my birthday this year.'

'Oh no, I'll make it right. It's so important.'

'Maybe, but I wasn't expecting to start the day like this. I prefer we don't celebrate it this year,' he says, his tone flat.

I feel bad. Of course, it's hard, but it's hard for us both. I knew it was wrong to wake him, and I could have waited to share my feelings with him, but I needed the support.

The rest of the morning is rather sad, and there's tension in the air, but everyone is trying to move past it. But now it's ruined the birthday mood.

Ced desperately needed to sleep. He's been doing so much at home and with us. Plus, he's going back to work soon, and I know he's got a lot on his mind.

At noon, we have an appointment to see the professional studio photos we took last Friday. It was a gift from my work and had been organised before Eliott was born. It felt trivial to attend, but we agreed that it could be fun. And it was.

I'd asked to avoid flashes because we don't yet know if that could trigger seizures. Eliott actually slept through most of it. The three of us laughed throughout the session when the photographer suggested poses we felt were quite unnatural — we like natural photos, but it was still enjoyable.

The session was quite long, and after a while, Eliott had to feed and take his medication. He also needed a change, and as per his newest habit, he weed everywhere in the fancy studio!

When we go to review the photos, Eliott has to feed again. I'm trying to get more confident and breastfeed in public with a wrap, but my back is starting to hurt, so Ced comes up with a new technique: I lean back on him, and this way we're back-to-back, and I feel supported. Mum takes a picture of us and laughs at Ced's creativity! We choose two pictures from the studio, one that will be in Eliott's room, and one that will be used for his birth announcement.

Slowly throughout the day, the air clears between Ced and me. After apologising numerous times, Ced reassures me that he's okay, and of course he gets it, but celebrating his birthday is no longer on the cards.

In the evening, we change the routine slightly so Eliott can stay with Ced and Mum while I try and get some early rest, and then we do a good feed before we all go to bed. Eliott has started to sleep for longer stretches and even manages to sleep for five hours straight! Good thing Henry told us to let him sleep!

He still cries when we change him though, so we are starting to think that he might be getting cold and look for strategies to keep him warm, especially when we're out. Maybe he just doesn't like to be changed and is letting us know.

Day 31

Eliott is 1 month old

Eliott

Dad went back to work yesterday. So now it's just me, Mum and Mamie during the day. Mamie says we have some doctor's appointments for Mum because she's still tired and in pain after my birth.

Yesterday, we went to see our family doctor, Ewan. Mum told him she's not doing well, so he gave her information about how to get help. Mum and Dad seem to be doing great, but I know that they're not as happy as they used to be. When I was in Mum's belly, I'd hear them laugh a lot, but I don't hear that much laughter anymore. We also go to the hospital because Mum has some pain that won't go away. I stay with Mamie while Mum is in the doctor's office. Mamie smiles and sings to me. I like it when she sings; she has a lovely voice.

When Mum comes out of her appointment, she says she feels better and whispers something to Mamie. Mamie takes one of her calming deep breaths before kissing Mum on the forehead and saying, 'Oh my poor darling, I'm happy we came. You'll be better now'.

I'm glad everyone is better.

Day 32

Eliott

Today is *Mum's* birthday. It's funny how close it is to Dad's.

I hope today is better than Dad's birthday. I take my medication nicely; very soon I'll have less to take — Mum tells me every day.

Dad has made a brioche (I can't try it because I'm too little, but it tastes great in Mum's milk). He's also invited some friends over for Mum, but they wish them both a happy birthday. I've met most of these people already and everyone seems happy to see me.

Mum, Dad and Mamie say that today was a good day, and Mum thanks Dad for organising it. They say that they feel very lucky to have the friends that they have.

Day 35

Eliott

These past few days I've been so hungry and eating A LOT. Mum feeds me mostly, but Dad and Mamie have been giving me some of her milk in a bottle so she can sleep a bit more — I'm quite a slow feeder, and now that I am extra hungry, it's taking longer than usual.

This morning we went back to the mothers group. I like to see other babies. Mamie comes with us, and she helps Mum get me ready to be weighed. Everyone wants to weigh their babies, but it's not easy because it's so cold, and the babies aren't happy to be naked. It's the middle of winter!

When it's finally my turn, Mum puts me on the scale, and it shows that I've gained 360 grams! Mum is very happy. She's laughing and saying it's no surprise because I'm always hungry.

To celebrate, we take a long beach walk. I really enjoy it, and I sleep against Mum the whole time in the carrier. I like the gentle rocking; it feels a lot like it did in her belly.

Day 36

Maman

I'm always worrying about something these days. I know this is normal for new mums, but everything seems to be a struggle, and I'm not coping. I know our circumstances are quite extreme, but every other minute of my day is spent praying for the worry to stop.

I've made an appointment to go and see my psychologist, Donna. I met her about ten months after we moved to Australia. That first year in Australia was challenging; Ced was working long hours and was out of town a lot, so I felt lonely and had a hard time adapting to our new life.

Donna helped me change the way I view challenges.

One day, during a session, something clicked, and I hadn't felt the need to see her again. But when Eliott was born, I called her in tears. She remembered me after all these years and made time to see us while Eliott was still in the NICU. Ced and I have seen her a few times since, but today is the first time that we have seen her with Eliott, and she's really touched when she meets him.

We brought Eliott with us so I can feed him, but we leave him in the waiting room with Mum while we speak with Donna. However, after a short while, Mum knocks on the door and apologises for the interruption — Eliott is already hungry! After the feed, he needs to be changed, so Ced and Mum take him back to the waiting room.

I stay with Donna and chat some more, but through the door I can hear Ced and Mum giggle, probably making jokes about how they must be careful that Eliott doesn't pee everywhere in the waiting room! I can't help but smile at the sound of them laughing together.

Day 37

Maman

Mum and I meet with a lactation consultant today. It's been amazing to be able to breastfeed Eliott, but I'm not sure I'm doing it right. Like everything, it's very much a learned skill, not quite the natural harmony I was expecting. And it hurts, so much. Australia is in favour of breastfeeding, so there's a lot of support offered to new mums.

I'm expecting a lot from this visit. Every Thursday, there's a two-hour session, which anyone can attend. You come with your baby, ideally ready to feed, and they help you with positioning, looking for feeding clues, etc. I think part of the problem is that Eliott is sleeping so much, due to the medication. I often have to wake him to feed, and then he tends to fall asleep at the breast.

It ends up taking ages to feed. In itself, it doesn't bother me, but I worry that he doesn't have a routine, that he isn't getting enough to eat, and that he seems to be able to feed for hours on end at some times of the day, and then not at all. To make my point, I tell the nurse about the two-hour feed from the other day, and she's not impressed.

'What do you mean two hours? He was actively feeding for two hours?'

Well, of course he wasn't. But between sleeping, waking him, feeding, sleeping again ... Every time he was at the breast, he was falling asleep, and every time I tried to take him off, he cried. I try to explain it, start crying, and I can see she's not moved by all the emotions that are now overwhelming me. She's probably thinking, *just my luck, another emotional mum.*

I don't feel any wiser by the time we leave. I'm a little flat, but at least I know I'm not doing anything wrong, except letting him sleep on me. *Well, after not being able to take him in my arms in the early days, I'm okay with that.*

It's pouring when we leave, we run back to the car, rush to put Eliott in his capsule and fold the pram into the boot. Mum and I are soaking wet by the time we hop into the car.

Mum — being her exceptional self — breaks the mood by saying with a laugh, 'Well, she wasn't at all helpful. How about we go get a muffin and then we can snuggle at home for the rest of the day?'

Yep, sounds like a plan!

Day 38

Maman

We have an appointment with a paediatrician today. Yet another doctor, but the NICU doctors asked us to make an appointment with someone to follow Eliott's progress on a more *global* level.

I'm also hopeful that the paediatrician will have some answers for us. She comes highly recommended by Henry, and I like that they know each other. It makes me feel like there is alignment between them. Her practice is in a house that has been converted into a medical office. It's different to what I've become used to, but it has a welcome feeling to it, more reassuring than the usual general practitioner offices.

Mum, Eliott and I are in the waiting room when Ced walks in. He gives me a smile that says, 'Well this is different!' and kisses Eliott. He's telling us about his day — that he's happy it's the weekend — when a petite blonde lady, a child and another lady all enter the room and make their way towards the reception desk. The blonde lady makes a joke with the child and grabs a folder on the desk. She waves the child goodbye and then she turns her attention to us.

'This must be Eliott?' she says. 'I'm Mary.' Her voice has a nasal quality to it, and it manages to be both soft and enthusiastic.

Eliott gives her a smile. He has only just started smiling, nothing too determined yet, but it definitely looks more intentional — this last one being one of the best yet.

'Hi, yes, this is baby Eliott. I'm Cedric, this is my wife Claire, and this is my mother-in-law, Eliott's grandmother.'

'It's nice to meet you all. Let's go to my office.'

I look at Mum, who gestures that she's going to stay in reception and wait for us.

Mary sits behind her big wooden desk and invites us to sit on the two chairs opposite her. On the left is a doctor's table with a box of toys underneath it. 'I'm sorry to hear that you've had such a hard time,' she says. 'I spoke with Henry for over an hour yesterday so he could brief me. I wanted to make sure I was up to date on everything.'

I warm to her straightaway. She's lovely and gentle, and it's such a welcome change not having to repeat everything. The fact that she's talked to Henry to get up to speed before meeting us tells me that she's thorough and concerned about her patients.

58

She examines Eliott, asking questions as she proceeds: about his sleep, his nappies, how he's feeding. I go through the feeding issues, and she says it's all quite normal and should get better. She weighs him, measures him, and he smiles at her again. Throughout the whole consult, Eliott is calm, and when she tests his eyesight and puts toys in front of him, he follows them.

She puts him on his stomach to check how well he's holding his head up. 'He's doing really well, but he could do with more tummy time,' she suggests.

She then tells us that he has a big head, so we just need to monitor it — that could be why he's not holding it as well as expected, especially given he spent his first two and a half weeks lying on his back in the NICU.

We share with her the nurse's advice of waking Eliott every three hours and Henry's recommendation to let him sleep longer. Mary says Eliott is now at a healthy weight, so we can let him sleep as much as he needs.

This is great news!

She's happy to hear that he's started smiling and says that it's quite early for a baby, but in the normal range.

'He is growing and developing beautifully,' she says at the end of the appointment.

Ced and I are overjoyed; it's the best news we've heard in weeks. He's such a happy baby, and it's amazing to hear someone from the medical field say that he's developing 'beautifully'.

Before the appointment, we'd prepared a whole list of questions for her.

'He is due for his six-week immunisations next week, but I'm concerned about how his body could react,' I say. 'Could that trigger more seizures?'

Mary tells us that the immunisations are important, and that it's highly unlikely that they would cause seizures. She says we could give him paracetamol to prevent fevers and pain that may occur due to the immunisations, but with his medication, it's not recommended.

I dress Eliott and we're ready to leave when Ced asks one last question about Eliott's legs. He thinks they are arched and wants her opinion. Mary comments on the fact that babies usually have arched legs, so that could be normal, but she agrees that the right one is more curved than the left one.

She writes us a referral to get an x-ray done so we can check it out. It's probably nothing, but with everything that has happened, we can't be too cautious, and it might be a vitamin D deficiency. Vitamin D helps the body absorb calcium and ensures strong bones.

She informs us that one of the side effects of the medication is that it prevents calcium from being absorbed, so that could be it. She asks if we already have a referral for the next blood test, which we do. We're due to check his Phenytoin levels before we see Henry again next month. I carry it with me in his blue book, so she adds a vitamin D check at the bottom — we might as well do it at the same time.

The rest of the day and the weekend go by quietly. We've started watching *MasterChef* during one of Eliott's evening feeds. It's one of the only TV programs Mum can watch, as she doesn't speak much English, and it's good to help take our minds off everything. It's funny to think that he's feeding to the sound of a cooking show in the background! Maybe he'll like food and cooking when he grows up!

Day 41

Eliott

Mum tells me I'm having an x-ray today — I have no idea what this could be.

I close my eyes in the car on the way, and when I wake up, I can smell that we're at the hospital, but I don't know this room. Mum is carrying me gently and trying to put me

60

down on a table. But the table is cold, and I don't like it. She's wearing a funny vest too; she says it's for the radiation, and she'll stay with me for this test. That's nice, because often she's not allowed to stay with me.

But I want a cuddle, and I don't want to lay down, so I wriggle and cry. The lady who's doing the x-ray asks one of her colleagues to help and tells Mum that she needs to remove my nappy to put my legs flat on the table.

I can tell that Mum is getting frustrated, and she says that I can't keep still for that long, so maybe we could reset with a quick cuddle. But the ladies keep asking that I be still and that Mum take my nappy off.

Mum says that I might pee on the table because that's what I keep doing lately. She knows that I don't like being on this table, and she speaks softly to me; she thinks I might be afraid of the big machines.

After the ladies finally take the x-ray, Mum wraps me up in her arms for a big cuddle, and when she puts me back down to dress me again, I pee on their table. She was right!

Mamie comes into the room to help, as it's not easy for Mum to do it all: clean up the mess, change me, get the bags, all while I'm still naked and she's holding me to try to keep me warm. Mum and Mamie ask if they can change me on the table, one of the ladies says, 'Yes, but hurry up!'

And then I realise I need to do a poo!

Now they can't hurry us.

Suddenly, I'm hungry, so we find the feeding room, and Mum and Mamie laugh about me peeing on the table. They say the ladies should've been more understanding and let them change me on the table from the start.

Once I'm fed, they change me again, and I pee everywhere, except this time it really cracks them up.

In the middle of it, Mamie tries to protect everything and grabs a clean nappy to cover me up.

'No,' cries Mum, but she's laughing. 'We don't have enough clean nappies!'

They're still laughing as we drive home!

Day 42

Maman

Today we went to the mothers group again. I'm keen to keep hearing the tips and tricks that everyone shares, but I also want to make sure I weigh Eliott regularly, especially now that we're not waking him for feeds.

He's put on 260 grams in a week! Well, at least one thing must be working!

After the session, I'm chatting with Mum when one of the other mums walks up to me. She tells me her name and asks if I remember her. She looks vaguely familiar, but I can't place her. She tells me that we went to school together — she was in the year above me — in Normandy, France. *What a small world!*

One of our mutual friends told her that I recently had a baby and came to this group. She has a gorgeous blond baby, who is sleeping peacefully in his pram. Max is only a few weeks younger than Eliott.

'We should catch up for coffee soon,' she suggests.

Coffee with a fellow new mum is appealing, so I agree, and we exchange numbers. Organising an outing that isn't a doctor's appointment and having a chat with someone from 'home' sounds so good. I'm still holding on to my dream of a normal experience of motherhood, and spending time with normal mothers is one way to get back on track.

Day 43

Maman

Mum and I are about to sit down with a cup of tea after putting Eliott down for a nap in his room, when I hear the phone ring.

'Hi Claire, it's Henry.' His voice sounds different from what it usually does — more concerned.

'Is everything okay? Do you have some news for Eliott?

Have any of the tests come back positive?'

'No, I haven't received any test results yet. I understand you went to see Mary on Friday?'

'Yes, she was fantastic.' I can't help wondering why he is starting with this question.

'I understand you asked for an x-ray of his legs. Did you have any concerns?'

This is strange ... What's going on?

I answer hesitantly, 'Yes, Ced was worried, as he thought his legs were really arched. We asked Mary for her opinion, and she thought it could be a vitamin D deficiency, so she suggested an x-ray. We did it yesterday.'

'I know, that's why I'm calling. The arching can be perfectly normal for babies. But I have reviewed the x-ray, and Mary and I agreed that I'd call to give you the results.' Henry sounds upset.

'Okay ...' I've walked to our bedroom, and am standing next to the bed, looking out the window at the gloomy sky; the baby monitor on the chest of drawers is by my side. I can see the little light indicating that it's on, so I can hear if Eliott has a seizure or stops breathing.

Henry continues, 'Eliott has a fracture just above his right ankle.'

My heart skips a beat. 'What do you mean, a fracture? How could this have happened?'

'We don't know, and that's why I'm calling. This could be one of three things. It could be an injury from one of the seizures, but I don't think that's the case, as he was never restricted in his movements.'

I nod, which of course he can't see, and manage to say, 'No, he wasn't. He was always in his bassinet or in my arms.'

Henry continues, like he's reciting a memorised monologue. 'It could be from the cannula when he was in hospital, but I'm not sure. Did he ever have it on his foot?'

'No, he's had it on both wrists, but not his feet.'

'Yes, that's what I thought. Unfortunately, I'm going to need you to come to hospital as soon as you can so Eliott can have a skeleton survey. Go to the radiology department just like you did on Monday. I'll leave a script there. What we're trying to rule out is osteogenesis imperfecta. It's a rare condition where your bones break easily.'

I can't understand the words — all I hear is 'bones break easily'. 'Like in *Unbreakable*, the movie?' I can't help but think that's a stupid comment, and I don't think Henry hears me, as he doesn't even reply.

'The fracture has healed now. It's been reviewed by an orthopaedic surgeon and has healed properly. The team has managed to date it to about two to three weeks ago. But I'm going to need you to come here this afternoon, as we need to make sure that nothing else is broken. They'll have to take x-rays of every single bone in his body, including his skull to make sure that he doesn't have more fractures.'

We hang up, and I collapse on the bed. It takes everything I have left to go back into the living room. Mum turns around, and I can tell she's ready to tell me off for not resting while Eliott is asleep but stops when she sees my face.

Eliott

Mum wakes me from my afternoon nap. I'm still sleepy when she carries me to the car — it's strange, though, because Mum usually tells me about any appointments.

In the car, Mum and Mamie are quiet. Mamie watches Mum and wears her worried look. Mum is clenching her teeth. No one is smiling. We get to the hospital — I recognise the car park, the lighting, the smells, as I've been here so many times. Before Mum puts me in my pram, she gives me a long cuddle.

We're back at the x-ray place. Mum is talking to the receptionists; she's getting frustrated. She's not yelling, but she's firm. She says 'it' will be done today.

A radiologist comes and asks Mum how old I am, what needs to be done, and tells us to follow him. He says he'll do it. I'm given priority, and that sounds serious.

Maman

When we go home, I'm stressed, sad and lost. I call Ced to fill him in on everything throughout the afternoon, and he says he'll come home soon. Thankfully, Mum is here — I have no idea how I could manage without her.

Henry thinks the fracture happened about two to three weeks ago. It doesn't mean anything to me, but Ced suddenly realises that it's exactly when Eliott had the blood test, which was so distressing.

It wasn't just a painful blood test; they fractured his ankle. I feel so bad — he was crying on the changing table because he was in pain. His ankle was fractured, and we kept holding his foot to change him, singing and trying to distract him. But he was trying to tell us something was wrong, and we couldn't understand.

I am deeply upset.

Day 45

Maman

It's been a rough day. Mum and I have spent the morning worrying. Mary calls around midday, and it's good news — everything is okay, and nothing else is broken! I'm so relieved that I cry. Mary is empathetic and says no one could ever have guessed. It makes me feel a bit better, and I want to trust that no other parent could have guessed what was happening, but I feel so inadequate, so unequipped to face what's in front of me. I can't help thinking I should've seen it, guessed it, felt it.

Mary advises again that we should check sooner rather than later how his vitamin D levels are. The fracture could be because his bones are more fragile from the medication he's been on.

I feel so guilty and upset by it all, but I'm trying to focus on the fact that his ankle is healing properly.

Day 46

Eliott

Everyone's happy after yesterday's good news. I take my 8am medication well, and Mum gives Dad his belated birthday gift. She's organised a daytrip to Taronga Zoo. It'll be enjoyable for us to do something different.

It's such a great day, and we all have fun. I feed in the middle of the zoo, and that makes Mum and Dad laugh. Mum seems a little uneasy, but she says she's happy. It's wonderful to do something different.

Day 48

Eliott

After a quiet Sunday, we have an action-packed day today. Mum, Mamie and I go to IKEA to buy some mattress protectors for my changing mat. We need a few more because I keep peeing on them!

After IKEA, we head to the doctor. I'm seven weeks old now, so I must get my first immunisations done. The nurse gives me two needles, which hurt and make me feel funny. Mum asks the nurse to call the doctor because I've become pale. But everything's okay, and we go home.

It's 5pm, so it's already quite late for me. I'm so tired that I sleep through the 6pm Phenytoin dose, which they give me while I am asleep. I wake after the B6 and the Topamax at 8pm, and then I have a delicious feed with Mum, a bit of a top-up with Dad and go back to sleep.

Day 49

Maman

Usually, two of us give Eliott his medication — even for the 2am dose. Most of the time, I'm up because he gets hungry anyway, and I can feed him at the same time, but Mum and Ced manage some of the others.

It's been getting easier to give him his medication, so Mum offers to do the 2am Phenytoin dose on her own tonight. It's the first time she'll be doing it on her own, and I know she's stressed about it.

At 1.50am, I hear rustling in the kitchen, and then the familiar sounds of the syringe being taken out of the sterilisation tub, the bottle of medication being shaken, and then muffled footsteps on the carpet. I get up to see if she needs help and find her as she's about to enter Eliott's room.

She has the syringe with thick bright-pink syrup in one hand, her phone for some light and a little wipe in the other hand.

'Hi honey, did I wake you?'

'No, all good. I heard you in the kitchen, so I figured I'd come and help.'

Out of habit, Mum puts her hand on Eliott's forehead and gives him a gentle stroke on his cheek. Suddenly, she turns to me, anxious. 'Claire, he's boiling hot.'

I put my hand on his little cheek, and then his forehead. *He really is!*

Mum continues, 'What do you want to do? Do you have some baby paracetamol we can give him?'

'I don't know. They said it's not ideal to give him paracetamol with the Phenytoin, as it can interact. Maybe we can just remove layers and I'll check in an hour?'

'Okay, let me help you.'

We take Eliott's pyjamas off and give him his Phenytoin dose. I feed him, but he's so hot and unwell that he goes back to sleep quickly and barely drinks anything.

When I go back to bed, I set the alarm for 3am and tell Ced that Eliott is hot, but I get a muffled moan in response. I think about Mum and her look of concern.

I have this growing feeling that something's wrong, but nothing has been right for so long, and I can't trust myself. I can't listen to my instincts because my body is constantly in fight or flight mode. Mum has dealt with fever in kids before, and I know immunisations can cause fevers, but we've been through so much that we are completely thrown by this.

When I go back to his room at 3am, his forehead is a little cooler. As I fall sleep again, I decide that we should see the doctor in the morning, and also call Henry just to double check whether there actually is an interaction between paracetamol and Phenytoin. I'm lost in thoughts again about our life, our future, and slowly drift to sleep.

Suddenly, he is screaming. It's the most horrible scream, like he's in pain, scared, and calling for us all at the same time. We both know what's happening. We don't have to stop and think about it — in seconds, we're in his room.

This was the scream of a seizure.

Chapter four

Moving from a day-to-day existence
into the rest of our lives
(July-August 2015)

Maman

When we turn the lights on, we find Eliott on his side. He's bright red and having a seizure.

Ced takes him out of bed and looks at me. 'He's burning hot.' He lays Eliott on the change table and starts to remove Eliott's onesie. His hands are shaking. 'How do I get this thing off? Give me scissors, I'll cut it.'

'I'll do it,' I say, stepping in front of Eliott as Ced steps aside. 'I'm sorry, he was hot, I didn't know what to do.' I knew this could happen, but we had a month without a seizure. I was desperately hoping they were gone forever.

The seizure stops, and Ced takes Eliott in his arms. Mum is at the door coming to check on us. My brain switches back on.

'Mum, go grab the phone. We need to call an ambulance.'

Just as I'm finishing my sentence, Ced yells, 'He can't breathe.'

I turn around and see Ced on the feeding chair, turning Eliott to face down on his lap and gently rubbing his back to try to open his airways. He's not seizing anymore, but he doesn't seem to be able to breathe. I look at Ced's hands and recognise these movements we learnt just a few weeks back at the kids first aid course, hoping at the time that we would never have to use them.

Mum is still standing in the doorway.

'Mum, go get the phone.'

She looks at me, then looks at Ced, then at Eliott, then at me again. And suddenly it hits me — she's frozen. She can't move.

I rush past her to get the phone in the living room and dial 000. 'Please send someone, my newborn is having a seizure,' I yell as soon as someone answers.

'Police, fire, or ambulance,' the voice answers, but I can't hear it.

'Please send someone quickly. He's having a seizure.'

I hear Ced scream from the bedroom, 'He's having another one!'

I talk to the operator again, not having heard a single word of her response as I'm walking back to the bedroom. 'Our address is ...'

With a firm voice, she manages to say, 'I can't do anything until you tell me what type of emergency it is. You must tell me what you need first.'

'Oh, ambulance, I need an ambulance, quickly. My son is having a seizure.'

'Okay, calm down. What's your address?'

After I give her all the information, she assures me help is on the way and asks me to tell her when Eliott is breathing.

'Inhaling, exhaling, inhaling, exhaling.' But he's now having a lot of mini seizures. 'Oh no, he's clustering. Where are they?' I yell at the operator. I feel so anxious.

When the ambulance finally arrives, they assess Eliott and decide to take us all to hospital.

'Is your bag ready?' one of the paramedics asks.

It's not.

In seconds, we get something ready — changes of clothes, nappies, wipes, toys, and Eliott's blue book, which is full of all his medical and birth information. I jump into a pair of jeans and pull a sweater on. 'Okay, we're ready to go. I'll go with him.' I turn to Ced. 'Can you meet us there?'

The paramedics help me get into the ambulance. Eliott

is in my arms as I sit on a stretcher bed. They take all his vital signs and ask about his history. He looks so fragile, my little seven-week-old. So vulnerable. I can't even imagine how I look — shattered, probably.

When we get to hospital, Eliott is still burning hot. As I'm about to stand to get out, they ask me to stay on the stretcher bed, as they'll transport me into the Emergency Room (ER) this way; this is the protocol. It feels so weird, as I've never been to the ER in an ambulance. In fact, I've only been to the ER three times in my entire life.

We go straight in, and one of the paramedics does the handover with the nurse. He asks me to confirm a few things, and I feel like I'm repeating all these words I learnt only a few weeks ago.

'He's a newborn with a history of neonatal seizures. He's on Phenytoin, Keppra, B6, and Topamax. He's had lots of metabolic testing done, and nothing has come up; his neurologist thinks it might be genetic. He had a fever after his immunisation and started having seizures and clustering at about 5am this morning.' All these words have now become part of my identity.

How has this become my life?

When Ced arrives at the ER, he also looks like he's been hit by a train. An ER doctor introduces herself. 'I'm the ER paediatrician on call this morning and will be looking after little Eliott. I've read the notes from the handover and his stay at NICU. You guys have had a rough time. Do you want to tell me about this last seizure today?'

All I can do is cry.

I wish I could go back to what it was before, when I only had a vague idea of what the word seizure really meant: mental images of people losing consciousness with their body shaking, not my baby experiencing them.

The ER paediatrician seems genuinely concerned, but there's something that I instantly don't like about her. I just put it down to me being tired, stressed and lost. She's looking at Eliott like he's an interesting case, but I don't want

71

that; I want him to be a boring baby with nothing worthy of a doctor's interest. Nothing to be excited about.

Ced recounts the events from the last twenty-four hours. He stops to let me talk about the immunisations, and I tell the paediatrician about how Eliott had a weird reaction but then got better on his own, so we weren't too concerned. I also share how Mary told us not to give him paracetamol for fear of an interaction with the Phenytoin, and how he got hot overnight.

'Can you call neurology? Maybe Henry could come and see Eliott?' Ced suggests.

We both trust Henry and could do with a familiar face to talk us through what's going on. We need to see someone who's going to tell us that it will be okay.

The paediatrician answers, 'Yes, we will. But you've come to the ER with a high fever, so we need to run a few tests before we call neuro.'

She asks a lot of questions about the previous few days, and when I suggest that the fever may be linked to immunisation, which I always thought was a normal reaction, she disregards it. 'Immunisations don't cause fever.'

My grandmother has always said they do. And I vaguely remember my cousins having high fevers after theirs. But she's a doctor, surely, she's right about that.

She continues, 'I'm afraid this could be an infection. Fevers don't come about like this.'

'But he just had his immunisation yesterday, so are you sure it can't be linked?' I try once more.

'No, I don't think so. Sometimes you can have a mild fever, but not a high fever like this. We're going to have to run some tests.' She looks serious and studies Eliott's monitors again.

'Should we give him some paracetamol, given he's still hot?' Ced is trying to steer the conversation back to why we were brought here in the first place.

'I wouldn't suggest that, as it can skew the results. Let's do a quick blood test first. It should only take about thirty minutes to get the results back.'

'Okay,' I say, 'let's do it. But I don't want you to do it on his heel, as they broke his ankle last time.'

She looks a bit surprised but doesn't argue.

Eliott screams when they put the needle in, and I think I'm going to faint, watching him suffer like this. Hopefully the results are good, and we can go home soon.

While we wait for the results, Ced goes home to get Mum; she must be worried sick. When they return, Ced walks into our little pod first and whispers, 'Your Mum feels really bad.'

'What? Why?' I look beyond him, to where Mum is standing back a little. She's looking at Eliott, who is fast asleep on the big hospital bed. I smile at her, and she walks towards me and gives me a big hug.

She starts crying. 'Oh, darling, I'm sorry I couldn't go and get the phone this morning.'

'Mum, that's okay. I get it, it's not your fault. You froze, anyone could have frozen. Don't worry about it.'

'I couldn't stop watching Cedric with Eliott on his lap and not breathing. I'm so sorry I couldn't help.'

I'm about to respond when the doctor walks in. 'We've got the blood test results. Unfortunately, the infection markers are high, so we need to do more testing.'

Ced looks incredulous. 'What does that mean?'

'It means that there could be an infection.'

'But couldn't it be the immunisation?' I'm desperate for the immunisation to be the explanation of everything. I can't figure out if it's intuition, or if I just desperately need it to be.

'No, I don't believe so.' The doctor's tone makes me understand that I probably shouldn't raise the immunisation point again. She's the doctor, and she knows best.

'What are the next steps?' Ced is good at thinking about things in terms of how we can take action.

'Given his age, we don't want to take any risks. I'd suggest a lumbar puncture to rule out meningitis, and to start a treatment of antibiotics straightaway.'

He's had two lumbar punctures already. I look at Eliott; he's probably exhausted from the seizure. He's so peaceful, with such gorgeous full lips and chubby cheeks. My perfect little bubba.

'That sounds a bit extreme. Are you sure it could be meningitis?' Ced seems as surprised as I am.

'Ultimately, this is your decision. I can only recommend what our protocols suggest. For a seven-week-old with a high fever, we must use antibiotics to minimise the risks of meningitis.'

'But you can't be telling us that you do that with every seven-week-old that comes to you with a fever,' I say.

'No, but you came to us after a seizure, and his blood test shows signs of infection. So that would be our protocol. Have a think about it.' She looks annoyed.

It's 8am, and some nurses are coming to give Eliott his medication.

'Ask the nurses to come and find me when you've made a decision,' the doctor says. 'But time is pressing. Let me know if you have any questions.'

We give Eliott his medication in his sleep; he doesn't even fight the Topamax. Mum is gently stroking his cheek, looking so sad and tired. It's too late to call George's parents in France and ask them for advice. I feel like we have no one to turn to for advice.

Ced looks to be deep in his own thoughts. 'Our own paediatrician was great ... maybe we could just call her?' he says.

We arrange for the hospital to get in touch with Mary.

It's good to talk to someone we know. Mary has all the results from the hospital and knows about the seizure and the immunisations. I pose my immunisation theory again, but she's on the doctor's side. Immunisations can cause fever, but the blood infection markers wouldn't be up. She says we could give him paracetamol and see how he goes. Meningitis is very unlikely, but if it is that, it would be disastrous. Her voice is soft and gentle, and I'm grateful for her time.

At the end of the call, she argues, 'It's your decision. But he's so little, and so precious, no one wants anything to happen to him.'

I'm still not convinced, but she's right — he is so precious.

Ced asks Mum if she can watch over Eliott for a few minutes. 'We need to go outside to have a quick chat.' He then takes my hand and leads me outside.

We sit on a bench, and Ced starts talking, 'Hon, it's our decision. Let's weigh the pros and cons.'

'I don't know. It's so hard.'

'I know.' He kisses my forehead.

I look around at all the people going about their day: doctors coming back to hospital with their morning coffees, people in suits waiting for their buses to go to work — all are completely oblivious to our personal drama.

How can the world keep going around?

'I feel so lost. I'm not ready to make these decisions. I don't want him to have another lumbar puncture. I'm sure it's the immunisation, as he can't possibly have contracted meningitis.'

'I know, but what was Mary saying?'

'She said that given the markers are up, we don't know what he has.'

'Okay, should we do it, and ask them to give us the results as quickly as they can?'

I answer, sniffling, 'Okay.'

We go back and give them our decision then ask if we should come with them to the treatment room.

The nurse looks uncomfortable.

Ced, clearly picking up on the vibe that they'd prefer us not to be there, says, 'We'll go and grab coffee.'

When we return, we find Eliott back in his bed, and it looks like he's been crying. My heart is breaking. They said in the NICU that lumbar punctures aren't painful for babies, as their tissues are so soft. However, could it be that now he's getting older, he can feel it more?

'It looks like he's been crying,' I say to the nurses.

'He cried a bit, but it went well,' replies one nurse.

'He cried a lot, so she had to re-do it three times,' admits another nurse.

Oh, my baby! I am devastated.

Eliott now has the antibiotics flowing in through his cannula. They started them while we were away, so he can now be admitted to the ward.

When we get to the ward, it doesn't feel as protected and sheltered as the NICU. We'd grown used to the room where all the babies were together. Even if I was anxious about the constant beeping of the machines, it had felt like a familiar environment.

This feels different.

Despite the drawings on the walls and the colours in the corridor, it feels more like an adult ward, with the separate patient rooms, the nurses station in the middle, and the fact that the nurses and doctors aren't constantly with us.

The nurses, who are kind and gentle, show us to our room. Eliott is transferred from the big stretcher bed into a cot. The nurses check the equipment, the notes from the ER, when the next medications are due, and tell us they'll be back later. We can call them if we need to.

I ask for a little bassinet like the ones they had on the maternity ward and in the NICU, but they don't have any left. Behind the curtain, partitioning the room in two, is another family. Coincidentally, the family is also French, and the baby girl is an eight-week-old twin also suffering from unexplained seizures. The other twin is well and healthy.

The day goes slowly. Eliott is exhausted and only wakes to feed. I am going to have to sleep here tonight, as Eliott needs at least forty-eight hours of antibiotics.

In the afternoon, Mum offers to look after him while Ced and I go home so I can have a shower and get an overnight bag ready. We can't leave him alone because the nurses can't stay by his side. If anything were to happen, we'd miss it.

Mum is being brave and smiling her gentle smile. 'Take your time. I'll watch over him.'

Eliott has been really hungry these past few days, and I feel like my milk supply is too low, so I even take the pump with me. I can pump and give him an extra bottle overnight.

When we arrive back at the hospital, Mum looks exhausted. She had to change Eliott, but he did a wee all over the bed. The nurses were occupied and couldn't help her, so the grandmother of the other family in the room went to grab clean sheets for her and helped make Eliott's bed. By the time the nurses came in, Mum had already managed to do everything. It is such a different environment to what we had grown used to in the NICU.

In the evening, Henry comes to check on us. We're grateful to see him. He's happy with the course of treatment. Given the fever, he's leaving it to the ER doctors to make the decision. His concern is the fact that Eliott had a seizure, and he gives him a small loading dose to increase the Phenytoin levels in his blood, and he increases the doses that we have to give him. He thinks that the Phenytoin is working, but Eliott may need a higher dose. He's been growing, so the doses will need to be reviewed carefully, and often.

While he's here, he's keen to review the medication. He's received the B6 results, and Eliott doesn't have a B6 deficiency. We can stop that straightaway. I'm a bit surprised that we don't have to ween him off the B6, like the Keppra, but he explains that given it's a vitamin, it can be stopped immediately.

One less medication to give Eliott!

We also want to check the timing of them all.

Henry looks hesitant when I list them. 'Do you give him 12am and then 2am doses? Do you put the alarm clock on?'

'Of course. You told us to, and the doctors gave us the instructions when we left NICU four weeks ago.'

'Oh no, you must be exhausted. We can change that so it's more manageable.'

What?

I thought the medications were given at different times because of potential interactions. I feel let down. Surely someone could have thought about this and the impact on our lives before. We're not doctors, and it's hard enough being new parents and feeling like you're completely out of your depth. But I can't be mad at Henry.

To be fair, I shouldn't be mad at the NICU doctors or the nurses. Their job is to make sure we're safe and that the medication is given on time while in the hospital setting. But in these situations, when the new parents are already at a loss with what to do, emotionally and physically exhausted by what has happened to them and their baby, whose job is it to make sure the plan has taken all factors into account? If medication can be given at the same time, and at better times, why not discuss it?

We all agree on a better schedule.

8am: Topamax (which we will drop a few weeks after Keppra). We will also give him Phenytoin at the same time.

12pm: Keppra (for another couple of weeks).

4pm: Phenytoin.

8pm: Topamax.

12am: Keppra and Phenytoin.

What a change. I can see a more manageable future and feel more positive.

However, this positive feeling is short lived.

The doctors tell us that the IV that was put in Eliott's arm needs to be replaced. It wasn't put on properly. Maybe he was moving at the time, and the tube is at risk of being blocked. They need to do it again.

They've done it a few times in the NICU without any issues, but I'm still trying to shake the bad feeling I had from our episode in the ER. It needs to be done straightaway. Eliott is asleep, so hopefully he can sleep through it.

I sit on the armchair so I can be in a comfortable position, and Ced picks Eliott up from the hospital cot to put him in my arms.

The doctor and the two nurses wake Eliott up as they start the process. They try to put the needle in deeper into his tiny chubby wrist, and he starts to scream.

I'm holding him and have tears rolling down my cheeks. 'Stop. You're hurting him. Stop.'

They stop and look at me. 'We're going to have to do it again; sometimes they just don't like it.'

I'm trembling and about to faint. 'Look, last time someone told me this, they broke his ankle. This morning, she messed up his lumbar puncture and had to do it three times. If he's hurt, we'll stop.'

It must strike a chord because they pause and nod. 'You're right. Let's take a five-minute break. Give him a cuddle, maybe give him a bit of milk so he feels better, and we'll wait in the corridor. Call us when you're ready.'

When they come back, they try again without any luck. Eliott's now screaming every time they touch him, and I'm sobbing uncontrollably. Mum is standing next to me holding Eliott's little arm, and I'm cradling him as close to me as they'll let me. Ced has offered to hold him, but I can't let go of him.

After some unsuccessful attempts to simply straighten his arm, one of the doctors kneels, looks me in the eyes and says, 'I know it's difficult for you. I can see that. We must get the cannula in because he needs the medication. I think your stress is now affecting him. Would you be okay if we take him to a treatment room? I promise we won't hurt him. If he cries, we'll stop. But we can't even touch him here.'

Ced lowers down too, and says, 'Claire, I'll go with them. You stay here with your mum. I'll go and hold Eliott's hand. Don't worry, he'll be safe.'

I finally let go of Eliott, and Ced takes him away. They come back only a few minutes later, a fresh cannula in.

The doctor gives me a big smile. 'He did so well. We managed to put a good cannula in, and we won't need to change it again for the duration of his stay.

When I look up at Cedric, he gently puts Eliott back in

my arms and gives me a kiss. 'He didn't cry at all. They were very gentle.'

Eliott

I woke up this morning because my body was doing the thing again, and we are now back at the hospital. I am scared, and it doesn't help that I have to do more tests today. It has been painful, and I don't know how to tell them.

Mum said that she's staying with me tonight; I'm happy she gets to sleep in my room.

Maman

We stay in hospital for another couple of days before they come to our room and say they have the test results. 'All clear. No sign of meningitis.'

I'm exhausted, as we haven't really slept for two days, and I feel betrayed. I am even now more convinced it was the immunisations that led to his fever. I've let him down. I didn't give him paracetamol, and I didn't stand my ground enough to avoid the unnecessary hospitalisation with all the associated trauma. The only positive coming out of all this is that we can change the medication routine, and I know that this is going to have such a positive impact on our life.

I've also spent a lot of time alone with Eliott and feel more confident in my ability to look after him. This sounds like such a minor thing, but it is incredibly powerful. I feel more confident as a mum, being able to look after my baby on my own. If I'm honest, I don't just feel more confident as a mum, I feel more like a mum. I've had the luxury of having Ced and Mum around to help and haven't yet had an opportunity to spend time just with Eliott. It's hard to imagine, but I hadn't really felt like a mum yet.

But with the forced hospitalisation, as both Eliott and I needed to get some rest, I've allowed myself to pump at night and give him a bottle. And I've set my alarm to go off before the time he feeds, so I can pump, clean everything up and get the bottle ready, feed him, change him, put him back to sleep, go clean everything again, and go back to sleep — all on my own. By doing this, I realised that he and I are a little team and make it work. I also have a lot of milk. No issues there.

Because of his feeding pattern, I was starting to believe that this was another challenge, but as it turns out, he just drinks a lot. It's definitely a silver lining. I still need to pump a lot, but I know he's getting what he needs. And I'm providing this to him. I'm able to give him what I believe is the best, and we're connecting this way. We need this connection so badly. I need him to need me. And I need to feel like I can be there for him. Feeding time is where just him and I can be in a little bubble, so who cares if it takes two hours for him to have enough.

A week after we leave the hospital, Ced and I have an appointment with our psychologist, Donna. We take the chance to offload and tell Donna all about our recent events, and she empathises and gives us some advice.

I've always liked her approach. She's a good listener, asks questions that make me think and dig deeper, and when she gives advice, it's always practical. She never suggests ways to handle a situation but suggests 'wellbeing' activities: going for a walk, taking a deep breath, or buying a new mug. It's never something impossible or unpractical, such as 'go on a holiday', which would potentially help but isn't necessarily feasible.

She challenges me to think about the small things that make a difference.

I've organised for a private lactation consultant to visit later that night. I've done seven weeks of breastfeeding, with all the ups and downs, but it's tiring, and it's stressful not knowing how much he's getting, but most importantly, it's now become excruciatingly painful.

In a short week, I've gone from regaining confidence

and feeling positive about breastfeeding to dreading every aspect of it because of the sudden physical pain it brings me.

The lactation consultant arrives, wearing a skirt which almost touched the ground and long earrings dangling from her ears. When she walks into Eliott's bedroom, I'm sitting on the feeding chair, cringing every time he sucks.

'How's it going here?' she asks, smiling. She then has a quick look at Eliott's attachment and how he's positioned on me and asks a few questions.

We let him feed as much as he feels like, and when he takes a short break, she looks at his tongue and his palate to see how well he sucks. After looking at him for a few minutes, she hands him back to me.

Everything is fine.

I've heard this so much before: 'He looks completely normal and responds well to all the tests. We don't know what's wrong with him.'

It doesn't help at all.

'Have you taken any antibiotics since the birth? Some women are more sensitive to them and can develop thrush,' she says.

As a matter of fact, I have, but that was six weeks ago, so why would I be in pain only now? But suddenly, I realise what must have happened. It started hurting on one side, and then the other. Eliott has just had a course of antibiotics and must have had thrush, then passed it on to me on one side, and then contaminated the other when feeding.

She suggests a cream, and thankfully in less than forty-eight hours the pain stops. Breastfeeding becomes easier once again.

A week later, Eliott needs to have more blood tests to check his Phenytoin levels. We're seeing Henry the next day, and he wants to check them. Eliott is just over two months old. He examines well, and Henry is happy with his overall progress and to hear that he's been fine since his last stay in hospital. Given we're about to stop Keppra, Henry also confirms we can start weaning him off Topamax as well. We're given a six-week plan to stop it. The Phenytoin, on the other hand, is low, so Henry wants to increase the dose.

We do another blood test on Thursday to confirm the levels after the increase, and then go for brunch with Mum to do something special on her last day before she flies back to France. It's crept up on us so quickly! It is also the last day that we will be giving Eliott his dose of Keppra.

It's 12pm, and I give it to him in the restaurant. Then I throw the tiny syringe in the bin. *Done!* We're down to two medications, four times a day!

Henry calls later to give us the results of Eliott's blood test. His levels are good, so Henry wants him to stay on the higher dose of Phenytoin.

I wish we could've kept a lower level and not increased again, because we've already increased them just after the seizure; however, we must follow Henry's instructions. At least we dropped one med today. *Small victories.*

It's now mid-August and time to say goodbye to Mum. She's helped us so much while being here, supporting us through a myriad of dark times. But in between all these horrible experiences, we've had some lovely moments together; she's seen Eliott's first smiles, enjoyed outings together, laughed so much every time he weed during nappy changes, sang to him, and relished many walks on the beach. It seems inadequate to say that we are really going to miss her!

Chapter five

Learning to be a family
(August 2015)

Maman

I've been emotional since Mum returned to France. Ced even had to come home from work early because I wasn't managing at all.

We've organised to go away just the three of us for a long weekend, to clear our minds.

We had to check with Henry to make sure he was happy for us to go, but seeing as it's in Kangaroo Valley, a short two-hour drive from Sydney, he sends us off with one instruction: 'try to have fun together'.

Eliott

We're playing in the living room of our holiday house (the three of us are on a mini-break before Mamie Francette — Dad's mum — arrives), but I feel annoyed, so I arch a lot when they carry me. My body feels weird. I'm not comfortable, but I can't figure out a way to tell them that there's something weird going on. We enjoy some nice walks, but I cry a lot, and Mum and Dad look sad.

Maman

Eliott's been arching his back frequently, and we just don't know why. It feels like he doesn't want to be carried in our arms. Everything has been such a challenge, but he's a happy baby, which has helped. If he doesn't like being in our arms and doesn't want contact, then it will make things even more challenging, unbearable even.

My mind has been thinking all sorts of things.

What if he is on the autism spectrum?

Can you even diagnose autism and similar disorders in such young babies?

Is this how it starts?

I asked a friend for her advice, as she used to work with babies, and she suggested that we take Eliott to see a physio to check his alignment, as it could be what is making him uncomfortable.

When we walk into the physio's room, I notice that it's airy with lots of gym mats on the floor.

The physio walks towards me, barefoot, and stretches her hand by way of introduction. 'Hi, it's wonderful to meet you. I'm going to put some music on, and we can start.'

I go through the already long medical history of his short life before she starts the session. Eliott seems happy and looks intrigued by this new person, but he still arches his back a few times.

The appointment is very different from what I was expecting. I thought she'd check his alignment, look at how he moves, and give me recommendations for next steps, and maybe even explain a bit more about the process in general.

But, instead, she does a few tests, plays with him, and at the end tells me that he's a bit delayed — he's eleven weeks old and should be holding his head better than he is. She gives me three exercises to do with him and asks me to come back two weeks later.

I don't really get it. There is no acknowledgment of the fact that he's had such a tough start in life, the medication, nothing.

I point out to her that he's got a big head; he's on the 95th percentile in terms of his head circumference. Surely all of this could be impacting his ability to hold his head and should be noted? Why do we have to come back in two weeks? I was under the impression that this appointment was a once-off.

Unfortunately, before she can explain why we need to come back so often, my alarm clock sounds; I'd planned the session so it would end around the time that Eliott's medication was due. I explain to her about his anti-epileptic drug schedule and that today is the first time I'm doing it on my own away from home.

I'm not too sure why I'm sharing so much — maybe I'm expecting her to ask if she can help. But she doesn't. She's on the other side of the room while I struggle to give a wriggling Eliott his medication. I'm battling trying to hold him and give him the pink syrup. I don't think the therapist realises the drama that's quietly unfolding — she just doesn't get it, and I haven't learnt how to ask for help for this kind of thing yet.

Eliott is cradled in the little diamond shape I create with my legs, so he has somewhere safe and comfortable to lie down. I lean over him and whisper, 'Please, baby, you have to take it. I know you don't want to, but you have to.' He and I must be a team if we're going to keep doing this effectively, otherwise we won't be able to leave the house anymore.

How did I end up here?

I feel so alone, sitting cross-legged in the middle of this big room (where I imagine lots of people come with their perfectly healthy babies) cradling my two-month-old baby who's fighting his daily dose of anti-epileptic drug.

When the therapist asks if she should book me another session, I say, 'No, thanks.' I'm just so emotionally drained, exhausted, and I don't get why I need to come back. I ask if she can just send the report from today to our paediatrician.

We see Mary the next day, and I share my experience of the physio. She's really surprised. She's also bewildered about why Eliott has to go every two weeks, given he is so young. When I tell her of our concerns about how he's been arching his back over the past two weeks, the surprised look quickly changes to worried.

Every time she's seen Eliott, he's always been such a smiley baby. So far, one of the things that's defined him is his low muscle tone, so hearing that he's been arching his back is concerning. And now his arms are sometimes doing little shaking movements and moving uncontrollably. I've filmed it, and so I show her the video.

Mary asks us to put Eliott on the observation table. He smiles a lot, but he arches his back a few times. She tests his reflexes, how he moves his limbs, and then she sits back at her desk. 'Look, I'm actually really concerned. When did this start?'

'About ten days ago. We went away for a few days, and he started doing it then. We tried to come and see you earlier, but we couldn't get in. The hand and arm shakes only started a few days ago.'

'When did you increase the medication? Let me have a look at the letters from Henry again.'

'Do you think it could be the medication?' I ask.

'Yes.' She writes down his weight and starts calculating the mg/kg. 'I don't want to scare you, but I'm going to ask you to get a level test done immediately. We'll finish the appointment early so you can go across the street to the hospital and get a blood test. I'll fax them a referral and give them a call right now. I think he might have what we call Phenytoin toxicity. It's very dangerous.'

We rush over to the hospital, and they prioritise Eliott. We then head home around 4pm, and once again we're left feeling worried.

I go online to search what Phenytoin toxicity is, and my head is spinning.

Mary calls just before 5pm.

Eliott doesn't have Phenytoin toxicity, but his levels are a bit higher than usual. She is still waiting to hear back from the neurology fellow on call but thinks we may have to reduce the levels.

Shortly after, I get the call from the hospital. Given the levels are within the therapeutic range, the neurology fellow feels that it can wait until we see Henry. He's away for the weekend, but they'll make an emergency appointment for us to see him on Tuesday.

I point out that his levels are usually well below, but they don't feel he's at risk. I then call Mary and tell her about the decision, but she's not impressed.

'Let me give them a call and I'll call you back,' she says.

It's a relief to have someone take control. Ced's been with Eliott while I have been on the calls, but now he's telling me that Eliott's getting hungry. I'm walking to the bedroom to feed him when my phone rings again.

'Claire, it's Mary. Here's what we're going to do. I want you to drop tonight's dose from your current 7ml to 5ml and keep them there all weekend. Monitor him closely, as this is a big drop, and then come back for a blood test on Monday in advance of your appointment with Henry on Tuesday. I'll fax another form to the hospital. Does that make sense?'

I tell Ced, and from the look in his eyes, I gather he's thinking the same as what I'm thinking. *What the hell is happening to us?*

Lowering the dose is very scary, as we don't know if that might put him even more at risk of seizures, but we're even more scared of a potential toxicity. We find comfort and reassurance in the fact that his back arching and arm movements may go away. If they're linked to the medication, they may stop.

Chapter Six

Wake up, survive, broken sleep ... repeat
(September-October 2015)

Eliott

Mum doesn't seem very happy. Dad rushed home from work again yesterday because she couldn't stop crying on the phone when she called to give him an update of our day. And today he is staying home with us. We're going to see Henry, and as usual, there's a lot to do between packing my bag, getting me dressed and ready, checking we have all the medication, and feeding before we leave the house.

Henry says he's sorry to hear that I've been unwell, and that Mum and Dad had such a big scare. He agrees with Mary that the levels were too high for me but says the results from yesterday came back and they were too low. He'd like to increase them again, but certainly not as much as they were before the weekend.

Then Henry plays a bit with me, looks at my head, my legs, my feet, and says that I am doing well, but he doesn't know where the back arching might be coming from. There's a possibility that the condition I have, whatever it is, might be causing it.

It is so hard!

Maman

We barely have time to think about our appointment with Henry before Francette, Ced's mum, arrives in Sydney —

89

she's going to stay with us for a whole month. I'm so grateful for the extra support.

Ced leaves the house early Wednesday morning to pick her up from the airport. He gives me a concerned look before he leaves, but I assure him that I'll be okay. The past several weeks have been tough, and I haven't been coping. But today, I assure him that it will be fine. Surely I can manage while he's away? Eliott isn't due to wake before 7am — when I give him his medication. We changed the schedule again.

Eliott wakes a little early today, so I have time to give him a feed before the 7am dose. At least we're starting the day nicely, no waking him and trying to give him the doses that he's starting to hate. He feeds well. He no longer arches his back; it's been almost a week since we've dropped the medication levels, and we've seen a big difference in his mood and his muscle tone. He's not as irritable and doesn't get as stiff when we carry him; he looks more comfortable overall.

This morning's feed is so calm, and it's such a boost to my morale to see him like this and for us to connect.

But 7am arrives, and when I go to give him his medication, he starts to cry and pushes me away with his little arms. And then he throws up! He hasn't even taken the medication and has thrown up all the milk.

With the worst timing, Ced calls to say he's in the car with Francette, and I'm on speaker. He sounds so joyful.

'Hey, I've just picked Mum up, so we'll be at home in about twenty minutes. How are things at home?'

I can't even try to hide it. I look at Eliott in his vomit-stained pyjamas and down at the stained carpet and start sobbing. 'Oh, he's fine, but he just threw up. It was such a good, relaxed feed. And now he's thrown up all my milk. I hate these meds. I just hate them.'

'Claire, I'm so sorry. I know it's hard. Has he had his meds now?'

'Yes, I gave them to him after he threw up. He took them

90

fine. I'm still in the process of changing his clothes and cleaning the room. And I need to take a shower.'

'Don't worry about the room. We'll be there shortly.'

Once I've changed him, I decide to feed him some more. I stroke his hair and his little cheek gently, and he manages to get some milk, which makes me feel better.

When Ced and his mum arrive, I still have vomit everywhere, and Ced takes over.

Francette, in her usual cheerful self, gives me a big hug, regardless of the vomit still on my clothes, and looks at Eliott like he's the world's most wonderful baby. He's her fifth grandson, but she manages to make me feel like he's her first. She takes Eliott in her arms and tells me I should take a shower, as she'll clean up with Ced. I sigh in relief and do as I'm told.

For a few minutes, I relax in the shower, knowing that help has arrived — at least for a month.

The rest of the day is great, and there are no other medical appointments scheduled for the rest of the week, which feels relaxing. Eliott is back to his usual happy and chilled self. I'm amazed at Francette's ability to resist jet lag, as she's up cleaning windows and skirting boards a mere few hours after having landed. Eliott is happily watching her from his bouncer.

Ced and I have decided that we should start introducing a regular bottle to Eliott. We've had so many ups and downs with breastfeeding, that at this stage it just feels like the right solution. It's been a great way to connect with Eliott, and knowing that I was able to do my best to give him my milk has helped me cope. It gives me a sense of having some sort of control over the situation.

That afternoon, when Ced's at work, Francette and I go to a pharmacy to buy formula. The choice is overwhelming, and we settle for one that has an enticing packaging. It's organic, so surely it must be a good choice. He tries it for his afternoon feed and loves it! A whole bottle swallowed easily. Part of me is sad that there's not more fighting, but it's a welcome change to have it easy sometimes.

However, when we give him a bottle again the next day, he throws it all up. And then again the following day. I'm concerned and call Mary.

After hearing all the symptoms, the fact that he's still arching a bit, and the throwing up, she suggests giving him anti-reflux meds, just in case.

Not another medical condition ... please not reflux!

Today is a big day for us. We have Eliott's first routine EEG. I'm so stressed about it, but Francette is coming with me. Henry mentioned that he'll be in the room next door working and will be able to give us the results almost immediately, which is reassuring.

This EEG is different from the EEG he's had before, where they had portable equipment they brought to the NICU. This time, we're back as outpatients, and entering this testing room feels more like a medical appointment.

We get Eliott ready, and even though nothing is painful, the paste they use to stick the leads on his head is cold, and he doesn't like it. Quickly enough, he's screaming the whole department down. I try to shush him, sing to him, but nothing will do. Finally, we manage to get him ready.

The EEG process starts, and I give Eliott a bottle of my milk to help him fall asleep. Unfortunately, I have to wake him ten minutes later because the operator needs to test Eliott's photosensitivity. He's going to flash lights in his eyes and see if it triggers a seizure.

I'm scared, properly scared, but it all goes well.

Francette is waiting for us outside and gives me a smile and a subtle nod to ask if everything is fine.

'He didn't have a seizure during the flashes. We just need to wait for the neurologist now,' I say.

We wait for about ten minutes, long enough for me to change Eliott. As I'm walking back from the bathroom, I see Henry walking out of his office — he's wearing his familiar colourful pants.

He gives us a huge smile, takes Eliott into his arms to say hello and asks me how it all went.

'He was a bit upset at the beginning but then settled down,' I say as we follow him to his office.

'I could hear you were not happy about the EEG,' he says to Eliott. 'You have a strong voice.'

I feel bad knowing that everyone could hear him cry. At the same time, he's only three months old and has had so many EEGs, blood tests, MRI, scans, etc. He's allowed to be unhappy and complain.

Henry has seemingly read my mind.

'Don't worry about it. He's allowed to tell us he's not happy. It's good that he didn't react to the flashing lights. Only a subset of people with epilepsy are photosensitive, but we needed to check. Let's look at the rest of the EEG,' he says, handing Eliott back to Francette, who is eager to give her cherished grandson a cuddle after his test.

I too look at the multiple horizontal lines with spikes and annotations of what Eliott was doing at the time. I recognise one of the notes the operator put up in the beginning, where the lines are all over the place 'crying'.

That makes sense.

'It's a normal EEG; it's the best he's had,' Henry says with another huge grin.

I've been praying so much to hear these words, to hear that there is improvement, that one thing in our lives is normal and there is hope for the future. I am so happy that I walk towards Henry and give him a massive hug.

He's clearly a bit surprised but hugs me back. 'I'm happy for you. We'll keep monitoring him, of course, but this is great news.'

I start packing up, ready to leave, when Francette reminds me to ask Henry about Eliott's eyes. They look like they're wandering and are often crossing. I tell Henry about it.

He says, 'It's probably nothing, as a lot of babies do that.'

But as if Eliott knew we needed to show Henry, his eyes start wandering.

Henry notices and says, 'Ah, I understood it was only the one eye, but both is more concerning. I'll refer you to one of my colleagues who's an ophthalmologist.'

Another doctor!

I make an appointment with this new doctor for the end of the month. Because we have a referral from Henry, and Eliott is so little, they're able to fit us in quickly.

It feels like it's never-ending — every time we get a victory, there is something else that happens, which brings us down.

Eliott

I'm starting to have better days, and it's nice to feel more relaxed. Ever since Mamie Francette arrived, we've had less appointments. I've really enjoyed spending more time at home and going for longer walks in the pram. We used to have up to two appointments each day — this week, however, we only have three in total.

The weather is so beautiful that we go on a picnic in the park; it's a thirty-minute walk from our apartment. I like being in my pram. I'm still in my bassinet, so I can see the trees when I look up. Mum, Dad and Mamie Francette are talking about how good the last couple of days have been, but Mum's a bit worried that I haven't put on as much weight this week, and that I'm still throwing up.

We saw Mary yesterday. Mamie is saying that Mary seemed happy with my progress, and Mum agrees. Maybe she's worried about nothing.

They're talking about the picnic, and about whether they could stay out and let me nap in the pram, when suddenly Mum gasps. 'Oh no, the Phenytoin! We left it at home. He's got to have his 3pm dose!'

'Don't worry about it. You guys keep going. I'll run home and get it,' offers Dad.

Maman

It feels like the days are finally starting to turn into weeks. We're still living day by day, but we have fewer medical appointments. We're even stopping Topamax this week, and we're starting to think about travelling, even looking into going back to France for Christmas to introduce Eliott to our families.

Instead of having medical appointments for Eliott this week, I'm the one with an appointment at a family centre to talk through the support they can provide us. I've heard nothing but good things about them, and during the hour, I do my best to open up to them about my struggles. I share everything, again. From the uneventful and healthy pregnancy to our last traumatic hospital stay, and the most recent challenges with feeding, settling and sleep. We have all the normal changes parents must learn to deal with, along with all our extra complexities.

The lady asks questions along the way. While Eliott is drinking his bottle, she watches him interrogatively. Maybe she knows why he's drinking so slowly.

After his feed, I change him, and as he's lying there, she suddenly sticks her finger in his mouth.

'What are you doing?' I ask, my tone probably not as polite and calm as I'd intended.

'I'm just checking to see if he has a tongue-tie. He was drinking this bottle very slowly.'

'But you should have asked me first. No one has ever talked to me about a tongue-tie, and we had some lactation consultants in the NICU and again at home. Plus, you don't stick your finger in a baby's mouth like that.'

She's taken aback and doesn't seem too impressed to be told off by a mum, let alone one she's been asked to assess because of her baby's medical needs.

'I'm sorry. I should have mentioned I was going to check,' she says.

I can't help but think that 'telling me' you're going to do

it still isn't exactly the same as 'asking' ... but anyway.

She continues, 'But I do think he has a tongue-tie, and that would explain why he's unsettled while you feed him. So, I'm going to give you the details of a great surgeon.'

I start to cry. *How is it that every time we see someone new, they find a new issue?*

She looks at me, crying over what she must see as a very common issue, and sits me down. 'Look, let's talk about the outcomes of our chat. I think you need to see a psychologist. I know you said you see someone privately, but I can imagine it's expensive, so I'm going to make appointments for you here. You can come more often, and it will be covered. How does that sound?'

'Okay, thank you,' I say, still sobbing.

'I think you have postnatal depression (PND). You're not coping. You're seriously depressed. You'll need weekly sessions.'

When we leave, I can't talk. Francette sits quietly in the car as we drive home and offers to look after Eliott for a bit so I can take a nap.

Lately, Eliott's been going to sleep before Ced even gets home. He doesn't nap well during the day so gets tired before 6pm, and often we do a feed around 5pm, then bath, then a quick top-up and he falls asleep at the breast. But today, he has a long nap in the afternoon and is awake when Ced comes home. It's lovely to see how happy he is to see his dad.

When Ced asks me about the appointment, I feel a heavy weight on my shoulders. Getting a PND diagnosis isn't making me feel better about it being recognised, as I feel like I've been put in a box. Ced says it's a good thing I can go every week. I can keep seeing Donna if I need to, and then see the psychologist at the family support centre more regularly to help with more day-to-day management.

Having access to weekly sessions is a blessing, but I feel like I'm not the person he married anymore. I used to be a

96

fairly positive and enthusiastic person, and now I'm crying all the time, barely holding it together. I am still hopeful about the future, but I can't seem to see the path forward. Tomorrow scares me.

Maybe I do have PND.

'And she thinks Eliott might have tongue-tie, so we need to make another appointment,' I add.

'What? What's that?'

'It's when their tongue can't move properly because the bit of skin underneath is too short. That might be why he's unsettled when he feeds.'

'But why is that coming up now? No one has seen this before. Let's ask Ewan or Mary next time we see them.'

Eliott

Today, Mamie Francette suggests we go for a walk and take it easy.

Mum took me to see another physio (I don't think she was impressed with the first one), and this new one has given me exercises, which I have been working hard to do.

Mum has even put a little headband on me; she and Mamie say I look like a mini tennis player.

Today, Mum puts a toy just above my chest, so I reach up with my hands and grab it! I'm so excited, and Mamie and Mum applaud.

Maman

When we see Henry next, he's thrilled to hear that Eliott is now starting to open his hands and grab toys. He still thinks Eliott might have a mutation of his KCNQ2 gene, the disease he and his colleague suspected when Eliott was in the NICU, but we're waiting for the results of the genetic testing to confirm. We won't get them back for a few months. In the meantime, all the symptoms fit.

When we first heard that name, I investigated KCNQ2

and found that what seemed like a random set of letters and a number formed a disease name. K is for potassium. CN for channel. Q is the subfamily, member two.

Some patients with KCNQ2 have a benign form, so Eliott could have this and still be okay. He may even outgrow the seizures.

Henry tells us he would like to wean him off medication completely. Eliott's been doing so well, it's worth a shot. If he doesn't need the medication, if there's a chance he might grow up fine with no long-term effects, then we all agree it's worth trying.

It would be so amazing to not have to give him medication anymore.

Could this all have been a bad dream?

I feel on top of the world, more positive, and more energetic.

The next day, I have my first psychologist session at the new centre. It's another person, so I have to go through everything ... again. I also find I have to take Eliott in the room with me, and I am uncomfortable saying everything in front of him. I end up stating facts without speaking to how I feel.

It's a busy week because we also have our appointment with Mary on the Friday. Last week felt so much easier with only one appointment. It makes me challenge whether I need to see that new psychologist every week, given it hasn't helped one bit.

The appointment with Mary goes well, but I talk to her about how best to get around the fact Eliott is still fighting most feeds.

Night-time feeds are relaxed, and both our favourite moments. He's usually smiley, cooing, and feeds nicely. Day-time feeds have become horrendous, and the reflux medication hasn't really made any difference. The formulas we've been trying have all been disastrous too – we've tried four. Once again, I feel at a loss with what to do. Lots of kids with complex medical conditions such as epilepsy and low muscle tone have feeding issues.

Mary suggests Eliott may have a dairy intolerance. I'm still breastfeeding, so she asks me to stop all dairy and swap to a lactose-free formula for the one bottle we give him. We also start giving him a heartburn medication, in case it's bad reflux. Stop one med, start another. It's relentless.

At least we stop Topamax on Sunday.

While the new heartburn medication is important, it doesn't need to be given at exact times. Even if we were to forget it one day, it wouldn't be too bad, unlike the anti-epileptic drugs, so I'm less anxious about it. The number of alarms set up on our phones is reducing. It feels good to know our lives are slightly less controlled by the clock.

After such a busy week, we have quiet one. We manage to go to mothers group again, and things feel a little easier. I've only been a few times in total and haven't connected with anyone from the group.

However, having some slower weeks has given me the opportunity to experience what other mums might be going through. I now have other things to talk about other than hospital stays and doctor appointments.

I can take part in chats about formulas, feeding, settling, and people are starting to talk about going back to work — when they might go back, full-time or part-time, day care or otherwise. It's stressing me that we're going to have to think about this soon, but it's also good to start thinking about next steps.

We finally book our flights to go back to France. We've planned that Eliott and I will fly to France early December, so I can make the most of being on maternity leave. And most importantly, Eliott will get to spend more time with everyone. I'm glad I can stay longer. Ced will join us for

Christmas, and we'll fly back together before I start back at work in January.

Eliott

We have an appointment with a new doctor. I don't like having to go to a new place again, but Mum tells me it's for my eyes.

After a thorough examination, he can't find anything. I am not surprised; my eyes are feeling a lot better than they were. I hear the doctor tell Mum that we should come again in six months and to call immediately if it gets any worse. I also hear Mamie Francette say that she too has noticed that my eyes are better.

It's been nice to have Mamie stay with us, as she has helped Mum a lot, and they have been having fun dressing me up in funny clothes. I have a new outfit every day. I don't think I need to wear them, but I like it. On a nice sunny day, they even put something on my face that makes everything look grey!

Maman

Francette has been so helpful over the past few weeks. She's been patient and supportive and has listened to me and tried to find solutions to issues, while at the same time helping me see past some of the hurdles. She's shared our joy when the EEG was normal and assisted me with all the new daily physio exercises.

But she's also made a point of making sure Eliott was wearing all the cool clothes that I'd bought for him in anticipation of his birth, and all the ones she brought over. It's a bit frivolous, but it makes us laugh and lightens everything else.

The family is also pleased that we're making the effort to dress him and that he's wearing all the presents they lovingly picked for him. When the weather gets warmer and the sun gets stronger, we even buy him sunglasses and take a picture of him smiling in his pram with them on.

On Saturday, the day before Francette leaves, Ced's organised to go with his mum on a whale-watching cruise early in the morning.

Initially, I said I'd stay home with Eliott to feed him. But the morning goes well, so at 9am, I decide we should surprise Francette and Ced.

'Come on, my love, we'll wait for Mamie and Papa at the wharf for when they get off the boat. What do you think?'

Eliott coos back at me, and we take the bus to the city. We arrive at the wharf just as Ced and Francette are about to disembark.

They've had a great time and are surprised and pleased to see us.

When Francette arrived, I was a mess, and now I'm managing to get Eliott across the city on the bus on my own. We go for brunch in the city and have a normal afternoon. It feels like stolen time after everything we have been through.

Chapter Seven

Losing everything, again
(October-November 2015)

Eliott

I'm four months old now and more aware of my surroundings. I'm not taking as much medication, and I'm feeling better. It's been good to be more active and alert and play more with Mum and Dad.

I have a lot of trouble going to sleep during the day though. Usually, I sleep one cycle of forty minutes. So, to help with my day sleeps, Mum puts me in the pram and walks a lot; sometimes we walk for hours.

It's so pleasant, but I know she's tired. It's not easy for me to adapt to all the new sensations, and we still have a lot of appointments, which means it's tricky to get used to a new routine.

Today, Mum is swimming at a local pool. It's sunny, and I stay with Dad while she's in the water. She's happy when she comes out, laughing and telling Dad that the water is chilly, but she loved it. Everyone is relaxed and happy, and they agree that swimming should become our new weekend routine! I love it when they smile at each other and laugh together.

Maman

We've had a few good days with lots of progress on Eliott's development. Francette was over the moon when I called

her to say how well Eliott did in his latest physio session —
she helped with his exercises so much when she was here.

But feeding — again — is getting more challenging.
Eliott doesn't like the new lactose-free formula, and the
throwing up is out of control. I've tried it myself, and it
doesn't taste nice, so I'm not surprised he doesn't like it. It's
a success when he drinks more than 50ml.

I'm worried he's not getting enough nutrition. He still
gets my milk two or three times a day, but I wonder if this is
enough. He hasn't been gaining weight for a couple of weeks
now either. I remember those early weeks when he was
putting on so much weight; I was proud and kept joking that
it was all my good milk.

We think that some of the problem could be related to
weaning him off the Phenytoin. Perhaps he's experiencing
withdrawals, as these are strong drugs, and it's a big change
for a newborn. We're seeing incredible progress with his
development. It's like he's suddenly more awake and aware
of everything, but it must be overwhelming for his little
body.

It makes me feel awful for putting him through this, but
I keep telling myself that at least we should be done with it
soon enough, and that gives me hope.

Based on the weaning plan that Henry gave us, we
should be done with Phenytoin soon. That would be life-
changing for us all — no more waking up in the middle of
the night for the midnight dose.

It's Sunday, and while getting ready for my friend Julie's
baby shower, Eliott is fussy; we're both having a hard time.
I'm feeling really stressed today, and Eliott's probably
feeling it. I try the breathing exercises Donna gave me. And I
try to be positive; however, seeing Eliott so unhappy is
making me feel horrible.

I am looking forward to the baby shower and want to be
there to celebrate Julie and her baby, but at the same time, it
hurts so much to be attending. It reminds me of my own only

a few months ago. Obviously, at the time, I had no idea that our lives were going to be turned upside down like this.

My friends made it such a special day. They organised lots of games, baked cakes, and one of them had printed a huge banner that read: *Welcome baby boy.*

My close friend Sophie had got in touch with both Mum and Francette and had recorded videos of them giving us baby-related advice. It was better than I could ever have imagined.

I vividly remember the smells of all the cakes, the laughter from everyone, and the horror stories told by my friends who were already mums: leaky nappies, sleepless nights, teething. It made us laugh at the time, because everyone goes through it, and these experiences are part of being a parent, but it's all worth it because you have a gorgeous, loved and loving, healthy cherub.

I'd been given advice around resting when the baby is resting, looking after myself, and knowing that we all do our best and 'they', the babies, grow up fine.

I was happily naive and ignorant.

How could I have imagined what was ahead of us?

I force myself to put on my shoes. Eliott is still in his pyjamas, so I guess we must pick our battles. I put him in the baby carrier, and we walk down to Julie's.

I helped organise the baby shower, so I know about the games, the food, and the guest list. I know half the guests as well and am confident that it's going to be a safe environment, but still, it's going to be tough.

They live down the street from us, so it only takes us a few minutes to get there. I am especially grateful for that today, as it's raining. It's not heavy rain — which would have given me an excuse not to go — but a little drizzle, which shrouds me in sadness as it reflects how I feel. I'm still mourning for that normal parenting experience.

I wanted to give birth and go to the postnatal ward with my baby. I wanted to sleep when my baby sleeps. I wanted to only see the doctors to check on my baby's weight and height.

When I get to the bottom of their apartment building, I'm almost crying. However, I pick myself up and decide that I can't ruin Julie's baby shower. There will be no crying today. I give Eliott a kiss on the top of his head and ring the doorbell.

An hour into the baby shower, Eliott is hungry. No wonder, as we spent the morning trying every kind of milk we have, him fighting and refusing to drink anything. So, I go to Julie's spare bedroom, soon to be the baby's room, and start breastfeeding.

'Eliott, my love, we're both struggling today, but we're not at home. I need you to be good, please. Mummy is trying hard. I didn't bring any bottles, and we only have the breast. Do you want to try it? We can stay here as long as you want. Take your time.'

To my surprise, he actually drinks and has a long, relaxed feed. Shortly after that, I call Ced to ask if he can come and pick me up, as everything is starting to feel too hard.

I then go back to the living room, give Julie a hug, congratulate her again, and wave goodbye to everyone. We managed to stay for two hours, but that included one full hour in the room feeding. Still, I'll take it as a win.

In the evening, Ced and I decide that giving him the formula is too hard — everyone gets distressed, and we've had enough of giving him things that he dislikes. I've already dropped a couple of feeds a day to introduce the bottle, so going back to exclusive breastfeeding will be hard work, but that will still be a lot easier than the constant fighting over every feed.

Back to exclusive breastfeeding it is!

And somehow, breastfeeding feels easier than it has ever been before. Maybe he's just happy that he doesn't have to drink that formula again!

Eliott

At the end of the month, we have a weekend away with George, Charlotte, their baby Iggy, and George's mother who's visiting from France. Mum and Dad have been talking about this long weekend away for a while, and everyone's really excited to go.

We've decided that Mum and I will leave on the Friday afternoon with baby Iggy, Charlotte and George's mum, and Dad and George will meet us in the evening. It takes almost the whole day to get to Jervis Bay. It's only three hours away, but between packing the car, picking everyone up, driving, and stopping for our bottles, our lunch, my medication ... it takes a while.

It all goes well though, and both Iggy and I manage to sleep in the car. When we get to the house, Mum gives me a tour and we settle in. Charlotte and Mum give us our dinner — well, a breastfeed for me — we have a bath and a play, and then I have another quick feed and go to sleep.

This weekend was meant to be the last time I have my afternoon medication, but we skip it. We're outside on a walk when I need it, and when I look at Mum and Dad, expecting it, they laugh and say, 'That's it, Eliott, you're not getting it today!'

When we come back from the weekend, Mum and Dad are so happy; it's fabulous to see them more relaxed. We're also getting more sleep because we don't have to wake up during the night for my medication, and Mum doesn't have to wake me for my afternoon dose when I'm napping. It's such an amazing change. I can sleep when I'm tired and not be woken up to drink that pink syrup anymore.

Mum talks a lot about going back to France for a holiday. Mamie Vero has sent us a little parcel with gifts: a beanie, scarf and little mittens she's knitted for me for our trip, as it will be cold when we're there. Mum's excited! She wants me to meet the family and her friends.

It will be good to meet new people; I have cousins I've never met, and uncles, and an aunt, and even three great-grandparents!

One week, Mum signs us up for something called GymbaROO. She says it's like a gym class for babies. We go with Mum's friend Julie for the first one. Mum is impressed by some of the exercises, especially when she has to turn me upside down.

I like the teacher; she's super energetic, and she explains that it is important to move me around in every direction. After all, she says, I just spent nine months doing somersaults in Mum's belly and then being upside down.

I really enjoy it, so Mum is convinced it must be the right thing for me!

The next day, we finish the week by meeting some of Mum's friends, Julie and Leonore, and my friend Luna — Leonore's daughter — who's a year older than me. They look after me while Mum goes for a quick swim. It's lovely to see friends and go for walks without having to worry about appointments or medication.

Maman

After the challenges of the past few months, it feels like we're catching a break. The weekend away was great. We had such a lovely time. Eliott was relaxed and slept and fed well. George's parents are both doctors and have been helping us since Eliott was born.

His mum, who happens to be a developmental paediatrician, spent a lot of time with Eliott over the weekend, and she mentioned that he was catching up. It's such a miracle to hear this. Of course, she can't give us complete assurance, no one can, but hearing such positive comments from someone who knows what they're talking about is amazing.

We are hopeful. Maybe I can finally let go of that dream I had of what the first few weeks with him should have been. If the future is looking positive, if he gets better and has normal development from now on, then it really doesn't matter. I know I can get past this.

One of the most difficult things to grapple with since Eliott's birth has been the uncertainty about his future, and all the extreme emotions of the past few months. The ups are really high, and the downs are the lowest I've ever experienced in my life. On the one hand, we are positive that it will all be well, but at the same time, it still has been so hard to manage the withdrawal symptoms that come with the drop in medication.

Throughout the next week, I'm trying to preserve the positive feeling we had following the weekend. If I focus too much on the day to day, I must admit to myself that everything is still hard.

Mary has suggested that we start Eliott on solids. He's old enough at five months old, and perhaps milk just isn't enough for him. That could help with the weight gain.

This is a big step.

The introduction to solids is a milestone, and I want to do it right. Food is important for us, and I endeavour to make sure we pass our love for food onto him.

We're not foodies, but we both love to cook and bake, and we have a true passion for fresh produce, colourful dishes, flavours and textures. I have this vision of Sunday afternoons cooking dinner and baking cakes with Eliott and peeling and chopping veggies for our weekly meals.

So, Ced and I decide that we'll start on the weekend so we can both be here, and in true French fashion, Eliott is going to try a homemade puree of carrots for his first meal.

The first Sunday in November, we explain to Eliott that he's going to try his first puree. We show him the spoon, the bright-orange puree, and give him another spoon to play with so he can hold onto something. He's clearly wondering what's happening and looks at us expectantly.

To our delight, he loves it! It is so much fun to see his little face light up when he tries it, and then he wants more, and more, and more. He eats three spoonfuls in total.

I still keep a note of everything: sleeps, food, nappies, weight and, above all, medication. I like to keep track, so I know how he's doing. I also do this to make sure I can quickly identify any allergies if he starts developing symptoms, but I also want to make sure I'm introducing a variety of foods and veggies, as well as different types of cereals, such as baby rice cereal, and nuts.

I feel that giving him good nutrition can only help his overall wellbeing. After all, don't they say gut health is key?

We quickly go from a few spoons of carrots, beans, sweet potatoes, potatoes, broccoli, to adding rice cereals, almond meals, and some fruits. I cook a lot and freeze it in small portions. I even try more unusual things like beetroot, cucumber sticks, and peanut butter. Eliott develops a love for lamb, which neither Ced nor I eat. He just doesn't like chicken so far.

At our next consultation with Mary, she recommends seeing a gastroenterologist, to check if Eliott has a dairy allergy and if that's why he isn't taking much to the milk. I'm not super impressed that we have to see yet another specialist, but we make an appointment for later in the month.

The day of our appointment, the specialist is running late, and Eliott is hungry and grumpy. I've given him some milk, but he wasn't that interested. He's thirsty, but he still can't manage to drink from a sippy cup; he doesn't understand that he needs to tilt it.

As he keeps playing with my water bottle, which has a straw, Ced just opens the top of the bottle and sticks the straw in his mouth. 'Go, baby, you can do it like Mummy, just sip, try to sip the water through the straw.'

And to our surprise, Eliott starts sipping. The look on his face is priceless — it's a mixture of surprise, happiness, and just a little bit smug.

When we see the doctor, he keeps making jokes and wants Eliott to do a high five. He asks the usual questions — we're now so used to it that we give him the full overview.

He's happy to hear that the introduction to solids is going well, and he's not concerned that Eliott hasn't put on weight at all last month, given he's already at a healthy weight. He says he looks healthy from a growth perspective and is alert and smiling, so he's not worried.

Ced asks him about the possibility of a dairy allergy — he's always so good at steering the conversation back to our immediate concerns. The doctor suggests we could probably stop the heartburn medication, which is a big relief. However, he also says that babies with dairy intolerances or allergies tend to develop allergies to other things, such as soy, egg and gluten.

Given he's still breastfed, the doctor recommends I stop eating these foods to prevent the allergies from coming.

What? Go off all those foods when we don't even know if he has an allergy?

Ced puts his hand on me, as he can see I'm about to cry, and he asks when we should start re-introducing dairy, and what the process is for testing. He wants to know if we can test first before making another drastic decision.

Eliott is in my arms listening to everything. Maybe he understands that we're talking about food. He's been loving it, so perhaps he's truly understanding and interested in the subject. *My sweet, clever baby.*

The doctor says there really isn't any tests, so we may have to wait until he turns two or three before we try.

By this stage, I'm getting emotional and can feel the tears.

Ced asks why we couldn't just do a test now, given we're not even sure Eliott has a dairy allergy.

'I guess you could try to give him some dairy, and then see how he reacts.'

That all sounds less than scientific.

Ced and I are both annoyed by the time we leave. I am deflated, as once again no one can give us clear answers. I start saying that I will give up all those foods if it makes Eliott feel better, but Ced suddenly says, 'That's enough!' He bends down to look at Eliott in his pram. 'You're getting yoghurt as soon as we get home!'

It's late when we get home, and I don't want to introduce new foods too late in the day in case he does have an allergic reaction, so we decide to try the next day … and he immediately loves yoghurt, but more importantly, he's completely fine. Ced was right, we just had to try.

One small victory!

It demonstrates that we may have to challenge doctors more, and we should feel confident in asking questions and probing. If Ced hadn't asked the question about testing one more time, we would have blindly followed the advice to cut all those food groups off and waited until Eliott was two or three!

Our next medical appointment is the following Monday. In just one week, we will have seen two new types of doctors. Given Eliott has a risk of a developmental delay, and he hasn't been good at responding to sounds, we go to the hospital for an audiology test. The results are inconclusive; they tell us that we'll have to come back, so I make the appointment for March.

Even though we're going back to France for a long period of time, I realise that I won't be the one taking Eliott to this follow-up appointment. I'm returning to work soon. I love my job, and a big part of me is looking forward to going back, but I feel like a completely different person than when I left, and I've been in a bubble for the past six months.

There I was, pre-baby, thinking I would keep in touch with my colleagues and keep abreast of industry updates. I thought I would come back ready to have it all: a fulfilling career and a happy home. Now I'm finding myself hoping I can make it past the first day without crying when people ask me about the new baby and motherhood.

Ced's decided that he'll take more paternity leave, and his work has been flexible enough to allow him to take six months off. He wasn't planning on it initially, but he feels that Eliott needs more time with us, and he wants to be a full-time dad to support him. It will be amazing for their bond, and good for Eliott to be at home a little longer before he has to start day care.

I'm also relieved that I can go back to work knowing that they'll be together and Ced can take Eliott to his medical appointments. Plus, we don't have to worry about the logistics of managing work and day care drop-offs and pick-ups while I get back up to speed with everything. What a luxury!

We're now only two weeks away from flying to France. The suitcase is ready with everything — I went completely overboard and bought a lot of winter clothes for Eliott to make sure he's comfortable and warm when we're there. In my carry-on, I've packed all the lovely things Mum knitted him, so he can wear them when we land.

We only have to give him 3.5ml of the Phenytoin twice a day. Considering we went up to 7ml three times a day, it's a drastic change. Henry also advised that we could start dropping the other two doses by 0.5ml every week until we get to 2ml. Then we can stop altogether, as this will be low enough that he'll effectively be weaned off it.

The big risk with weaning, is that if the drop is too sudden, then the body can react by triggering the effect that the medication was preventing. In our case, that would mean triggering seizures, just by removing the Phenytoin (and all the others before). This is because these drugs are so powerful and impact how Eliott's brain works.

So, we've followed Henry's plan to the letter to make sure this doesn't happen. And so far, apart from the mood swings, every time we've dropped the doses, and the subsequent withdrawal in the first few days, the seizures haven't returned. Henry thinks that he may have outgrown them.

We are excited by it all!

Eliott

Just a few days before we're due to fly to France, we go for a walk with Anthony and Julie and their new baby Lila, who's just a few days old. She's almost as heavy as I am already!

That evening, I'm a little hot and have a cough. There are quite a few babies sick at the mothers group, so I might have a cold like them. I'm a little tired, but Mum and Dad don't think too much of it.

Maman

At 5am, we wake to the sound of Eliott screaming. We rush in and find him having a seizure. We call an ambulance, but when they arrive, Eliott is resting. Following our usual plan, they take us to the hospital.

When we arrive at the ER, we repeat Eliott's history for the doctors. I keep thinking that they should have all our information in their records. The staff ask whether he is up to date with immunisations, which he is, and they ask if there are any other concerns, allergies, medication.

So of course, we mention the medication, and how we're weaning him off, and the possible dairy allergies and potential reflux.

We ask for paracetamol, as he's still boiling hot, but the doctors focus on the reflux and ask a lot about it. They want to know whether this episode could have been reflux. But we're adamant — no, it's a seizure. Unfortunately, we've seen too many before — no matter how much we want it to be something else, we both know what it was.

I'm worried about what this now all means, the fact that it could have happened on the plane, how it might indicate that he hasn't outgrown seizures. Thankfully, we can see Henry and his team later today.

We ask for paracetamol again in the morning, as Eliott is still hot, but it's a full-on day, and hours pass without him getting it. When he falls asleep for his morning nap around 9.30am, he looks so small and vulnerable in the large hospital bed.

His body twitches a little, but it's not too concerning. It looks like the movements people get when they dream, or when cats or dogs move their legs because they're dreaming of running. While I stroke his warm forehead, we wonder whether he will ever get paracetamol.

Suddenly, he opens his eyes and fixes them to the ceiling. He's seizing again.

I scream for help and jump to my feet. I put him on his side, stroke his hair, and tell him it's all going to be okay. I don't know what else to do; there isn't anything else I can do!

Ced asks the nurses and doctors to come, and they all come rushing. They start timing the seizure. And this time, it's not stopping. His body is stiff, head turned to the side, bright red. And it's still not stopping.

He keeps arching, gets stiff, and his legs pedal a bit. He's also having difficulty breathing and makes a guttural noise. I then notice his lips turning blue, and the rest of his face becomes a pale yellowish colour.

I hear one of the nurses asking us what he's been admitted for.

I scream back, 'Seizures, we're here for seizures.'

From the corner of my eye, I notice someone standing back, looking at the clock, and another one writing numbers down, making calculations on a pad and drawing medication.

At the five-minute mark, one of the doctors asks, 'We're going to give him emergency medication, are you okay with us doing this?'

I can barely nod and manage a sobbing, 'Yes.'

Within seconds of receiving the medication, Eliott's

whole body relaxes. He's asleep. We take him in our arms and give him a cuddle. He's still boiling hot.

Just as the doctors and nurses start asking questions, his body stiffens again — another seizure. It stops, but shortly after he has another one, and another, and another. He can't get out of them on his own — he's clustering, which means he's having multiple seizures in a short period, leaving his little body no time to recover.

He's swiftly moved to the resuscitation room and given another dose of the emergency medication. The doctors are struggling to put an IV in his arm; his body keeps arching, is stiff, and he keeps seizing, over, and over, and over again. There are now about ten or fifteen doctors and nurses around him — one is watching the time and taking note of everything, one is trying to put the IV in, whom I scream at because he's hurting my baby.

There's all these doctors and nurses, but no one can make it stop.

Ced and I are on the bed, watching Eliott's body, which looks like it has given up. We ask someone to call the neurology department, so Henry and his team can come.

Finally, they manage to get an IV into him. Then someone from the neurology team arrives and instructs the ER doctor to give Eliott 10mg of Phenytoin per kilogram.

That's 16ml!

The maximum he has ever been given in a single dose was 7ml. And because he is still seizing, they instruct to give another 5mg per kilo, which is equivalent of another 8ml.

That's a total of 24ml!

After an hour in the resuscitation room, once the Phenytoin has finally kicked in, the seizures stop, and he falls asleep.

However, the seizures might have stopped, but his body is full of drugs, and we are scared for his life.

A few hours later, the doctors sit us down to discuss what happened.

We are told that what Eliott experienced was called a

115

'status epilepticus'. It's a life-threatening condition, and because he has just had about thirty seizures in one hour, it's worrying. This means that when he wakes up, he could be a completely different baby, or regressed so much that all the milestones reached so far could simply be lost — maybe forever, or possibly with the hope that they can slowly be regained.

We were so lucky to have been in hospital when the status epileptics started. However, we will probably never know what the long-term effects could be. We just must wait for him to wake up and recover a bit.

If the ambulance hadn't taken us to hospital, or if we had been sent home earlier, it would be a completely different story. In fact, I painfully realise that it likely would have been the end of the story.

Scariest of all, is the fact that it could happen again.

Some people have epilepsy but always come out of their seizures on their own; they're all brief and don't impact their cognitive abilities. For others, every single seizure can be life-threatening, and it looks like Eliott might have ended in that latter camp.

We will need to be trained by Elody, the epilepsy nurse who trained us before we left the NICU, to be able to administer the emergency medication should we ever need to. It's called Midazolam, and it's an effective but dangerous drug. It relaxes the muscles, so it stops the seizure quickly, but it doesn't prevent them from coming back. And it could send Eliott into respiratory distress if too much is given.

It's not difficult to administer — it's simply a syrup that needs to be given in his mouth between the gum and the cheek — but the dosage is specific, and we would have to be careful not to give more than one dose. It also means that from now on we must always carry this emergency medication with us.

We spend the day in the ER, but at 5pm, Eliott is still asleep, and we need to see Elody, so we're admitted into hospital. They want to keep us under observation. Eliott is a neurology patient, so we're in the neurology ward, where only one bed is left in a room with five other patients.

A teenage girl is in the bed next to Eliott's and she screams a lot. Eliott's sleeping on my lap like he has been all day, and Ced is next to us.

Elody finally comes and shows us how to administer the Midazolam. I can't stop crying. She asks about our upcoming trip, and I admit that I'm now far too afraid to go on such a long flight by myself. Ced is also anxious about the flight, and we are thinking of cancelling.

A bit later, Mary arrives. She's not working in the hospital today but has come in after her day of consultations to say hello. She's extremely reassuring and says we've done everything right. However, I can't help feeling like this could all have been avoided if we had pushed more to get paracetamol because he was so hot. Mary, on the other hand, says that unfortunately there was probably nothing else we could have done.

We tell her that he wasn't given any paracetamol and the doctors didn't take us seriously — they thought it was reflux.

What do we have to do to be taken seriously, given he was already admitted for seizures a few months back and started his life in NICU?

Mary is a little concerned and says she's going to talk to the doctors in the ER.

She believes that the trip home to France could be good for us, as it would be beneficial to be near family, and as she says that, I start crying again. I already know deep down that we're not going back. I can't take that risk, and when I look at Cedric, I know he's thinking the same. Beyond the realisation that I won't see my family, I also realise that I must call them to tell them what happened, and that we won't be heading over to see them.

When Henry and his team come to check on us later in the day, we tell them the news, and Henry agrees that it's a reasonable decision. He also says we must increase the medication again and go back to 7ml twice a day. It's a hard thing to hear, especially given we were so close to weaning Eliott off it. He reiterates that what Eliott just had is serious, but he's positive and tells us that it doesn't take away the hope that one day he may outgrow seizures.

Elody comes back soon after and says we've been moved to a different ward, which only has three other babies, so it will be quieter, and we can get the rest we need.

I call Mum and start crying as soon as I hear her cheery tone on the other side of the line. 'Oh, Mum, something horrible has happened.' I tell her everything.

No one really understands the extent of it, but the status epilepticus condition will impact our life immensely.

When we go home on Sunday, a few days later, we start unpacking our suitcases. We have follow-up appointments with Mary and Henry, and more blood tests. After thinking that we were almost done with the medication — and having the prospect of catching up developmentally, as well as the upcoming holiday, and generally feeling that everything was falling into place — this has now stripped us of our last shred of security.

Chapter eight

Looking for joy in the little things
(December 2015)

Maman

I can't even articulate how I feel. Every feeling of hope has been crushed. Every cell in my body is screaming for it to end. For the pain to go away. After feeling like things were finally getting better, and having spent weeks planning and looking forward to the trip to France, this has been an impossible situation. I feel like I will never be safe again; I will never be emotionally capable of believing in better days ever again. How could I? I am left with no sense of security. Something bigger than us, epilepsy, has taken over our lives.

I'm not coping after that last hospital stay. Eliott could've died on that table. And the realisation that from now on, every seizure could end in a similar outcome is daunting.

I can't sleep, I can't eat, and I can't smile. But we must somehow keep putting one foot in front of the other. We have a tiny baby depending on us, and I'm still breastfeeding, so I must keep going or he won't get what he needs. I don't have the luxury to stop.

Every time I talk to Mum, I can't help asking her why — as if she could give me an answer, as if something, someone could explain what went wrong. My own religion and belief system doesn't give me any sense of understanding as to why and how this could happen to us.

How could we go from being a happy couple excited

about starting a family to where we are now?

I have a rational mind, which throughout my life has been an asset, except now, when I can't process any of it.

How could this happen when I did everything right during pregnancy?

Of course, Mum can't provide me with any answers, but as usual, she listens and tries to comfort me however she can. She knows that there isn't much to be said, so she keeps telling me she loves us more than anything, that Eliott is beautiful, and she wishes she could do more to help.

Eliott

I haven't been sleeping well over the past couple of days, and it's been hard for everyone. I still don't know what happened to me, and I don't understand why Mum is putting all my winter clothes away — she's crying a lot when she does. She was so happy only a few days ago when she was telling me about our trip to France, so I don't get why she's putting everything away.

Today I heard her speaking with Mamie Vero over the phone. She was talking about our trip, her maternity leave and how it's not what she thought it would be. Maybe she doesn't realise, but I'm slowly beginning to feel like myself. It's hard, though, as I can feel the medication fog again, but I can do the things I was doing before we had to go to hospital.

Maman

A couple of days after we left the hospital, Mum calls me.

'Look, darling, your brother and I have had a chat,' she says, sounding very serious. 'And I've discussed it with Grandma and Grandpa.'

'Is everything okay?'

'Jean-Mi and I have booked our tickets today; we're coming to spend Christmas with you.'

I cry, happy tears, as it feels like a weight has been lifted.

'Oh Mum, that's incredible. Thank you so much!'

'We can only stay for two weeks, so it will be a short trip, but we really want to be with you.'

This is an incredible gesture, and at this stage, I really need Mum. The fact that they would just drop everything, again, and come to the other side of the world is extraordinary.

Eliott

Mamie Vero and Uncle Jean-Mi are going to spend Christmas with us! I'm excited to see Mamie Vero again, and to meet my uncle, even if we're not going to France to see him. Mum and Dad have also told me that with the change of plans, they've decided to try and take two months off to go to France for my first birthday. It seems to make them more relaxed to have made that decision, and I'm happy to know that we haven't just cancelled the trip because of what happened. We're going to go later.

That same day, we go to the doctors because I'm still coughing, and Mum is worried that my cold isn't going away. Everything is fine and there isn't anything that can be done for a cold, unfortunately, so I just have to fight it. We also must go to hospital for a blood test, and we see Elody, who is there with another patient. It's a joy to see her.

Mum asks her about a rash I've developed after that last hospital stay, and Elody sends us to the ED to get it checked. Everyone is very reassuring, so we eventually leave.

I missed all my naps today, so Mum puts me in the pram, and we go for a walk so I can have a good sleep.

When we see Mary the next day, she's happy that I've put on weight this week: 400 grams!

I'm also teething, which isn't much fun! But now that I've got two teeth, Mum gets me a toothbrush. They say I must be even more careful with the pink syrup, because one of the side effects of the medication can be tooth decay. More scary words. I really like the toothbrush, and I brush my teeth with Dad in the morning and at night. I like the funny feeling on my teeth and my gums ... I also like chewing my toothbrush!

This weekend, we also try bottles again because Mum is going back to work soon. I don't mind this first bottle.

I'm also excited that I can now grab my feet! These things are quite amazing! They keep moving, and I see them when I'm lying on my back. And now I can grab them!

Maman

The past few weeks have flown by. Eliott's started waking up a few times a night again and is still not napping, so it's been really tiring, but we're holding up because help is on the way!

I feel the constant worrying is building up again, and neither Ced nor I are sleeping. Every time Eliott moves in his sleep at night, I'm on my feet, scared that he's having another seizure. I'm constantly teary and keep wondering if this is what post-traumatic stress disorder (PTSD) might feel like.

Eliott is back on higher doses of Phenytoin, and I can see his little body trying to adjust to all the changes, but I also notice that he's more affected by our mood. He seems anxious when we're anxious, sad when we're sad, and most importantly, happy when we're happy. I start developing this mental image of what his brain might be doing when he's happy. When he laughs, I visualise his neurons connecting, and this gives me hope. It feels like he's woken up from the status epilepticus the same baby, and I know I can be grateful for that, especially given we were told many times that it may not be the case.

We've had good weather lately, but today it's raining, and we can't do much but stay home and take it easy. I've been trying to get the house ready for when Mum and Jean-Mi arrive later in the evening. And when I put Eliott to bed for his afternoon nap, I'm expecting him to sleep for his usual forty minutes.

However, he sleeps for a solid two hours. Maybe it's the cooler weather, the gentle noise of the rain, and the muffled sound of the cars on the street. I even manage to cook his dinner, finish getting the house ready, and lie down for a bit before he wakes up.

When Mum and Jean-Mi arrive, Eliott seems excited to see Mamie Vero and meet his uncle. He's intrigued by the tall man who looks like him: same hair, similar eyes, same smile. But Jean-Mi has a beard that's itchy when he kisses Eliott, and there's surprise in Eliott's eyes every time he does it — which is often. It's also clear that Jean-Mi is smitten. He loves his nephew, and I love my brother even more for unconditionally loving Eliott.

Mum's suitcase is full of 'stuff' for Eliott. Between French baby creams, shampoos, toys, books, clothes, I don't know if she has more than two or three t-shirts and a pair of shorts for herself! Eliott is happy to see everything. He's curious about the new toys. And he looks proud when he shows his mamie all the new things he can do, the skills acquired through so much hard work over the past few months.

Drinking from his straw cup is one of the biggest changes, and he genuinely seems pleased with himself when she says proudly, 'Wow Eliott, what a big boy you are! You are drinking from your water bottle. You're not a baby anymore.'

We spend the first few days visiting local areas and parks. I appreciate being able to take our time and just wander around.

Ced also suggests that it's time to drop another day breastfeed so that we can keep working towards me going back to work.

I've read that you can drop one feed every three or four days to give everyone time to adjust. Eliott seems to enjoy it when Ced gives him his bottle — Ced makes funny faces, and they giggle after it. Mum is also helping, and he takes his bottle with her too. It feels like Eliott just needed the extra time, an extra couple of months of exclusive breastfeeding.

It's a relief that this re-introduction of the bottle is going so well. But I'm having a difficult time emotionally, which some of my friends warned me about — dropping feeds can impact hormones and make you feel like you're going through the 'baby blues' all over again. The trouble is, I don't know what the postpartum baby blues feels like. I sometimes make the joke that my body didn't have any time to consider baby blues when Eliott was born, so maybe this is what I'm experiencing now: full-blown baby blues with a six-month-old baby.

Either way, I'm not managing. I like the idea of dropping feeds, as it gives me the opportunity to do other things. I even spend one day with Mum, and we go for a swim together. But instead of feeling 'free', like I did when we dropped the first one in the initial weaning attempt a few months back, this time I feel like something has been taken away from me.

It's as if Eliott still needs me and I'm not there for him. I know he doesn't need me, and he's loving the extra time with Ced and Mum, but my whole body is aching for that contact with him. I'm emotional and having mood swings: happy one minute, about to curl into a ball the next.

So, we reinstate a feed and decide to try again in a few days. Everyone is understanding, but I can tell that Ced is concerned now that the date has been set for me to go back to work. Luckily, we still have a few weeks ahead of us, so he gives me space and time.

As a surprise to Mum and Jean-Mi, and to thank them for coming to spend Christmas with us, we've booked a house north of Sydney. When I booked the house, I told the host that my family was coming from Europe last minute. The lady was sweet and even offered us an extra night for free. A stranger paying it forward. We leave a few days before Christmas.

Just as we are about to drive off, I see the post office truck and shout, 'Stop!'

124

I had ordered a wetsuit and a little vest for Eliott so he can go in the water. I'm overjoyed that we didn't miss its delivery.

Everyone in the car, including Eliott, is looking at me like I'm crazy. But Ced obviously notices that this makes me smile — it's Eliott's first Christmas, and it's important to create happy memories, which will no doubt consist of splashing about in the pool. They all understand that this tiny and, on-the-surface, insignificant detail is important to me.

The house is magnificent! It's big, and everyone has their own room, including Eliott. It's such a change, given that Mum (on the sofa bed) and Jean-Mi (on an air mattress) are currently sharing the living room in our apartment!

We don't do much over the next few days, just make the most of the house and swim in the pool — which is, indeed, quite cold, so Eliott doesn't stay in for long but seems to enjoy it, proudly wearing the wetsuit. We go for a long walk in Seal Rocks, put Eliott in the baby carrier, and visit the lighthouse. Jean-Mi and I even go for a quick dip in the ocean. It feels like stolen time.

Eliott

I really like my first Christmas. Everyone sings, and there's a lot of cooking. I get to try new food; many pictures are taken; we swim in the pool. And we open gifts. I have some clothes, books and toys. Everyone is joyful. Maybe we should do Christmas more often!

Mum even bought me a little costume, so I'm dressed up as a mini-Santa with a white and red beanie. And they all wear a similar hat; it's funny! Theirs have lights that flash red on and off ... I like watching them.

When we're back in Sydney, Mamie and Jean-Mi visit the city, and Mum and Dad spend time with me at home so I can rest. One morning, Mamie and Jean-Mi look after me so Mum and Dad can go for a run together.

Maman

I haven't been for a run in so long, and I miss it. Mum has offered to look after Eliott a couple of times during her stay, and now that I've finally managed to drop that second feed while we were away, the timing is right. I'm scared to leave him, even for a few minutes.

Except for my swim at the local pool, when Eliott was with Ced, I haven't left his side for just over a month — since he had his status epilepticus.

Ced and I agree that it's important that we get back to normal, or at least our best version of normal so I show Mum how to give Eliott his medication in case he has a seizure.

We only go for a short run around the block, and it feels so good. It's hard, and my legs and lungs hurt, but I experience a feeling of freedom. A few times during the run, Ced looks at me and we smile — it feels right. Every aspect of what we're going through is hard, and I feel like I'm drowning, but we have each other. Not just Ced and me, but Eliott, Mum, Jean-Mi, our families and friends.

We're running back, and Ced is challenging me to finish strong and run just a bit faster. I can't, so I smile at him and make a sign indicating that there's no way. And that's when I see it — an ambulance is parked in our driveway.

We still have a good 400 metres to go, and I learn that I can run that bit faster, if needed. When we're about fifty metres away, we realise that the ambulance is parked in the driveway two buildings away; the paramedics aren't there for Eliott. I break into tears from the scare. I am still a bit emotional when we go back into the apartment.

When we walk in, I see Eliott on his mat having a nice time playing with Mum. I'm still shaking but relieved. Learning to let go and trying not to think of the worst-case scenario at every instant is going to take time.

A few days later, Jean-Mi, Ced and I are planning to go to the movies one evening. Mum is happy to look after Eliott on her

126

own. I show her the medication again and can tell she is doing all she can to look confident. She clearly wants us to be able to go out and enjoy some time together. But I also know she's stressed and anxious about what would happen if Eliott had a seizure. It's one thing to be there with Jean-Mi to help, but she'll be on her own tonight.

She likes to be prepared for everything, so I've written the instructions down again, and I can see her mentally rehearsing.

I appreciate that she's anxious about being prepared, and I know she still feels guilty she didn't react well the first time he had a seizure at home. She's apologised so many times, and I've reiterated that it wasn't her fault; Ced and I know that no one can anticipate how they will react in emergency situations.

Thankfully, Eliott is good all night; he sleeps well, and the next day, we're ready to celebrate New Year's Eve!

We go to the beach for a walk in the morning, have brunch together, and in the afternoon meet up with our friends Jasper, his wife Daniella, and their son Anton, who's just a little older than Eliott. One of their friends has lent them his apartment, which has an amazing view of the Sydney Harbour Bridge, so it's incredible to celebrate the new year while watching the fireworks.

Everyone has a spectacular time, and the fireworks don't even wake Eliott. At midnight, we all wish each other a happy new year and leave to go home.

Mum and Jean-Mi are flying home the next day. Unfortunately, the two weeks have gone by too quickly, and before we know it, Mum and Jean-Mi are boarding their flight back to France.

It's been so good to spend time with them, for Eliott to get to know his uncle, who he now adores, and Ced and I are more relaxed. We have regained some confidence and positivity, and we are enthusiastic about the trip to France in June.

Chapter nine

Planning for the future
(January-March 2016)

Eliott

It is the start of a new year, and I'm seven months old! After a great break with the family, we go back to our routine. Mum says it's not really going back to normal because she only has one month left before she goes back to work. She's going to go back three days a week for the first month, so we can all adjust. And while she's at work, Dad will be here to look after me. We're going to have a lot of fun together.

Not much happens in January. We have the usual appointments with various doctors, and I manage to roll from my back to my tummy. I've been able to turn from tummy to back for a couple of months now, but I couldn't do it the other way.

One weekend we go to the pool for a swim with George, Charlotte and baby Iggy, and I love it. The pool is warm, and it's delightful to be in the water and play with Mum and Dad. We all agree that we must do it more often!

My sleep is still a bit of an issue. I can't nap well, and in the evening I'm extremely tired from not sleeping enough during the day. So, we walk a lot, as I fall asleep in the pram more easily, and it's lovely to have the quiet time and enjoy the good weather.

Mum still feeds me occasionally to help me go to sleep, and Dad is worried because he won't be able to do that when she's at work. I'm now eating cucumber and broccoli, and

I'm starting to hold my spoon during mealtimes. Mum says it's good for my hands, and I have fun.

On another weekend, we go to a barbecue with the mothers group so the dads can meet each other. Dad has heard how good and how tough it's been for Mum, so we decided to go together.

When we get there, Mum introduces Dad to the other mums and says hi to all the dads. But I'm not interested in playing with the other kids, as I prefer to look around, observing the new house. Mum has prepared some lunch for me — zucchini with some cumin — and it's the first time I've had spices. It's yummy. I eat my apple puree for dessert, and Mum is happy that I'm eating well.

But the truth is I'm not feeling that well. And I can tell that Dad isn't feeling well either.

Maman

Ced isn't handling the barbecue well. It's painful to see how hard it is for him. It's the first time he is confronted with a room full of other babies who are the same age as Eliott, but who are all behaving quite differently. I'd warned him that it would be challenging, but also told him that the group has helped me feel more normal. Sometimes, we share similar issues, and it helps to hear they're all going through the same things.

Some of the mums have been meeting outside of our group weekly sessions, and I'm envious of the bonds they're forming and the experiences they're sharing. I was hoping that going to the barbecue would help me form stronger bonds with some of them. But I don't think Ced anticipated how bad it would be, how 'fluid' and effortless everything looks for them, and how hard and 'clunky' it feels for us.

After being there for only forty-five minutes, Ced approaches me. 'Can we go home? It's too much. I just can't do this.'

I look at him, smile, and pack our bags. We say a quick goodbye to everyone — who all ask if we're okay — and then we leave.

When we get home, we load the pram and go for a walk, just the three of us. Ced is quiet for the rest of the day.

In the evening, Eliott eats a good dinner, has his milk and falls asleep. But after thirty minutes, we hear a noise in the monitor and run to his room. We get there just in time to pick him up as he starts throwing up. We give him a cuddle, clean him up, change his pyjamas, sheets, everything, and then give him some water. But he throws up again. He just can't seem to hold anything down. He looks so unwell.

His Phenytoin dose is due at 7pm, so we try to give it to him in small amounts. At least he seems to be able to hold that down. But after ten minutes, he throws up again. We're at a loss with what to do and decide to go to hospital. The doctors have always said that it's important for him to take every dose on time, and we've never missed any. We know that being sick or unwell probably makes him more susceptible to seizures, and we're anxious about missing tonight's dose.

It's close to 9pm by the time we arrive at the ER, so I see the nurse at the admission desk, then the triage nurse, while Ced is parking the car. It's our first time coming through the ER ourselves, not in an ambulance. I wish I could be anywhere else.

Both nurses say that we can wait, as Eliott doesn't look too unwell — and they don't budge even after I tell them about his status epilepticus episode, and how he can't miss his dose of medication.

When Ced arrives, I give him Eliott, and the nurses ask us to see the triage nurse again. Eliott is so tired and looks like he's about to faint. When his head falls back a little, and then onto Ced's shoulder, the triage nurse thinks he's having a seizure and rushes us through to the ER.

As we walk through the doors, I feel the panic. The room has become too familiar in only a few months.

130

Ced's convinced it wasn't a seizure, and I trust him. Every seizure has been similar in how they've presented. Eliott is just exhausted now; he's missed bedtime, has been throwing up all night — of course he lost his head control a bit and wanted to rest on Ced. I am so scared of the status epilepticus, but I trust Ced more than anything.

The doctors say they'll have to put an IV in to give Eliott his dose of Phenytoin. However, they then mention that they're concerned about the seizure he just had and want to give him a loading dose.

Now, that's a big step!

So, we insist that they give him tonight's required dose only.

Later in the night, Eliott is still vomiting. The doctors ask about the last few days — where we've been, who we've seen, what he's been eating. But no one has been sick. Ced and I are fine. So, we're admitted on the ward again. That same ward. For the second time in a few hours, I wish I could be anywhere else.

We're placed in isolation because they don't yet know what's wrong. Isolation makes it easier for us to sleep, even with the constant beeping machines. I suspect Eliott just has gastro. We saw another baby for a playdate on Friday morning, who had had gastro the week before.

The doctors, however, don't agree.

The next morning, we see the neurology team. Henry is away, but the head of the department, who we also know, comes in with her team. She's heard about the debate we had in the ER about the loading dose and is curious to hear more. After telling her our version of the events, she agrees that if we're sure it wasn't a seizure, we were right to refuse it.

We're pleased to hear that, but we're shocked. If we had blindly trusted the doctors, we would have been pushed to make the wrong decision.

I start to think about all the times we've been to the

hospital, and I feel guilty that I didn't trust my gut instinct in many of those situations.

The doctors on the ward still feel that Eliott has something other than gastro. They test for a blood infection, a urinary tract infection, and for gastro. The gastro test will take a couple of days to come back, but everything else comes back negative.

Eliott

I'm not feeling much better today. Each time Mum feeds me, she is covering herself with towels in case I throw up, which I do every time. She says that the doctors are worried about what I could have caught. I don't have diarrhoea, and Mum and Dad aren't sick.

In the evening, I start to feel better and can hold down a little milk.

Mum and Dad are told that we'll have to stay an extra night to make sure I can feed before we are discharged. And suddenly, the diarrhoea arrives; however, apparently it's good because now everyone agrees it's most likely gastro, and even Dad starts to feel sick. I've got those little onesies that can be buttoned up from the front, and Mum keeps saying we're lucky Mamie got a couple for me! It's easy to get off! She's going to buy more when we get home!

We spend another night in hospital, and the next morning when the doctors come to do their morning rounds, there's a new paediatrician. He notices that we're tired and want to go home, so he suggests something different.

If Mum and Dad feel comfortable with this approach, they'll leave the tube for my pink syrup in my arm, put a big bandage over it, and we can go home. And then if I'm feeling better, I can come back only to get the tube out, or if I'm not better, they can easily give me medication.

Mum and Dad are happy with this.

When we get home, we all lie on Mum and Dad's bed in their room and fall asleep within minutes.

The next day, we go to hospital to take the tube out. They also have the test results: it was gastro!

First gastro done and dusted!

Maman

Eliott is eight months old now, and I'm due to go back to work next week. I've been taking the time to sort his room, as there are a lot of toys he's no longer using, and he's outgrown all his baby clothes.

I've also been working on his routine, to make sure that it's back on track. I'm now giving him bottles during the day and breastfeeding only in the morning and at night.

We have five doctors appointments this week — some for me, but most are for Eliott. One is with Henry, who we haven't seen since November.

He mentions that he'd like to introduce a new medication for Eliott, explaining that if Eliott continues to need medication in the long term, having something with a better side effect profile is preferable.

Henry says that it would only be for a couple of months, so we have another treatment option. We will try to wean him off Phenytoin again, by then Eliott will be close to turning one and hopefully won't need any medication at all.

Lamotrigine, the new medication, is similar to the Phenytoin in terms of acting on the potassium channel. And while it does have a better side effect profile, it comes with one big caveat. One of the most common and dangerous side effects is a bad skin rash. If you have the rash, you must stop taking the medication. Henry wants to make sure we understand this. So, we say that we'll look it up online. Henry laughs because he knows we've been trying to read as much as possible to understand what's happening to us.

We also talk about Eliott's development, and Henry asks if he's able to sit up yet. He's not. We've been letting Eliott learn to move, sit, and do these gross motor skills by himself, rather than forcing it to happen. It's meant to be better because babies learn at their own rhythm and their body's strength builds up. The GymbaROO lady has been advocating for this, and I really like the philosophy behind it; he needs to learn to put weight on his arms first and then prop himself up to a sitting position.

It's a good theory, except that he's not yet doing it on his own. And he's now at risk of missing the milestone for sitting independently. Henry suggests that we should try to sit Eliott up so his muscles get stronger. Henry can clearly tell that I'm disappointed and is very gentle. He asks if we can try and see if it works, at least.

It feels like I'm being stripped of every one of my mothering decisions. But I know that what's important is that Eliott sits, and the earlier the better. I'm still pondering all this when the genetics team arrive. Henry pulls the interim report, reads it, as I'm sure he's already done a few times after receiving it, and puts it back down. He looks at us and says it's not KCNQ2.

But I thought that was the most likely issue?

Henry admits that he doesn't understand it either, but the lab that ran the results has tried two different methods to check for a variant of the KCNQ2 gene, and it came back with nothing when using both methods. For better or worse, nothing at all shows up on these results. As usual, it's a good thing because that means it's not a potentially serious disease that we know of, but it also means that we still don't know. We're back on the diagnostic hunt.

I do feel relieved, however, as everything I've read so far about KCNQ2 isn't all that positive, but Henry says KCNQ2 could have been okay, as it's on a spectrum. Some kids have a benign form, so there was hope that Eliott could have that. But now it could be anything. It could be something already discovered, or not. It could be deadly, or seriously debilitating, or it might not be.

Ced softy takes my hand in his, as Henry continues,

'Unfortunately, we still suspect a genetic epilepsy, even if the technology doesn't allow us to prove it at this stage.'

I'm trying to think ahead. *What does it mean?* I know Eliott has been stable since November, and we must see how it plays out for him. But Henry is not telling us about the next steps.

'Henry?' I risk. 'When can we test again? When will we be able to find out?'

Henry turns to his colleague, Daniel, letting him speak about his area of expertise.

'Well, given we just did the epilepsy panel, that means that at this stage, the scientists don't know any other genes causing epilepsy. They're discovering new genes every month. That being said, it's unlikely we'll want to retest before three to five years because the chances of finding something would be too low before then.'

My ears are buzzing. *Three to five years of not knowing? Ced is quiet, why is he so quiet?*

'Do we know if it's coming from us?' Ced suddenly asks.

'No, we have only tested Eliott, and we haven't found what is causing it, so we don't know,' Daniel replies.

'But you had our blood, couldn't you test all of us?' I ask.

'We did get your blood, but we decided to do the epilepsy panel only for Eliott so we could get the results back quicker,' Daniel explains.

Henry starts talking again. He's not smiling, and he genuinely looks sad. 'Ced, you asked a good question. Unfortunately, we don't know if it's inherited or not at this stage, which means you could pass it on if you were to have other kids.'

'I don't want to go through this again,' I say.

'Neither do I,' Henry replies. 'If it's a disease like KCNQ2 that's on a spectrum, having another child with the same condition means that he or she could have a better outcome than Eliott, especially now that we know which medication works, but you have to know it could also be a lot worse.'

I look at Eliott sleeping in his pram. We can never get this baby to sleep, and now he's asleep. I don't want another child with this same condition. I can't go through this again.

135

When we drive home, Ced asks, 'How are you feeling? What do you think about that conversation?'

'Oh, I'm okay. I mean I don't want to sit him up, but I guess I just have to get over it. Like everything.'

'Hmm, did you not hear what Henry said?'

'Yes, it's only one approach, and I know it shouldn't matter. But I'm still attached to things like that. I will let it go and make sure I sit him up at times, I promise.'

'No, Claire.' He's looking at me, then the road, then me. He looks really concerned.

'What?'

'Did you hear what he said about the fact that we don't know what is causing it, and what it means for our family?'

'Yes, I can't go through this all again. It's just too hard.' I look intently at him.

'Claire, I don't think you're getting it. I don't think you've heard him.'

'What do you mean?' I continue, and now just feel like I've missed something big, and I don't know what.

'That means we can't have other children.' Ced's hand is searching for mine.

And it finally dawns on me.

My brain had blocked this.

But now the fog is clearing.

Ced is right. It's one thing saying I can't do it again, but the only way to avoid it happening again is to never have any other children.

The image that I've been holding on to for as long as I can remember, the picture of our family — three gorgeous, healthy kids running around and giggling together — is gone.

'Oh no, you're right. Oh no, Ced,' I say, and then I burst into tears.

When we arrive home, Ced takes Eliott and his nappy bag and supports me upstairs. I go to Eliott's room, where some baby clothes are still next to a plastic box. I was tidying up this morning, putting baby clothes and toys in boxes for the next child, which we may never be able to welcome into our lives.

Maybe the three of us is all we get. Nothing feels real, and I keep thinking of that nightmare I had the first night back in hospital. When I woke up and realised it wasn't a dream.

Later that week, Brooke, one of the doctors from the genetics team, calls. Eliott's having a nap in his bed for once! She and I have a long chat. She has lots of empathy and takes the time to answer all my questions. She then explains what the results mean for family planning.

She says that unfortunately we don't know what the risks are, but they can be as low as the general population, if this is not genetic epilepsy, or up to fifty per cent, if it is genetic epilepsy and is a disease that only needs one gene of a pair to have a pathogenic mutation. Usually, you only need one copy of your two genes to be fine to function properly, but in some instances, if one of the genes has a mutation, it can be enough for you not to function well. That's very rare, but if that's what Eliott has, the only way to have another baby would be adopting or through in-vitro fertilisation (IVF).

As if that wasn't complex enough, Brooke wants to make sure I understand that it wouldn't be a 'usual' IVF process. She explains that they couldn't do genetic testing on the embryo, given we don't know what to look for, and we would have to get an egg donation, to ensure that at least a full copy of all the genes is 'safe'.

Of course, we can also wait a little longer and do a full genome sequencing as a trio, with both of us being tested as well in a few years, to see if they can find anything.

She then asks me about what our intention was, and when I share that we wanted other children, I burst into tears. For now, looking after Eliott is more important, so maybe waiting is good.

Before we hang up, Brooke makes me promise to give

her a call if we have any questions, or if I get pregnant! This is very important — if I find out I'm pregnant, I am to tell Ced first, and then call her or Daniel. She repeats that I need to tell Ced first, and I realise that she's trying to lighten the mood, and it works a little.

This is so much to take in, so Ced and I start with more research and try to find a way to keep going, telling ourselves that we can always reconsider later. It's so hard to imagine that this is what our family life is going to be, that we will never have another chance, we will never experience what other parents have, what all our friends have.

Every time I speak to friends, their experience is so removed from what I'm living, feeling, and mine often just feels like a dead-end. But for better or worse, life must go on. On the Sunday we go to the pool again because Eliott just loves it. And then, on Monday, I set up my alarm clock, get ready and head to work. Eliott spends the day with Ced, who is officially starting paternity leave.

Eliott

Today, Mum had left for work by the time I woke up. Dad and I have a great day — we go to the playground and for a walk so I can nap. Dad even cooks carrots for my lunch, and we do some physio exercises!

Dad sends a lot of videos and pictures to Mum, and it's great to see her in the evening.

On Wednesday we go to GymbaROO, and I think Dad feels a bit lonely because he's the only dad there, but we have fun together. Dad even starts moving things around in the house. He's taken the full-length mirror from their bedroom to the living room and puts it sideways on the floor so I can see myself when I play. I really like it, and I keep touching the mirror when I see my reflection.

Mum works three days, and then we have four days together. We go to the playground and the pool, so they can

138

swim, and I can dip my toes in. It's great to spend time together. I'm doing my best to eat well, and to make progress, and I can almost sit up without support! Mum and Dad are very excited.

Maman

Going back to work feels different, so different. Up until having Eliott, I felt defined by my work. It's such a huge part of our week, and it had been a priority in my life.

But going back is difficult, and leaving Eliott is hard, even if it helps to know that he's with Cedric. I miss him a lot, but I know he's in good hands. I also feel that it's important for me to go back to work and regain some of my identity.

It's confronting returning to the office, yet at the same time, liberating. I get ready in the morning, and for a full day I get to focus on something else. At least, that's what I thought would happen before I started. In reality, the first few weeks are tough.

I'm still breastfeeding, so my body feels weird, and I can't stop thinking about all the ideals I had before I left the office to go on leave.

Every one of my colleagues who welcomes me back asks me if I had a good time with the baby. How can I say no? Most of them don't want to know; they're asking because it's the usual thing to ask. But, how could I say yes? I can't give them the usual answer, 'Oh, it was wonderful, thanks.' It's still too painful, too fresh, too raw. I can't lie, as I don't have the strength to hide the truth. So, I try to be as honest as I can, without getting the 'pity look'. I want to be open about it, but I'm not ready to be.

Sometimes I share too little about everything, I sound cryptic, and they rightly move on, not understanding how bad things have been. Sometimes I share too much, and I make them uncomfortable.

I get a lot of responses from people who have only good

intentions, such as: 'Babies grow at different rates, it will be fine, don't worry about it.'

And then one day, I realise that I'm not coping well with it at all when I firmly respond, 'You don't know that. Actually no one does. It isn't *fine* for some people, and we don't know if it will be for Eliott.'

It is a wake-up call for me. So, I decide that I need to come up with an equivalent of the 'I'm good thanks, and you?' answer — I certainly don't want to start alienating everyone.

In the first weeks, I also have a chat with my boss and somehow manage to summarise the whole situation. I know I can be honest with him. We've kept in contact and had a few chats over the past few months. I even came to the office with Eliott once during maternity leave, so my boss is aware of the big picture. I tell him about the status epilepticus that happened last November, managing to hold back my tears.

When he asks what he can do to help, I'm honest.

'I'm going to need to take two months off to go back to France. I need to see my family. And we need time to start building ourselves back up,' I say, aware that I literally just got back to work.

'Of course, that's fine. Take all the time you need.'

'We're thinking that we may even consider moving back home. I don't know what the timing looks like, but I'd like to start talking to the French team about a transfer.'

He looks at me, and I witness so much empathy. This man, who has been one of my strongest supporters in the firm, who bet on me all these years ago when he hired me, who has mentored me ever since, who came to our wedding reception, and who was genuinely happy to see me become a mother, is desperately trying to help, and he's clearly hurting too.

'Of course, let me make a few phone calls,' he responds.

We're trying to figure everything out, and to see what our options are.

Eliott

One week, after Mum finishes her three days at work, we go on a plane to a place called Noosa! It's my first time in the sky, and it's very new and exciting.

We drive to the hotel, and the staff are lovely. They've even set up a porta-cot for me in Mum and Dad's bedroom. The hotel has a couple of pools — one for babies, which we go and try immediately.

The next morning, we have brunch in one of the cafés near the beach. I try some of Mum and Dad's breakfast, and then I want more, so Mum orders toast, just for me. It's the first time that we order something just for me and, somehow, it feels like a big milestone.

We spend the rest of the day at the pool, and I watch some teenage boys playing with a ball. They're yelling, splashing water around, and the ball is going up and down; it's so much fun. Mum is filming me and looks thrilled because I manage to stay in a sitting position for a while. But it gets tiring, so I end up lying on my stomach.

It's a joy to spend some relaxed time with Mum and Dad, not worrying about appointments or hospital trips!

But the next day, as Mum and Dad undress me for my bath, they notice that I have a big rash in my nappy area. They say it could be sand, heat, humidity, but they're scared it might be the new medication I am taking.

They call the neurology fellow on call at the hospital, who says it's risky to stop giving me the medication without them seeing the rash, and he recommends we keep going with the usual dose. The doses are low, anyway. We were meant to increase it slightly to build it up, and they say to keep it the same and see them next week.

Mum calls Ewan and lets him know what the neurology fellow has recommended. He explains that the issue with the rash and this medication is that it can be serious.

It's like an allergy, and the rash is the body's reaction. If you expose the rash for too long, or if you stop the medication and start again, that is when you can have a dangerous reaction, which is potentially fatal. If we stop because we think this rash is due to the Lamotrigine, I can never go back on it. So, Ewan also suggests I keep taking it, not increasing it, and that we see him early next week. Mum and Dad put some nappy cream on me and are happy that the rash hasn't spread further.

The next day, we fly back to Sydney. It's been an amazing few days. When we get home, we find that the rash has already started to disappear, and when I see Ewan, it's completely gone. Ewan looks at the picture that Dad had taken of it and says that it was a bad nappy rash. What a relief it isn't the medication!

Maman

During the third week back at work, it is with mixed feelings that I realise that Eliott and Ced will continue creating their own routine while I'm away during the day. I know it will be beneficial for us all though. And soon, I'll be back at work full-time.

Thankfully, I won't have to travel much, and the coming months are still going to be a little bubble outside of what our routine will be once Ced also has to go back to work. In the meantime, I'll enjoy having Ced at home watching over Eliott and taking over for a bit.

My boss has reached out to our team in France to see if they would be interested in my profile, and the partner in France has emailed to organise a formal phone interview. It's an important step to have that first interview, and it makes the decision to move back to France so real.

We've been in Sydney for seven years and never seriously considered going back. But now we've agreed that we need to at least give it some thought. It's been hard being away from our families and having to manage everything on our own. And we're just so, so tired ... all the time.

Not being able to go back last Christmas, when we needed it the most, felt like we were being kept hostage. We have a great support network in Australia, and our friends have been amazing in helping us through the challenges, but it's bittersweet. They've all had a normal experience of parenthood, so even though we exchange on some challenges, for most of them, the worst medical experience they've had to experience is their kids' immunisations.

A lot of people sometimes hurt us with their comments, without realising it. They say things like: 'I don't know how you do it'.

To which my answer is: 'I have no choice'.

Or they say: 'He couldn't have better parents' — as if it should make us feel better that our peers think we're the best people for the job.

I would have been a great mum to a healthy baby too.

Eliott

I am almost nine months old now, and I can hear Mum and Dad talk a lot about 'day care'. They've decided I should go to one near where we live. We visited two different places this week, which was interesting.

The lady at the first one seemed panicked when Mum and Dad told her about my seizures. But a lady at the second one knew exactly what to do — put me on my side and call 000!

When we get home, Dad packs the car for another weekend away! We're going to a place called The Entrance with Leonore, Matt and baby Luna; Anthony, Julie and baby Lila; Sophie, Ethan and baby Chiara.

The house has lots of space and an outdoor swimming pool. It smells a bit weird, like the windows haven't been opened in a while, but after we've settled, gone outside and started cooking, it smells more like it does at home.

The rest of the weekend is fabulous — we go to the pool, we take lots of pictures, and I play with Lila, Chiara and

Luna. I'm more tired than usual this weekend, and Mum has commented on it a few times; she seems a little worried. But we have such a nice time with all our friends — I hope we can do it again!

Maman

Eliott starts his first day at day care with a couple of hours of orientation. We've filled in all the documentation, have investigated creating a seizure management plan and reached out to nurse Elody so she can be the staff's point of contact if they have any questions.

Ced and Eliott go to the centre to meet the room leader who will also be Eliott's key educator responsible for filling in his development book and to be our contact for questions and concerns. All the girls are lovely, and Eliott has a blast. We're worried about him falling and hitting his head, because at this stage we don't know whether that could trigger a seizure, so we tell them to be careful and put cushions behind him when he's sitting. He can still fall back at times, so this way he won't hurt himself on the hard floors. They're all very understanding.

On Eliott's first full day, Ced drops him off around 8.30am and picks him up at 2.30pm, after nap time. The educators inform us that he had an amazing first day and Eliott was our usual smiley baby.

When they send the daybook with all the pictures, it's hard to imagine making a better choice for a day care, as he's obviously loving it. In half of the pictures, he's reading a book, deeply absorbed in looking at the pictures, touching the fabrics and materials, and when we share them with the rest of our family, they comment on his love for books.

It's such a big achievement.

Being separated from him for a day where he doesn't have either Ced or me is tough. It's stressful leaving him with strangers, but we're confident we've made the right choice.

It's also a relief for Ced, who can have a few hours to

himself, prepare Eliott's dinners, organise the house a bit. We sometimes laugh about the fact that I too was in much need of time to rest and do other things when I was on maternity leave, but the truth is that at the time, it felt insurmountable to find a day care centre, especially when life was already so full of appointments, hospital visits, breastfeeding, and general newborn matters.

Putting him in day care for one day a week is perfect for us. It's good for him to get used to being there, and in the Sydney market, we're lucky to have found this place at short notice.

Ced has been looking after Eliott for a month now. It's been good to make the most of my short weeks at work in that first month while we were all transitioning into our new roles. And except for the past week or so when Eliott has been a bit withdrawn, overall, he has been better.

He's always been a super bubbly, chatty baby, and in the past month, he's made a lot of progress; he's more interactive and is now sitting up well. However, in between the wins, such as day care, and the relaxing time away, the day-to-day goings-on continue to be hard. Every milestone is hard fought for.

Ced is also experiencing first-hand that even though dads taking parental leave to care for their baby is more widely accepted, promoted and recognised, it's still rare. He's the only dad in the GymbaROO class, at the playground during work hours, and doesn't have the support of a fathers group.

The delays in Eliott's development are becoming more obvious. We're witnessing this every time we meet our friends, see other children of Eliott's age, and we notice it at day care. At this stage, Eliott isn't getting any additional support beyond the six-weekly physio appointments.

Of course, he has more than his fair share of specialist appointments, but these are to target and address his neurology condition, for his epilepsy. No one is really encouraging Eliott to progress and develop further.

We often look at what the alternative would be in France. And when I ask my friends there, they advise me that Eliott would see a speech therapist, an occupational therapist, and a physio at least two or three times a week.

So, we make an appointment to see Mary. We trust her, and she welcomes us with her usual warm smile and takes Eliott in her arms for a cuddle.

'How are you doing?' she asks. 'Is that a new pram? That looks like a new pram. I really like it.'

It isn't, but I find it a funny comment to make, and I feel instantly at ease and somehow reassured, like every time I come and see her. She's a lifeline.

Ced completely opens up to her. He shares his worries, he shares his loneliness, but most importantly, he shares his concerns about Eliott's development. He mentions that Eliott is more withdrawn than usual, even more so than I realised.

'I'm starting to worry that he may have autism,' Cedric says.

I wasn't expecting this.

Mary turns to me and asks if I'm worried too.

I wasn't really worried, but then not one bit of our parenting journey has gone according to plan, so I feel like I'm always worried about what the next big thing will be. I've observed him being more distant than usual, and I know that autism is one of the biggest co-morbidities with epilepsy.

Mary says that she doesn't think there is any reason to worry at this stage, but she also says that this is something we need to keep watching. 'He's too young for anyone to be able to diagnose this, but we should revisit this around his second birthday, if we're still worried,' she adds.

I feel like the only thing getting me up in the morning is Eliott's gorgeous smile — it makes me want to take him in my arms and tell him it's all going to be fine — and the way he looks at us, the way he seems to be saying that he gets it, and that he's fighting. If the phase he's now in isn't a phase, and if his smile goes away, well, what's left?

Mary moves on to talk about Eliott's development. When we share what we now know about the French system, and that we would like to have a similar level of support here, she explains that that's not how it works here in Australia. She's confident the physio would agree to see us more often, given we're paying her privately. But she does assessments every six weeks to review Eliott's progress, and also gives us exercises and advice, so doing it more often may become counterproductive.

And that's exactly where the issue lies: we don't want more frequent assessments, we want therapy, and we want someone who can help Eliott do the exercises more often. We feel like bad parents having to admit that we just can't do it all — we need more support. Even though everything we do is about achieving the next milestone, it's like we're not doing enough, we're not doing it well enough, and we're losing it.

Mary, however, says he's making so much progress, and that we're doing a fantastic job. She does a mini test of Eliott's abilities and says that at this stage he is a little delayed, probably about two months. Yes, he should be putting weight on his arms to lift himself up, which he isn't and thus can't get into a sitting position by himself, but he's still too young to be properly assessed, and she is confident he'll improve.

She then talks to Ced about how it is normal to feel lonely. 'Being at home with a child is an amazing gift but can be tough and lonely, and even mums go through that.'

I can see Ced disengaging, and I know that he just wants to take Eliott and leave the room. No matter how extraordinary she is and how incredibly supportive she's been, she doesn't know what it's like to walk in our shoes. She's missing the point, and she's failing to see just how much we're struggling.

We're faking our degree of coping with everything

because we don't know where to go to for additional, much-needed guidance and support. And when Eliott is safely tucked in bed at night, and the craziness of the day has stopped, we can't imagine what the rest of our life is going to be, because we never planned to have a child with potentially lifelong health issues.

Ced is quiet when we leave. I'm aware he's suffering. I have to go back to work that afternoon, and it's hard not being able to stay, but I'm off the next couple of days, and we'll spend time together before I go back full-time next week.

That evening, Eliott comes down with a fever, so we're once again setting our alarm clocks for every two hours to make sure he's not too hot and not having seizures. He has a good night, and even though we are exhausted when it's time to get up in the morning, the fact that we didn't wake up in hospital makes it all worth it. The feeling of waking up in our own bed feels surreal — surreal that we should be grateful to have lasted another night without calling an ambulance, but grateful nonetheless.

It's a glorious sunny day, so we go for an afternoon walk while Eliott naps. We reflect on what Mary said to us. Ced feels like he's been treated unfairly, like she was telling him to stop complaining. This isn't what she said, but I get it. And I don't believe that there's nothing that can be done to provide more support to Eliott, and that the health system is so closed that no one can assist us. We're willing to find creative solutions — could we do therapy at home, could we do it over Skype? We feel lost trying to understand an unfamiliar system with little support, and we're wasting precious time.

I decide to call Ewan.

'Claire, I'm glad you called. I've been thinking a lot about you guys, as I have a few things I'd like you to consider.'

He tells me about a clinic at the hospital that does developmental assessments. Seeing them is the first step in

148

getting access to the right support. In Australia, going through the public hospital system is usually a better option than private.

'I'd like to fill in a request for Eliott to go there to be assessed around his first birthday. They rarely see kids that young, but given his history, I feel it's important we do that.'

'Yes, absolutely,' I reply. 'Thanks Ewan.'

'I feel this is the best way forward. We'll have to think about other therapies for him as well.'

'Thank you again, Ewan. We need more support, as we feel completely lost.' I barely finish my sentence before the tears start to flood my eyes.

'Of course,' Ewan replies.

I think he can hear that I'm crying now.

'I'm always here if you need me. I think we need to start actioning things, and I'll get on with it. Don't worry about it, and please tell Ced and Eliott I said hi,' he says before hanging up.

I put the phone back in my bag and feel like something big, something positive has just happened.

Chapter ten

Can we ever let ourselves feel hope again?
(March–May 2016)

Maman

It's March already, and we have Eliott's christening tomorrow. It's an important moment for us. We haven't had the opportunity to do it sooner, and because we wanted George and Charlotte to be Eliott's godparents, we've decided to do it in Australia. We're surprised by how well our families in France took it.

I get home from work, preoccupied with thoughts of the bonbonnières that I need to get ready for the next day, and when I walk in, I sense something is wrong. Eliott and Ced are both in the living room — Eliott is playing on the floor, and Ced looks tired.

'It's been a really tough day,' Ced says. 'Eliott hasn't been interacting much.'

When I pick him up, I notice that he's not smiling or looking at me.

Ced then gets up, stretches his legs and leaves the room to grab something from our bedroom. I put Eliott back on the floor, trying to forget about whatever was going on at work, trying to forget that I must finalise all the bonbonnières for tomorrow, and bracing myself for a couple of mentally challenging days at home.

I initially think that maybe Eliott just needs a good night sleep and will feel better tomorrow; he still isn't sleeping well, so maybe he's just overtired. I start playing with him, and Ced comes back to get Eliott's dinner ready.

At this moment, I notice the smallest thing — Eliott's eyes aren't focusing. When I present him with his toys, it looks as if he's not watching them, not interested. His eyes are glazing over. I ask Ced if he noticed anything, and he says no.

I do a few 'tests', and Eliott is definitely not focusing on anything.

Suddenly, it hits me: we've been increasing the doses the Lamotrigine — the new medication we've been giving him. They're small increases, which were meant to be insignificant. So, I go online and check the potential side effects. The rash is the main risk, but blurred and double vision are possible too.

I call Ewan but he's not in the office, so I text Mary, who says it could be a side effect, and to call the hospital straightaway and to talk to the neurology fellow on call.

We're in crisis mode, again.

I leave a message for neurology to call me back and keep doing research and exchanging text messages with Mary. When the neurology fellow calls me back, it's 8pm and Eliott is in bed.

The lady who calls knows Eliott's case; in fact, she says his case is quite famous in their team, and I feel that drop in my stomach every time a doctor says they know Eliott's case. I go over some background and how tonight, I realised he couldn't see.

'Sorry?' she says. 'How can you be sure he can't see?'

'I just do, somehow. Call it mother's instinct,' I tell her. 'I think it's the Lamotrigine, so can we please stop it?'

Her concern is that Henry isn't on call this weekend, and it's a tough decision for her to make without getting his input. She doesn't want to disregard my concerns though. 'Let me get back to you, as I have to speak to someone else before I can make that decision. Blurred and double vision is a side effect, but it's incredibly rare.'

She calls me back five minutes later.

'Claire, we've discussed it with the team, and we have a plan. Let's stop the medication over the weekend. But I want you to give us a call on Monday so we can reassess, depending on how he goes. Give me a call if anything changes over the next couple of days.'

Eliott

Today is my christening. Mum dresses me in a new outfit: grey linen pants with a matching white linen shirt. It's a beautiful ceremony. Mum and Dad look so proud, and we're surrounded by all our friends. It feels very special.

Because the weather is still spectacular, Mum has organised cakes and quiches, and we have a picnic. The picnic area has shade, is right by the beach, and has a playground. I'm not feeling very well, though, and I can tell that Mum is worried. I usually love to see people, and I love smiling at everyone and babbling, but today I'm not in the mood to be around people and want to be left alone. I don't smile all day, and I just feel funny.

Maman

When we return home from Eliott's christening, he starts to vomit. Thankfully, this round of gastro isn't nearly as bad as the first one. Eliott vomits a lot but can take his Phenytoin, and within thirty-six hours he is already clearly feeling much better. We're glad it doesn't last for too long, because we've got the Phenytoin weaning process on our mind.

Over the next couple of days, since stopping the Lamotrigine, Eliott starts to focus on his toys again and look at us with that look I love. The look that shows just how much he gets it, and how cheeky he is. And within a week, we have our super happy, super chatty baby back. It's hard not to wonder what could've happened if we had kept giving him the medication, not making that link.

This drug didn't work for Eliott, but it works for so many others. It sounded like a good option, but it could have been disastrous for our baby.

Now we must face the Phenytoin-weaning process again.

Ced and I are in the living room. I'm lost with my thoughts, recalling the last meeting with Henry when we agreed to reduce the medication again. The plan is to try to start weaning him before we go to France — given we're planning to be there for two months — which means we must start now (we're at the end of March).

During our last consultation in February, before talking about the diagnosis — or lack thereof — and family planning, we'd asked about lowering the medication, and Henry agreed to give it another try. We had an open discussion about the risks of medicating Eliott and how all the side effects are frightening us.

Eliott was progressing so much better when the doses were lower before his last seizures in November. And it has become so hard to give it to him twice a day. The thought of having to do this for the rest of his life, our life, if there is the slightest chance that he no longer needs it, is unbearable.

In our research, we have found that a lot of kids with neonatal epilepsy outgrow their seizures, so there's a real possibility that he no longer needs the Phenytoin. That was our hope when we tried to stop in November and, despite landing in hospital and going through the scariest hours of our lives, we still believe the potential benefits of stopping the medication outweigh the risks.

But Henry was abundantly clear: if there's a relapse, he'll put Eliott back on the Phenytoin for at least twelve months before weening him off it again.

He also warned us about the risk of SUDEP. When you have epilepsy or have a loved one who suffers from the condition, this term is usually all too familiar — it may be one of your worst fears. The acronym stands for Sudden Unexplained Death in Epilepsy. It all comes down to one thing: you may suddenly and unexpectedly have a seizure and not wake up.

We must be ready and accept that without the medication there's a greater risk of this happening, as Eliott doesn't have the protection of the anti-epileptic drug. We're mitigating the risk by the fact that he's too young to ever be on his own, so we would hopefully catch any seizure, and at night when he's alone in his cot, he has a baby monitor with breathing pads, which would catch any 'weird' movements and beep if he were to stop breathing.

In the meeting with Henry, I experienced a strange deja vu, a dream-like impression. In front of me was this smart doctor wearing colourful pants who was examining my chubby nine-month-old. He then looked at Cedric and me and told us that we had to make a decision that meant our baby could possibly die.

However, none of it has ever felt like a decision. It's never felt like any of this was ever in our control.

Ced's voice brings me back to reality, to *our* apartment, to today. 'Eliott's feeling better, and he hasn't had a seizure since November, so I think we can go ahead with the plan to start lowering the doses tomorrow.'

Are we ready? I don't know. I feel like we're doing the best we can, but it's never enough. We know that Eliott is doing better without the medication. He's more alert, he moves more, and he's not lost in his thoughts.

As parents, there is nothing harder than looking at your child who is blissfully unaware of the complexity and gravity of what the adults are discussing around him. To think that twice a day, you are consciously giving him a substance that simultaneously saves his life and ruins it. And he's such a good baby, that twice a day, he looks you deep in the eye and takes his medication without a fuss, because there's no one else in the whole world that he trusts more than you.

I know it is the right way forward, but that doesn't help the creeping anxiety about how the weaning process will go. We're so scared that he might have another seizure. We're scared of another status epilepticus. We're scared of SUDEP. And we're scared of the withdrawal symptoms that Eliott experienced last time.

He's nine and a half months old, and he's older than the last time we tried, so it could be different, but we're just so scared.

This weekend it's Easter, and it's a long weekend in Australia. We spend Sunday at George and Charlotte's, who have a lovely garden. We all smile as we watch Eliott enjoying the freshly cut grass on his little chubby feet. It's a joy for us to be able to spend the time outside in a calm space.

We bring too many chocolate eggs for the kids, and George laughs when he sees us arrive laden down with them, but we have a ball hiding the eggs all over the garden for the two boys to search.

Iggy is about sixteen months old, and he's a very smart baby. He looks for the eggs, shows us all the eggs he's able to find, and is having a blast. It's much harder for Eliott, who doesn't quite understand what's going on. He loves being outside, so we know he's having a good time. He wiggles his little toes in the grass, which at times makes him giggle!

On Tuesday, a week after recovering from gastro, Eliott is sick again and has a big spike of temperature. We lowered the dose again just yesterday. *What should we do?* He started at 7ml twice a day, then we lowered it to 6ml before Easter, and we just lowered it again to 5ml the day before.

Seeing as this is a big and fast change, and he's in such a bad shape from his fever, we decide to increase the dose back to 6ml so his body can focus on fighting the infection or whatever is causing the fever; teeth or otherwise.

It is three very long, very tiring, and very stressful days. But we get through them without seizures, and by Thursday, he's finally back to normal. We then lower the medication back to 5ml on Friday.

The days turn into weeks. We started lowering the medication on Monday, 21 March to 6ml, and just like that, on Thursday, 28 April — a few days before turning eleven months old — Eliott swallows his last dose of Phenytoin.

He is medication free and is a completely different baby. He has started to climb onto furniture and commando crawl. Life's a bit easier. It almost feels like we could start dreaming of a better future again.

It's been a bustling few weeks, during which I'm offered a transfer to the French team. Ced and I discuss what our lives back home would be like: being closer to family and friends, having better support networks, and a better knowledge of the system that we'd need to navigate. But, on the flip side, we've found good doctors here, and work has been flexible; I often start early, finish early, and log on again at night, which seems to work for our family.

We talk to family and friends back home, to George's parents again about what the medical journey would look like, and one concern is that we may have to start over: get referrals, go on waitlists, and lose precious months trying to get into a new routine. A few of our friends also warn us that we should expect less flexibility.

So, overall, we feel that the timing isn't right. Eliott needs all the help we can get him now. As a result, moving no longer seems like the best option for our family, and we decide to stay in Sydney another year at least, while we wait to understand a bit more about Eliott's condition and perhaps get a diagnosis.

Eliott

Mum and Dad are going out tonight. Leonore, Matt, and baby Luna are moving back to France, and it's their farewell party. I have a babysitter coming to look after me. I have a long nap in my pram this afternoon, but when I wake up, I'm boiling hot, and everyone is worried.

156

Mum and Dad give me some paracetamol, take my clothes off, and give me a cool bath. I can hear them on the phone with the family back home, trying to get advice on how to make the fever go down.

Mum cancels the babysitter, and by the time I go to bed, the paracetamol has kicked in and I'm feeling much better.

Mum and Dad have a chat, and then Dad comes to give me a goodnight kiss and says he's happy to see that I'm feeling better. He says he's going to see Matt and Leonore to say a quick goodbye, so I have to be a good boy for Mum.

I fall asleep quickly, but I don't sleep very well — something doesn't feel right. Mum checks on me often, and I feel her welcome cool hand on my forehead. At one point, she moves my arm to put the thermometer under my armpit. I enjoy the cold metal end of the thermometer touching my hot skin. But something's still wrong.

Maybe Mum feels it too, and that's why she keeps checking on me.

After a couple of minutes, the temperature reading is complete, and the thermometer goes *beep beep beep beep ... beep beep beep beep ... beep beep beep beep.*

I feel my body stiffening and turn to the side; there's nothing I can do to control my body anymore.

Mum switches on the lamp. She's touching my back, telling me that it's going to be okay. She's crying when she says, 'Oh, Eliott, my baby, no! I'm here, Eliott, oh baby, please no.'

My body is still very stiff, and just like that, I stop breathing.

Maman

This is one of those life-defining moments.

I'm standing in the dark when the thermometer beeps. I feel Eliott moving, and I know, deep down (even though I'm praying for it not to happen) that he's having a seizure, and I'm all alone with him. I don't even stop to think that turning the light back on may wake him, because I know that he's no longer asleep.

I'm looking at him when his lips turn blue. It lasts two minutes but feels like a lifetime. My mind races, yet I feel calm — like I am having one of those out-of-body experiences you read about or see in movies. My whole body is shaking; however, I've rehearsed this moment so many times in my head that I'm on autopilot.

I grab his medicine. *Why is this happening?*

I grab the foil envelope. *Are his lips still blue?*

I tear open the envelope. *Can he hear me?*

I grab one of the plastic ampoules. *Oh God, please let him live!*

I open the plastic ampoule. *Go faster, his lips are going even more blue.*

I draw the 0.4ml in the syringe. *Please be okay — quick, quick, quick!*

I squirt the liquid in his mouth and wait for him to wake up.

Slowly, his body relaxes, he can breathe, and his lips turn a healthy pink again. It took a very long twenty seconds for the medication to take effect.

I take him in my arms, go to the living room and call the ambulance on the landline. Meanwhile, I dial Ced's number on my mobile. I hope that he will hear me speaking to the 000 people and understand what is happening.

What I don't realise is that he's missed my call, and that voicemail is going to be the most horrible voicemail he'll ever have to listen to.

By the time the ambulance arrives, I've packed our bags and Eliott is sleeping. We drive to the hospital in the ambulance, and Ced bursts into the ER a few minutes later. I erupt into tears, and yet again, we sleep in the Emergency Room.

The next morning, the neurology fellow on call comes to see how we're doing. We're still in the ER, and Eliott has been good overnight. They did a chest x-ray to check whether the fever could be a chest infection, as Eliott's been coughing lately, but it was clear. It was just a normal cough and nothing to worry about. The fever seems to have broken, and he's now having his morning nap.

Henry is away, so the neurologist asks us a lot of questions to make sure she's up to speed and not missing anything. We're tired, scared, emotionally exhausted, and desperate to go home. She's about to discharge us when Eliott's eyes suddenly pop open — he's staring at the ceiling, and within a split second he's having another seizure.

This is what happened in November. Exactly.

We yell for the ER doctors, but by the time they rush around him, the seizure is gone — he's managed to get out of this one on his own.

The neurologist comes back after briefly speaking with the ER team. She looks at Eliott and strokes his hair, then looks at us — at me who's crying, again, and at Cedric who looks like a bus just hit him — and says, 'I'm sorry to say this, as I know you want to take him home, but I think it's unlikely for today. I'm going to ask that they admit you so we can at least keep him under observation.'

Neither of us has the strength to answer, and we give her a faint smile before she leaves Eliott's bedside.

The ER doctor then arrives to check on us. Ten minutes have passed since that short seizure. She looks at Eliott interrogatively, 'Do you feel like he's back to normal?'

'He's usually pretty tired after a seizure, so he may need to rest,' replies Ced.

'But does he look like he's recovered to you?' She seems worried. 'I'm afraid he might still be having a seizure,' she says.

'What do you mean? I don't know. Could he? His seizures are usually tonic. He gets stiff, so they're easy to see.' Ced's watching Eliott, then he looks at me, then back to Eliott.

'I'd like to give him a dose of Midazolam to be sure he's

not having one. Are you okay with this?' she asks.

'Yes,' we both murmur — we're feeling incapable of making yet another decision.

The doctor gives him his second dose of Midazolam in twelve hours.

The neurology fellow finally comes back. She's spoken to another paediatric neurologist, who works closely with Henry and knows Eliott's case very well. Because we aren't aware what triggered the seizures, and we don't know why he had a fever, we're going to have to put him back on Phenytoin. Henry warned us this could happen, and he also warned us that Eliott would then be on it for 'at least twelve months' before we could try weaning him off it again.

Being prepared for it doesn't help. We were so close to being free of the medication.

'How much are you going to give him?' I ask. I remember when he had his status epilepticus, we'd given him 24ml — 15mg/kg — which was a large dose. And the maximum he's ever been on has been 7ml three times a day, so 21ml daily.

This time, they say we need to give him a loading dose, because he hasn't had a proper dose in a few weeks. They give him 33ml — 20mg/kg. This is an enormous amount to go into his tiny body.

We're then admitted to our usual ward, but this time we're in the room with five other patients. It's the room I like the least, as it's always noisy — it's one of the first rooms as you walk onto the ward, so there's a lot of traffic, but they put us at the far corner, and today it's exceptionally quiet.

We see a tall, thin doctor arrive. He has a reassuring aura surrounding him. He shakes our hands and looks at Eliott, who's asleep in the cot. 'I'm one of the neurologists working with Henry. How's Eliott?'

'He's doing better now, but we're worried about what this all means,' I reply.

'How has he been lately, developmentally? The doctors downstairs said he had been sick and coughing. Can you tell me about this?' He looks at Eliott again. 'I'm sorry you guys are going through this, and Henry's in Europe for a conference, but I know Eliott's case well. In fact, everyone in the team does.'

Ced and I tell him how he had been doing so much better than when he was on Phenytoin.

The neurologist is reassuring, speaks slowly and very gently. 'Tell me about the seizure last night. What happened?'

I hold my tears as best I can and tell him the whole story.

'How quickly did you give him the Midazolam? the neurologist asks.

'About one minute altogether,' I reply, feeling like I wasted so much time. 'That's long, isn't it?'

'No, I'm impressed! This is very fast for someone who's not trained to do it. You did well.'

It sounds like a compliment, and he is smiling, but I'm not feeling particularly proud of myself; I still feel that the thermometer triggered it.

The doctor reassures me that there's no way of knowing, and, if anything, I was there with him when it happened and reacted quickly — that's what matters. If I hadn't been in the room to react straightaway, the outcome could have been different.

He tells us that he's going to have a think about what the treatment needs to be going forward, and we'll be able to confirm with Henry as soon as he's back.

As he turns around to walk out, Ced stops him. 'Wait, can we have a think about this?'

I look at Eliott, who's sleeping peacefully in his cot.

Ced shares what he's been thinking about all morning. 'Eliott seems to only have his seizures when he has a fever. Thinking about it, there were the immunisations back in July, then November when he had bronchiolitis, and this time again, he had a fever. But he's also had lots of fevers without seizures, and these ones happened when he was on the higher doses of medication. But he's doing so much better without a daily dose. Could we just dose him when he's sick?'

He's right, I've noticed that too, but my brain has turned to mush, and I haven't been able to properly process the information, nor formulate that it could be part of a management plan.

The neurologist is silent for a while before he replies, 'We have a few patients who manage their condition this way. It's rare and unorthodox. Eliott is a bit young to try this, as his epilepsy was so hard to control initially, so we don't know if it could work. When do you think you would give it to him?'

There is so much hope that we look at each other, and Cedric carefully says, 'We could give it to him as soon as he has a fever. Would that be enough to protect him?'

The neurologist clearly weighs the options. 'Yes, but I feel Eliott is too young to try this method of management. Sometimes the first symptoms of an illness are the seizures, not the fever.'

'But he's been fine without the Phenytoin when he's healthy. And he's been doing so much better from a development perspective. Aren't there more risks to his long-term development by giving it to him when he may not need it?'

'Possibly. Unfortunately, there is no way of knowing this for sure. There isn't a way to run conclusive tests for this.' He pauses, looks at Eliott, then turns back to us. 'You could give it to him at the first sign of a fever. You'd have to be careful, though, and it will require more attention. The risks are also greater. But as long as you know how to react when he has a fever, it could be manageable.'

I can see from his body language that he's mentally formulating a plan.

'We can try it, and if it doesn't work, we can always put him back on Phenytoin. Of course, we'll have to confirm this plan of action with Henry when he's back.'

I'm starting to feel hopeful and scared at the same time. 'How do you know when to stop, or how much to give him?' I ask, trying to understand what this could mean for us.

'We'll have to calculate this based on his weight. If you give it to him for a couple of days, there won't be enough in his blood that you'll have to wean him again, you can just stop. When you're discharged tomorrow, for example, and he's better in thirty-six hours, just skip the next dose. That could be a good plan for Eliott. How do you guys feel?'

How do we feel?

My head is spinning — from lack of sleep, emotional exhaustion, and so much new information — but it feels like this could be a way forward. We could keep Eliott off daily medication long-term and possibly have a shot at a normal(ish) life.

The rest of the day is uneventful. By mid-afternoon, Ced has decided he'll stay with Eliott tonight. I've always stayed with him, as I was breastfeeding, but it's quite draining. Ced says I should get a good night sleep for once. But before that, I should go home and have a shower.

I call Sophie and ask if she can pick me up from the hospital and take me home. By the time we get home, I've caught her up on the latest developments.

When we arrive home, I'm okay, but as soon as I walk past Eliott's bedroom and see everything scattered across the floor in broad daylight, the memories of last night come crashing in. Eliott's clothes are everywhere, the plastic ampoules and the used syringe are in the bed, and I find the thermometer, which I had thrown on the floor in the action ... It still reads Eliott's temperature in flashing digits: 39.3.

I'm on the floor crying.

Sophie comes and picks me up. 'Come on, hon, let's get you ready. I'll clean this up.'

After my shower, I find that Sophie has organised Eliott's room a bit and closed the door. I go in and pick a few things for Eliott, put a bag together for Ced, and grab a few snacks for them. Ced has always prepared snacks and treats when I've had to stay in hospital by Eliott's side, so I know he'll appreciate that I do the same for him.

When I return to the hospital, Eliott is awake. It's almost time for his dinner and bottle, but he's agitated. He doesn't eat much, and when it's time to go to sleep, he's screaming his head off. We don't know what to do, and as the nurse comes in to remind us that his next dose is due, we say we don't know if we should give him more medication after the large loading dose, given how distressed he is. We ask if she can please get the doctor back in here.

By that stage, it's past his bedtime, and he's exhausted. He's in my arms, and I can see he's trying to go to sleep, but he can't. It feels like something is happening to him — he's scared, his eyes seem to be looking at things that don't exist, and he's frantically scratching his face. I gently hold his hands to stop him from hurting himself. I pat him, rock him, sing to him, but nothing works.

Ced tries too, but the sound of my voice singing to him seems to be the only thing that calms him.

And then it starts again.

Hysterical screaming.

When the doctor arrives, Eliott is beyond distressed, and we don't know what's happening. We're so scared. She says he needs to have his dose, and we say there's no way.

Is the medication making him like this?

We know he's sensitive to it, and we suspected a toxicity back in August last year, so could it be this again?

She admits that it looks like he's having a reaction, but she doesn't know. She's incredibly patient, empathetic, and takes all the time we need to answer our questions. But at one point, she takes a deep breath and says, 'Look guys, I'm sorry I don't have the answer to this. I don't think anyone has; maybe the neurology team does, but I've spoken to the fellow, and they recommend he has his dose. Of course, it's your decision.'

We keep probing, but she doesn't have the answers.

After an hour of screaming, Eliott finally goes to sleep.

I've cried so much again watching my baby scratch his own face and scream, when he's usually such a laid-back baby.

164

'These drugs are meant to make people sleepy, but some people can have a paradoxical reaction, where the opposite happens,' the nurse explains when she comes back later. 'It's like we've given him a bad trip.'

What? My eleven-month-old baby was having a bad trip?

We don't give him his dose that night, and when we're discharged the next day, we can't wait to go home, have a rest, and recover from this experience.

In the afternoon, Ced goes to the shops. I stay home with Eliott, and we play. When Ced comes back, he is carrying a gorgeous bouquet of my favourite flowers. I'd completely forgotten that today is 2 May, and it's our second wedding anniversary.

Chapter eleven

Making the impossible possible
(May–June 2016)

Eliott

Mum and Dad give me my medication for another two days. On Wednesday, they don't give me my morning dose. I don't feel like myself, and my head is still a bit fuzzy. Towards the end of the week, I'm feeling better and smiling again.

On Friday night, while Dad massages in my lotion before putting me in my pyjamas, I can't stop babbling. I tell him everything that springs to mind. He laughs as he tries to reply to me, but I just keep going; I can't talk yet, but I like to try. I haven't said anything in days, so there's lots to catch-up on! I like feeling like myself again.

When Mum comes home from work, she tells me, 'Eliott, my love, we've finally booked our tickets to go to France. You will meet everyone soon! And we have another surprise for you — we're going to Western Australia before, just the three of us!'

What an exciting day!

Maman

We've started taking Eliott to a new physiotherapy centre that delivers an intensive physio program.

The place is like a giant gym, and once I've filled in all the required forms, two physios come to take us through everything. They give Eliott lots of toys to play with. Telling them all about Eliott makes me a little emotional, but it's great to watch Eliott show off all that he can do — he's having a great day. The session is tiring for him, but he is keen to keep going. Both physios comment on his excellent attitude.

'We'd love to see Eliott twice a week. Would that be okay for you?' they ask.

'Yes, it's been wonderful seeing Eliott try new things,' Ced answers. 'I'm on paternity leave, and there's nothing more important for us. We could do two sessions a week until we go on holiday in four weeks.'

One day, Cedric comes home and says he's heard a comment that made him quite uncomfortable.

'While we were in the physio's waiting room, I was watching this family,' Cedric starts. 'A mum was with her daughter, probably Eliott's age or a bit younger, but the little girl has cerebral palsy.'

'Ah yes, I heard that they treat a lot of kids here with the condition. How was she doing?' Somehow, not knowing anything about this other family, the fact that she's close to Eliott's age, I can imagine how the mum must be feeling, taking her daughter to therapy. Instantly, I feel so much empathy for this family.

'She was okay, but the physio was a bit rough with the mum.'

'Oh, what happened?'

'The grandma was there. The mum was crying, and so the grandma asked the physio to avoid saying "cerebral palsy", because the mum is having such a hard time accepting the diagnosis.'

'That's sweet of the grandma,' I say.

I can picture my mum, the fierce protector, trying to make it easier on me and helping me fight the right battles. Sometimes that means avoiding the labels for a bit longer.

'Yes, but the physio took the mum aside, and said "Look, you must pull yourself together, as your daughter needs you.

She has cerebral palsy and it's hard, but it's not about you. You have to be strong for her."' Ced's looking at me, clearly trying to gauge my reaction.

'Wow, that's tough,' but as I'm saying this, it gets me thinking — it's like she's talking to me directly. When I look up at Ced, I know he's been thinking the same thing; it's not about us, it's about Eliott.

I realise that up until this point, we've thought a lot about how we're going to manage, how this is impacting us, affecting our lives, our hopes and dreams for the future. Yes, we've been doing everything we can to support Eliott, but again, *we* have been acting like this is about *us*. The truth is that Eliott is the one living with the condition, and we need to be strong for him and give *him* everything *he* needs to fight. We want *him* to be strong enough to grow up to be independent, stand up for himself, and be whoever *he* decides to be.

The following Monday, we have an important appointment at another hospital. We're meeting with another paediatric neurologist who specialises in epilepsy.

We haven't yet told Henry that we're getting this second opinion here in Australia, so I feel a little uneasy; somehow, it doesn't feel right.

We get to the new hospital, and it feels so unfamiliar — 'our' hospital has become familiar to us and, weirdly, even feels welcoming. This new hospital feels more like an adult hospital — the waiting room isn't as bright, but when the doctor welcomes us, he's friendly and has read all the referral notes.

We still go through Eliott's whole medical history and tell him how wonderful Henry's been but that we still don't have a diagnosis and how Eliott's development is delayed. Of course, I cry again.

The doctor looks over the documents we brought him, examines Eliott and asks questions. We discuss his routine, the medication, his sleep, his development, and the milestones.

'I think Henry has it covered,' he says. 'I'll give him a call to have a chat and so he knows he can reach out if he needs anything. I agree with him that it may still be genetic, and I'm sorry to hear that the sequencing didn't bring you any answers. Have you heard of the research work that is happening down in Melbourne on KCNQ2?'

'Yes. Henry got in touch and sent them a video when Eliott was in NICU. They really thought it was KCNQ2 too,' I say. It's amazing all these experts felt that it could be this, and the results still came back negative.

'Ah, yes, that research is incredible. But they're not just looking at KCNQ2 in Melbourne, so one piece of advice I'd give you is to follow their work. Henry and the genetics team can tell when it might be worth doing another test. We're discovering new epilepsy genes almost every month. In terms of his development, what are the next steps?'

'Our GP got us an appointment at the developmental clinic next month. We have an appointment before we fly to France,' I say.

'That sounds like a good plan,' he replies.

We leave feeling better and worse at the same time. We're still lost in the fog, trying to find our way to a destination without knowing the directions and constantly hindered by reduced vision. We get a sense that we're going in the right direction, but sometimes it is hard to tell. Will we ever know if we're doing the right thing? Talking to the right people? Getting the right support? I constantly have this nagging feeling that we're never doing enough.

On the drive home, we decide not to seek additional opinions. We're seeing Henry again tomorrow, and we'll still see a French specialist when we're in France, so we have a point of contact, but we've had enough opinions. They're not conflicting, but they're not giving us answers at this stage.

We need to spend our energy on Eliott, on getting him the support he needs to reach milestones, but also focus on our family, on us as a couple, on work, and on ourselves as individuals.

We're hoping that the clinic next week will give us a starting point for what to do next. And then we want to focus on us as a family while we're in France. No appointments, just family and friends.

When Eliott was first born, Ced often commented that it was hard to be at work knowing that Eliott and I were struggling. He'd also say how much easier his daily life was compared to mine because, selfishly, going to work provided an escape — a connection to our previous, simpler life. Work is important to us, and we often say how we both need to keep our jobs because we are relying on both salaries to pay for all the therapies, doctor visits, medication, but it also helps our mental state to focus on other things.

Earlier in the year, we made the decision that if we were both going to go back to full-time work and stay in Australia, we needed to have things to look forward to. Even when we were planning our family, we'd agreed that having kids wouldn't prevent us from travelling. So, despite Eliott's condition, we made an effort to continue. That's the main reason for booking a week in Exmouth in Western Australia, just before we go to France.

Ced's been dreaming of going there and swimming with the whale sharks since we stepped foot in Australia, so now seemed like the perfect time to do it.

We have our appointment with Henry to go over the paperwork for our trip to France and make sure that we have everything we need. We haven't seen him since the last seizure, and he's pleased we've come up with a plan that everyone is comfortable with. He's happy we're seeking more opinions too — the more we can find out and help Eliott, the better, given we still don't have a diagnosis.

'Have you considered giving Eliott a loading dose of Phenytoin and a maintenance dose for the trip, as a preventative measure?' he asks.

'Not unless he's sick,' Ced replies.

I know we're both still traumatised by that vision of Eliott screaming and scratching his face frantically.

'Last time, he had a large dose; 33ml was a lot for him, but the loading dose you'll give him is much lower.'

'But what about our trip to Western Australia? Does that mean we'd have to give him two loading doses in a week?' I ask.

'No, only the one to France.'

I don't get it. 'Is that because it's a long flight and there's more risks of developing an illness on the long haul?'

'No.' Henry pauses. 'It's because to go to WA, you're flying over land. When you go back to Europe, you fly over the ocean at some points for hours, so if Eliott had a seizure, then it would be hours before you could land and get medical assistance.'

Who could've thought that even the flight path would become a consideration in giving Eliott his medication?

On the last Monday in May, we fly to Exmouth. We take two flights, about eight hours in total, which is a big test before we go to Europe. Eliott does incredibly well; he seems enthusiastic to be on the plane.

We've travelled a bit with him, and it's been wonderful witnessing how discovering new places clearly brings him joy. His little face lights up, and we feel he relishes spending more time with the two of us.

Our time in Exmouth is special. Halfway through the week, a bus picks us up at the hotel, and we embark on our day excursion to swim with whale sharks. This has been Ced's dream for years.

'Hi,' we say as we are about to step aboard the boat. 'We just wanted to mention that our son has a medical condition, and we were wondering what your emergency procedures are?'

'What do you mean?' the young skipper asks. He waves at his colleague to come over to help provide answers and then retreats swiftly as soon as the person in charge arrives.

'Our son has epilepsy. It's very unlikely that he'll have a seizure, and we have all the emergency medication with us, but if anything were to happen, we need to know you have a good emergency procedure in place.'

'Okay, we have a radio and would ask for help. What's the likelihood of it happening?' she asks, looking at Eliott anxiously, then us, then all our gear that we excitedly prepared for the day.

'Unlikely, but if it were to happen, will you call a helicopter to come and pick us up?' I ask. I know deep down that they probably wouldn't do that. It's a risk that we must accept, but we're hanging on to our ability to do 'normal' things — we've come such a long way to do this.

She replies, 'Yes, of course we'd do that.' She has a huge confident smile, so we don't ask another question.

And off we sail.

Thankfully, everything goes well. We have a magical day. We take turns swimming, and Ced even swims with dolphins before we swim with the whale sharks in the afternoon. It's such a good day, and we promise ourselves that it will be a memory we will cherish for a long time.

Eliott

This weekend, my friend Chiara is coming for a sleepover. She brings lots of toys and books, which she shows me before we have dinner and a bath. It's fun having a friend around. Mum and Dad play with us and ask Chiara a lot of questions: is she hungry; is she thirsty; what toy does she want? She's very good at telling them what she wants.

When Chiara's parents pick her up the next day, they tell me we'll all see each other again in the afternoon.

Mum and Dad then tell me that today we're going to celebrate my first birthday! Mum bakes a few things, while Dad assembles a wooden rocking horse that arrived from France this morning. It's from Mum's best friend, Pauline (her daughter turned one last month, and she got the same one). Mum shows me a video of Pauline's daughter on it. She looks like she loves it, and when I finally try it, I understand why! Mum says Pauline is crazy to have organised such a gorgeous gift, but I see that she's touched.

Shortly after, we leave for Centennial Park, where Mum booked a space in the restaurant, and when we arrive, George, Charlotte, and baby Iggy are already there. They wish me a happy birthday, and I have more gifts to open. I give them a big kiss just like Dad taught me, and before I know it, twenty friends have arrived.

All the friends we've seen this year — those who brought food to Mum and Dad when I was born, those whom we've met so many times for coffees at playgrounds with all the kids who are around my age — are there.

After lunch, Mum disappears for a bit, and then suddenly, I hear singing. Everyone is crowded around me. Dad's carrying me, and I can see Mum walking towards me with a cake and a candle on it. Everyone sings 'happy birthday'.

Once the song is finished, I kiss everyone, and I get lots of cuddles and kisses back. Mum and Dad then give a little speech. I'm not saying much and staying quietly in their arms. They thank everyone for the support this year. Mum doesn't cry but is holding me very tight.

When we get home, I play with my new toys. Not all the presents are toys though — one of my presents is a frame with some leaves in it. I've loved looking at trees and the wind blowing in the branches, so our friends thought they'd find different types of leaves — a green one, a red one, an orange one, and a yellow one — of different shapes and sizes and put them in a frame for me to have with me when I go to sleep. It's been a wonderful day!

Maman

The day before we're due to fly to France, we finally have the first clinic assessment. We're feeling a little nervous, but the social worker and psychologist are lovely. We spend a lot of time talking about the first year of Eliott's life and mention our challenges with getting him the appropriate level of support here compared to what we would get in France. They're surprised that we've been struggling and say we should be getting more support in the future.

Eliott's brave and tries everything in the assessment.

The last task is the hardest for me to watch. There are objects in front of him, and the psychologist is testing his receptive language; how well he understands what we tell him. She asks him to pick the spoon up, and he doesn't. She suggests that he may be tired, and asks if he would usually know this, but I decide that lying wouldn't do him any favours.

'No,' I reluctantly admit.

When the test is finished, we leave the room so they can compile the results.

'Thanks for waiting,' says the psychologist when we are called back in. 'Firstly, I'd like to say that we don't usually test babies this young, but we've done it because your GP requested it. The results are probably not a great predictor of what Eliott can achieve, but they'll give us enough to make recommendations about therapies you could explore. It's also good that he continues day care,' she says, looking at us, clearly to make sure we're listening and following what she's talking about. 'Do you know how percentiles work? I'll give you his age equivalent for areas we've tested, but also the percentile.'

I do know what they are, because of what I do for work, but also because we've had to look at percentiles for weight, height, and head circumference for one year now, so we're both well versed in understanding what they are.

Bottom line is: if you're in the 90th percentile, it means ninety per cent of the population is scoring lower than you, so if Eliott's weight at one is ten kilograms, and he's in the 75th percentile, that means that seventy-five per cent of one-year-old babies are lighter than him.

This is looked at again and again in the first few weeks of life, especially if the baby is not putting enough weight on, but what we're looking at now are his mental and physical abilities, and that's a whole new level of concerns. The hope is that he's at least 50th in every category — average, normal, that's what we're praying for.

But he's not 50th, and this is a confronting discussion.

So, they recommend more therapy and refer us back to the hospital for more support.

'Don't forget he's still very young, and these results are not always great predictors,' the psychologist says. 'The one that is most important is his problem-solving skills, and he did okay on this one, it's one of his highest results.'

I look at her and start to cry, as the one she just referred to is his second highest score: 16th percentile. That means eight-four per cent of twelve-month-old babies perform better than him.

He's also in the 1st percentile for fine motor skills, which is bad.

On a positive note, he's in the 25th percentile for social skills, which — when considering his start in life — is nothing short of amazing. And it's a good strength to have, so I'll hold on to that.

'Don't get too attached to these numbers,' she continues. 'I understand, Claire, that you work with numbers, but the important thing to keep in mind is that if he progresses, it's positive. We're also looking at it across the board. As long as his overall result doesn't drop below the 5th percentile, he'll be fine. We'll see you again next year and do another assessment.'

I do work with numbers, and they feel comforting somehow, even if they're bad. It's important to me to know where we stand. But she's right, Eliott is Eliott, and this coming year, we must focus on helping him develop even more, now that we will have these windows of time when he doesn't need to be on medication.

The next day, everything is packed for our two-month trip, and we're ready to go! We're carrying so much stuff! We're not sure how we are going to manage with it all; we have suitcases, bags filled with food for the plane, bottles, nappies, wipes, change of clothes, toys, books, medication. But we manage to board, take our seats with a baby bassinet — thankfully — and we're eager for the journey ahead.

Eliott has a restful sleep on the first flight, and he's in a good mood. The second flight is rather empty, which means that the flight attendants are super attentive to our cute little baby who's giving everyone smiles. When they ask how old he is, I almost feel guilty when I admit, 'He's turning one today, and we're going home to see family.'

They shower him with gifts, so we leave the plane with various souvenirs: three stuffed animals that turn into a blanket, colouring books, crayons, and a picture of his first international flight. Somehow, this little human being has survived his first year, and so have we. He has taught us resilience, to keep smiling and laughing in even the hardest of circumstances, and to keep fighting.

Chapter twelve

A family dream
(June-August 2016)

Eliott

When we land in Paris, Mamie Vero is waiting for us. She gives me a big cuddle and wishes me a happy birthday, and then she drives us to Caen, in Normandy, where she lives.

Arriving at her apartment, we see that she's organised a changing table with the same products I use at home, some toys and books, and she's even cooked purees and snacks for me.

In the afternoon, my great-grandparents come to visit. Grand Papi keeps saying how gorgeous I am, and that I'm quite a big boy, and he's happy to see me. He puts his hand on mine; it's big and has patches of different coloured skin.

Grand Papi and Grand Mamie are like no one I've seen before; they both have grey hair and wear glasses.

'This is the first time Eliott's met older people, and he looks intrigued,' Dad says, with a chuckle.

At the weekend, we go to their house in the countryside. The whole family is here to meet me and wish me a happy birthday: Uncle Jean-Mi, Great Aunt Estelle and her two children Lucie and Anselme. They sing 'happy birthday' for me — the candle, everyone looking at me, the singing — this is a lot of fun!

After a week in Caen, we go to Paris. We're staying at Pauline's place — I get to meet her husband Freddie and their daughters in person. They're lovely but a lot more active than me! Manon is three years old, and she runs around the flat showing me all her toys. Mum's happy to spend time with her friend. She has missed her a lot, and we spend a lovely evening with them.

The following Thursday, Pauline and her family leave for a long weekend in London, so we have their apartment to ourselves for a few days. I settle in Chloe's cot — she's Pauline's younger daughter. Her room has a lot of pink, and I like it; it's cosy, and Mum keeps saying how beautiful it is and how well I'm going to sleep. And she's right!

During the day, we walk around Paris. Mum and Dad know it well because they used to live here before moving to Sydney. We even buy my first pair of shoes!

Maman

Eliott has been amazing! He's growing and developing more, he's more alert, he's just such a happy baby being surrounded by new people and going to new places. Jet lag was tough but only lasted a few days.

Now we're in Paris, and this afternoon we have an appointment with the paediatric neurologist for another opinion as to how we can look for a diagnosis, but we also want to have a neurologist in France who knows Eliott's case, should anything happen while we're here.

He's running almost three hours late, but Eliott's been so good while we've been waiting. When the doctor finally arrives, I thought I'd be a little more impatient and annoyed, but he apologises for running late, and it seems he genuinely wants to help us. He asks questions and does a few tests with Eliott, mainly checking his posture for muscle tone and his reflexes. He's talking gently, and Eliott instantly seems to like him.

'Thanks for coming to see me. Tell me a bit more about life in Australia,' he asks.

We tell him about our life, how different it is, and we mention the lack of access to therapy for Eliott. 'We were considering coming back to France, but we're afraid we may not be able to spend as much time with him as we currently do.'

'I think your team has done a great job, and at this stage, I can't think of anything else that would bring you a diagnosis. When is his next MRI scheduled for?'

'In the next six to twelve months, so his brain has time to mature.'

'That's perfect. I think that's going to help you understand what's causing it. But as your doctors probably told you, the main thing at this stage is stopping the seizures, so you need a good management plan, and that will help him achieve his developmental milestones. What medication is he on again?'

'Well, he's not on any presently,' we say, and naively add, 'and we're happy about this.'

On hearing this, the doctor's face and body language indicate that this concerns him. 'What do you mean he's not on anything?'

We go through the whole medication journey again.

By that time, we've been in his office well over an hour, but he's one of those doctors who are in the moment; when they're with a patient, their mind is solely focused on them.

He gasps a bit when we recount the status epilepticus and gives a seriously disapproving look when we say we tried weaning him off Phenytoin four months after that. He's no longer smiling when we tell him our new plan of only giving him the Phenytoin if he has a fever.

'If you'd been a patient in France, if you'd been my patient, I would never have let him come off the Phenytoin this young; he'd be on medication for at least three years.'

'But he's doing so much better without it. His development was suffering from being on medication.'

'I understand, but the risks are just too high. Sometimes seizures can come back without warning, so just be prepared if that happens. Are you always carrying his medication with him?'

'Yes, they're always in his backpack.'

'Okay, that's good. And be careful about Phenytoin; they don't make it in a liquid form here in France anymore. If you have a bottle of it, you're lucky, and you should be careful. Don't lose it or break it. We only have tablets, and they're incredibly difficult to dose properly.'

'Oh, thank you for that. We'll make sure to look after the one we brought with us.'

He probably can observe all the pain, the suffering, the anxiety we have been experiencing, and realises that at the end of the day, we're just trying to do our best.

He then looks genuinely concerned again when I ask, 'What about the diagnosis? Our Australian medical team thinks it's genetic, and they're advising against having other children.' Tears prick my eyes.

Ced reaches out, passes me Eliott for a quick cuddle, and holds my hand.

The doctor sits back and looks at his notes again. 'I have to say, there's nothing I can see that would point to it being genetic. Not more than other alternatives. And I think the MRI is going to give you more answers. I don't believe it's genetic, as you've got no family history and you're both healthy. If it is genetic though, you should stay in Australia, as they're leading the way with research.'

Shortly after, he thanks us for coming to see him, gives us his email address so we can email him some additional information, and tells us not to hesitate to contact him if we need anything while we're here.

All up we spent five hours at this hospital in the middle of Paris. We thought this visit would be a quick 'tick the box' exercise for him, as he was doing it as a favour for one of his colleagues, but we're leaving his office with lots of new thoughts about what it means for Eliott, as well as doubts on our medication management plan, but also hope for the future of our family.

Eliott

After spending a few days in Paris, where I have met so many new people, we pack up and drive to Bordeaux.

We're leaving at my bedtime, and Mum says she hopes I will be okay for the drive, but given the time of day, I should fall asleep soon. Turns out, it's so fun driving around the city. It's still daylight too, so I don't fall asleep that easily! It's 10pm by the time I finally close my eyes!

I wake up the next day in a new place. Mum and Dad show me around and say this is Mamie Francette and Papi Jean-Claude's house. Dad grew up here! We'll be staying for a couple of weeks.

While I'm having breakfast with Mum, Dad, and Mamie Francette, I hear a deep voice behind me. I turn around and Papi is here. I've seen him on video calls, but this is the first time I see him in person! He has dark hair like Dad, and he's looking at me and says, 'Oh, this is the little one! Come and give me a cuddle!'

I don't know Papi very well, but I like his voice, so I reach out, and Papi takes me in his arms. I put my head down on his shoulder and give him a cuddle. Everyone is laughing. Mamie Francette says she's jealous and wants a cuddle too. But no, Papi is the only one I want to cuddle. He's laughing and making a joke that he's very special.

Maman

After a few days here, we pick Mum up from the airport. We're spending a weekend at Ced's brother's house, and then Ced and I are going away for three days so Mum will stay with Ced's parents, and they'll all look after Eliott together.

We have an exceptional weekend catching up with Ced's brother Yannick, his sister-in-law Nathalie, and his niece Marion. We go for walks in the nearby forest, have long dinners and enjoy spending quality time with them. Eliott has a blast, as he's the centre of attention. It's clear that he adores meeting new members of the family. He sleeps well, eats well, and is a happy chappy.

When Ced and I leave for three days, it will be the first time we've been away from Eliott for an extended period. We're simultaneously anxious and excited. It's not much work to look after him, but we're scared that he could have another seizure. I'm glad our two families get along so well, that they both loved the idea of looking after Eliott together.

I've prepared a few pages of notes, going through his daily routine, from the amount of milk and the breakfast he has in the morning, to making sure they check for fever before they go to bed in the evening.

There's also a one-page seizure management plan, describing what the seizures look like, and what to do if it happens. Mum has seen it happen, but the management plan since then has changed a lot. They're very conscientious and listen carefully.

Francette is focused on what Eliott will want to eat, what he might need in terms of his routine, timings, etc. but gets uncomfortable when I go through the management plan.

She has a medical background and doesn't get fazed by anything, but she just doesn't seem to want to talk about the risk of seizures; I think she believes that by ignoring it, it may go away.

I want to do that too, so much, but my mind is wired differently. I tend to play out each catastrophic scenario in my head, just in case. And I know by experience that the best way to be prepared when such scenarios occur is by practising, being trained, and going through the steps over and over and over. Because when something happens, your mind needs to be able to go into autopilot, like mine did back in May.

That's why some professional training, such as safety training for flight attendants, is renewed every year, and why they're asked to mentally go through a checklist of what to do if they need to evacuate at take-off and landing. Because, in the unlikely event that something happens, their bodies and minds won't have time to think — it must be automatic.

Therefore, doing CPR training when you're a parent is so important. And every time Eliott is sick, I go through our checklist: check that Eliott is safe, grab bag, check time, get Midazolam, check if Eliott is breathing, draw 0.6ml of Midazolam, check Eliott, administer Midazolam, call ambulance, draw 18ml phenytoin, give it to him when he wakes up, hold him and check for potential clustering. Repeat.

And I know Mum needs to go through the same process.

When we leave on the Monday, Ced's niece Marion, his sister Karine, his parents, and Mum are all there to say goodbye. We're driving three hours east of where his family live to a little town called Sarlat, which is a historical village. The main activities there are: eat duck liver pate, drink good wine, kayak on the local river, visit castles and other gorgeous properties, and go to the famous Lascaux caves.

And that's all we want to do!

We've booked a charming hotel within walking distance of the historic village centre and appreciate not having to eat at set times, not thinking about naps, or preparing food, and having the luxury of not carrying a medication backpack everywhere.

We have the best weather and spend time doing activities that we would have done only thirteen months ago, when it was just the two of us. We also talk a lot about what happened in the neurologist's office, about our plans to get better, to fight for Eliott, what our family plans would be, and how to get on the road of recovery.

If we were to have another child, it could help us feel normal again, but if the child were to have the same condition, what then? Would we keep going? Would we move back to France? Would we change lives completely and go raise goats in the middle of the French countryside? We also talk a lot about the coming year: work, logistics, how to find a nanny for Eliott, for how many days? How are we going to afford it? But thankfully, we also talk a lot about a myriad of other things, and it's a refreshing change.

When we arrive back at Ced's parent's house, we don't hear a noise when we enter the house. We look at each other and make a joke: so much for a warm welcome after being away!

We head to the garden and see Eliott on the grass. Francette is jumping and dancing in front of him, and Mum is sitting next to him. He's holding her hand and watching his other mamie do whatever she can to make him laugh, and he's giggling. It's a picture-perfect representation of what his last three days have been like.

At the sound of our voices, they all turn, and we get the biggest cuddles ever — from Eliott, who seems happy to see us, and from the two grandmas. They're keen to hear about our trip, but also to tell us and show us all the great things they've been doing with him. It's been such a positive short trip for everyone.

Mum leaves the next day, just before we have Eliott's third birthday party for the year! Ced's sister, Karine, has organised a barbecue at her house to celebrate his birthday.

We spend our last week in Bordeaux enjoying the peaceful relaxing time in the French summer. We also celebrate Ced's birthday with his family, go for shopping trips to Bordeaux, just the two of us, catch-up with some of Ced's friends, and even go paintballing (a first for me!) with the whole family — nine of us run around shooting paintballs at each other, which turns into one of the best family-bonding activities.

We visit my grandparent's house for my birthday. It's the house I spent a lot of my childhood in; I went there every holiday, spent every summer there, and we used to visit every other weekend. Some of my best friends growing up lived on that same street in this tiny village. I have so many fond memories of bicycle trips, picnics with my grandparents, being outside during the long summer days and spending the evenings by the fire in the winter.

We arrive on the Monday before dinner and, after getting Eliott to sleep, we spend some quality time with my grandparents, talking about our lives, our hopes for Eliott, and anything in between.

The next day, Eliott and I go for a walk with Grand Papi around the village. The weather is not the best — the sky is low and filled with clouds — so we put Eliott's cute French yellow rain jacket on, put him in the pram, and wander along the small village roads I've walked thousands of times, just enjoying each other's company, as I've done with my grandfather so many times before.

When we get home, it's time for Eliott's lunch. He doesn't eat much, so I put him down for his nap. However, when I go back in to get him up, I can feel something's not right.

The way he's crying for us is more of a moan, and my heart sinks. I touch his forehead and he's hot. 'Ced, can you please come up?' I ask. 'He's hot. I think we may have to give him his Phenytoin.'

'Are you sure? What's his temperature?'

'I don't know, but he just feels hot,' I say.

'Okay, let's not stress about it. Let's take his temperature. I tell you what, if he's above 38 degrees, we give him his Phenytoin.' He reaches for the thermometer. 'He's 37.8.' Ced looks up at me.

'I don't know what to do,' I reply.

'How about we monitor him and check again in thirty minutes? Maybe he was just hot from his nap?'

I nod at this suggestion; it sounds like the most practical thing to do. I don't want him to have a seizure, not now, not ever, not just before we go on a weekend away with our friends, not while we're at my grandparents. However, I certainly don't want to give him his loading dose of Phenytoin if it's not necessary.

Ced's been playing with Eliott to make sure he doesn't get worried, and suddenly, as if he'd read my mind, he asks, 'How good is the local hospital?'

I don't really know, but I do know that the one in Caen is better. If anything were to happen while we're here, it would take an ambulance at least thirty minutes to get to us.

'I think it's okay, but we're probably too far, so we should go back to Mum's.'

We check his temperature again, and it's still 37.8. It hasn't gone up, and it's still a low-grade fever, but it's not going down either.

'I'll go tell my grandparents,' I say. 'They'll be devastated that we have to leave. I wanted to come and stay here for a few nights with you two so much.'

Ced takes my hand. 'It's the best decision. Go tell your grandmother, and we can always come back before we leave.

My grandmother is understandably sad to hear that we can't stay; she's disappointed that we don't trust the small country hospital, and that Eliott isn't going to eat the food that she bought. I call Mum to let her know that we're coming home, and as usual, she immediately finds the right words. 'Just pack up and come home. I'll get the room ready. Don't worry about anything else.'

We drive back to Mum's house and put Eliott to bed. I set the alarm clock throughout the night so I can check his temperature; it fluctuates between 37.5 and 37.9 degrees. It's been a tiring night, and when Eliott wakes at 5am, I'm grateful that Mum comes in to grab him.

Eliott

Mamie takes me with her in the living room to play so Mum and Dad can rest. At 8am, she puts me down in the cot next

186

to them in the spare bedroom, and I can hear Mum asking if I'm okay.

'Yes, he's had some breakfast, but he's really tired,' whispers Mamie.

But I don't find it easy to sleep, and after a few short minutes, my body does this thing again. I start screaming, and Mum — as if she already knew — turns the big lights on and grabs my bag.

My body is getting so stiff, and I turn to the side, unable to do anything. Mum asks Mamie to call the ambulance and to prepare the Phenytoin. Dad is by my side, telling me it's all going to be okay. Mum is moving stuff around me, and then I can feel the liquid in the side of my cheek. Shortly after, my body relaxes.

I cry and give Dad a big cuddle, and Mum says she's going to give me my Phenytoin. She squirts small amounts of the sugary pink syrup slowly into my mouth, and I swallow it all.

The ambulance arrives and takes us to the paediatric emergency room. When the doctor and nurse hear our story and are convinced that Mum and Dad know what they're doing, they ask, 'How can we help?'

'We'd like for him to stay here a few hours in observation, as we have no idea what triggered this seizure, so we want to make sure there's nothing too serious going on. It may be his molars coming through.'

'Sounds like a plan. We'll run a few tests as well, just to check that there's not an infection, but you may be right, it could just be the molars triggering the fever. Let us take care of all that, so you can just rest and cuddle him. You don't have to help with the medical stuff, we've got it covered.'

Maman

The experience in the French hospital is so different to what we're used to in Sydney. They tell us that they won't be drawing blood unless absolutely necessary and have put a numbing patch on his arm in case he does need it. They've also put a urine collection patch on him, so we don't have to hold a cup near him for hours; him laying exposed without a nappy while we wait for him to go.

The principle is that unnecessary procedures must be avoided at all costs, and so the comfort and convenience of numbing patches and the urine collection patch make for a more relaxed experience.

Most surprising of all, is how amazed they are that we are so fully across all his medical needs, so well informed, and were 'hands-on' with his medications.

Their vision is different. Parents must be able to parent, provide love, reassurance, and confidence to their kids. The doctors oversee supporting their patients, giving them the proper due care, medication, and answering their questions. Both systems are different, with their own advantages and disadvantages.

We've felt so alone in Australia, navigating a health system we knew nothing about, with little support, and having to create our own opportunities to support Eliott's development. We feel we are part of Eliott's medical team, and that comes at a cost, as there's the pressure of not doing enough, of having to step up, do research, and be advocates for him. But that also comes with the huge benefit of having a voice in the medical conversations.

In France, we're told — just as my French friends had advised me — that we would have a team supporting us and working out a plan to give Eliott the therapy he needs. He would probably have had speech therapy, physiotherapy, and occupational therapy a few times a week from birth. But like the Parisian neurologist said, he also would have stayed on medication for another two years, regardless of what we wanted.

It's a tough morning. We're feeling guilty for not giving Eliott's medication early enough as a prevention, and we promise each other that we won't hesitate next time. We'll give it at the first hint of fever.

Hearing the doctor and nurse say that we're doing incredibly well, and that only a few parents would have been able to react the way we have makes us feel a bit better. And when they share that they're sorry we've had to endure this and that we've had to be so involved in the decisions, this gives us a sense of recognition that what we're having to deal with is not normal — it's harder, and we're doing a good job.

After a day in hospital, all the tests have come back negative, and they think that his fever was caused by teething. We're discharged and able to go home. Eliott has slept most of the day on Ced or me, and Mum and my brother have come to visit and check on us.

I decide to cancel the booking for the house we'd organised for Bastille Day and call our friends who were going to join us. We're meant to go the next day, and this is obviously not reasonable at this stage. Not for Eliott, but also not for our friends or their kids, as Eliott may have an infection that he could pass around.

The next day, his fever ends up over 39 degrees, so we visit the GP to do further blood tests to check for infection, but it all comes back negative, and when we see the little white spots, we know his molars are causing this.

Mum has been so supportive through these long worrying days, and when the fever finally breaks after five strenuous days, our friends decide to come and spend the weekend with us. Pauline, Freddie and their two girls rent a little apartment and stay for three nights, and all the other friends who were meant to join also come for the weekend.

We have a picnic on the Saturday for lunch, a dinner on the Saturday night, when everyone has organised babysitters, and then we go to the beach on the Sunday. We are grateful that in such a stressful situation, they've all come to spend time with us.

The following Tuesday, with less than two weeks left in France, we take Eliott to the museum. But first, we have lunch in a delightful restaurant, just the three of us.

I've been meaning to tell Cedric something all day, something that's been bothering me, and I'm not quite sure how to tell him how I've been feeling. I'm overwhelmed and know I must share what's going on. However, I want to wait until after our meal, but as we walk into the restaurant, I burst into tears.

Ced stops straightaway. 'Hey, are you okay? Wait, let me carry Eliott. What is it?'

'I have something to tell you ... I ... I ...'

'Claire, what's happening? Are you okay? You're scaring me.'

'I don't know ... I'm pregnant.' I start to cry.

We both knew it was a possibility. After seeing the neurologist in Paris and hearing his views that it probably wouldn't be genetic and the risks of having another baby with the same conditions were low, we decided to just let fate decide. Not to 'try' for a new baby, but to stop using protection.

I did a pregnancy test mid-cycle, at the time hoping it would be positive, but it had turned out to be negative. It helped me realise that rushing into another pregnancy without knowing what Eliott has was reckless. We needed to focus on the three of us first, and Eliott needed us.

I also felt I had to have some time to myself, to let my body and my mind heal, and to enjoy a glass of wine after a long day when I wanted. I didn't have a single drop of alcohol during pregnancy and continued without alcohol all while I was breastfeeding for fear of interaction with the Phenytoin.

Over the past two months, I'd enjoyed a few glasses of wine, feeling like I had my body to myself again. I was even about to tell Ced that I didn't trust fate to do the right thing, and I wanted to wait a bit longer before 'letting things happen' when I noticed that my period was late.

This morning, a week after that first negative test, I took

another pregnancy test, and this time, the pink double stripes appeared so quickly — there was no doubting what I already knew.

Baby number two was on its way, just when I'd realised that it was too early for us to consider otherwise. I then felt stupid for rushing into it, because all the rationalising thoughts I had been formulating over the past week were front of mind.

I feel lost now and sob as I try to explain that I'm actually miserable when I should be so happy about this new life. Having Eliott has been difficult, and I can't quite believe we're doing it again and taking this huge risk.

'Claire, I thought you wanted this, so what is it? Talk to me.' Ced is looking at me anxiously, and I can't stop crying.

I go through everything: the fears, Eliott needing us now more than ever, my body not belonging to me again.

Ced is alarmed, but as always knows what to say. 'I think it will be great for Eliott to have a brother or sister, and I'm really happy we're going to have another baby.' He takes my hand and gives it a kiss.

The next day, before we share the news with family and friends, we call the genetics team. When Brooke answers, I take a deep breath. 'The last time we spoke, you asked me to call you if our circumstances changed ... I'm pregnant.'

'Well, first, a massive congratulations, this is very exciting for your family, and Eliott will be such a good big brother.'

I start to cry.

Brooke is the sweetest person, and I've learnt to trust her so much. Somehow, I was expecting her to tell me how reckless and selfish we were, that we're just asking for trouble — all the things I've been telling myself over the past 24 hours. But I hear genuine love and care in her voice; she's truly happy for us. Despite her profession in genetics where she sees terrible odds, the promise of a new baby is the same to her as it is for most people: it represents hope.

It makes me realise that getting pregnant can be a positive thing. And as I'm starting to feel a bit better, I hear Brooke continue, 'I understand this must be stressful for you. Let me chat to Daniel and get back to you.' Before we hang up, she asks one last question, 'I'm sorry to ask this, but it's going to inform how we decide on the plan ... have you thought about what you would like to do with this pregnancy? I mean, if we were running a more thorough test on Eliott's DNA and could find what condition he has. We could then test the baby and find out whether he or she has the same condition. You don't have to answer right now, but make sure you and Cedric have a chat about what you would do, as this will impact how we go about this.'

This is such a horrible question to have to confront, but I know deep down that this is part of why I'm so uncomfortable about this pregnancy. If they run more thorough tests, and we find out the specifics of Eliott's condition, we can test the baby in-utero, and if the baby has the same condition, we could terminate the pregnancy to avoid having two babies with this horrible disease ...

The following twenty-four hours are stressful. Thanks to the eight-hour time difference, we have a full day ahead of us before we can speak with Brooke and Daniel. We arrange to meet Mum for our daily afternoon tea. We want her to be part of this, even if we don't know what the future holds. We tell her we have a gift for her, to thank her for everything she's done for us. When she opens the box, a pair of tiny baby shoes are in the box.

She looks at us a bit incredulous. 'Oh, they look like the shoes you sent me when you were pregnant with Eliott. Are you ... are you?'

We smile and nod. And being the most amazing and supportive Mum that she is, she's thrilled with the idea that we're having another baby. We share some of our worries, and she's equally empathetic.

When we go home, I dial the number of the hospital, and

192

after hearing the familiar ringtone to Australian numbers, I hear Brooke's voice.

'Thanks for giving us a call back,' she says in her usual soft voice. 'I'm here with Daniel, and we have a plan we'd like to walk you through.'

They're going to run more genetic tests. They can send everything to the lab right away so they can do a whole genome sequencing, as a trio. They already have our samples from last time, so this can be done while we're in France. They'll sequence our whole DNA to look at every potential gene, not just the ones known to cause epilepsy. And by looking at the three of us, they may be able to better identify the potential cause.

If Eliott has a mutation but we also have it, it's unlikely to be causing his symptoms, and if he's the only one with the mutation, then it might be pathogenic.

We also must choose between two options related to the time it will take and the cost associated. But it's also bigger than that, as it impacts how the pregnancy is managed.

'One option is a lot faster and would take about two weeks to get the results. The other takes about ten weeks. The difference in cost is quite significant, and the hospital wouldn't be able to pay for it, so you'd have to cover this yourself.'

I swallow and manage to ask, 'And what if we were to find something, how do these two options impact the pregnancy?

Brooke jumps in, 'There's no need to decide right now, but as we discussed yesterday, we will only go ahead with the tests if you and Ced would consider terminating the pregnancy, should we find out that the baby has the same condition as Eliott.'

I feel my throat tightening, 'We would ... We can't go through this again.'

'I completely understand. You can also change your mind at any time. We believe that the chances of finding

193

anything are slim. If we were to find something though, with the accelerated process, we should be able to get the results by the time you're back in Sydney. If we find what Eliott has, we'd test the baby too. That can only be done at ten weeks gestation and takes another two or three weeks. So, you'd still be able to terminate the pregnancy. With the normal pace results, it'll take about ten weeks to get the results. Again, we don't expect they'll find anything. But if they do, then we'd test the baby just like in the first option. However, if we found that the baby had the same condition and you want to terminate the pregnancy, you'd have to go into hospital and be induced to deliver the baby; because you'd be over the twenty-week mark.'

I may have to be induced, deliver the baby, and see him or her go away. That is not an option.

Despite all my fears, when I hear her saying this, I find myself putting my hand on my stomach, and I realise that no matter what I've been telling myself about not being ready, I already love this baby very much. I look at Ced and see a reflection of all the pain I'm experiencing.

When we discuss it later that night, the only words I can pronounce are, 'I can't.'

We decide that we'll pay to get the results faster. It's a very substantial amount of money, money we had saved up as a deposit for a house, but this is more important.

When we chat with Daniel and Brooke again the next day though, they tell us that they've managed to secure funding to pay for the test to be performed for the normal delivery timeframe. We understand that because they're not expecting to find anything, paying to get the results faster won't deliver any value, and we finally agree to the normal turnaround time.

It's going to be a long ten to twelve weeks.

The next day, I have a message from my boss in Sydney about a conference happening the following week in Prague. Ced and I decide to go together, with Eliott. We change our flights and book a hotel so we can spend the weekend before the conference in Prague and then all fly home to Sydney.

We've just gained an extra week of leave in France with family, and a couple of days visiting a new city just the three of us, as well as a slightly shorter trip home.

Most importantly, we've just gained an opportunity to focus on something else other than the bigger picture.

Eliott

Mum and Dad have packed all our suitcases, and we've said goodbye to everyone. We enjoy some family time in Prague, walking around the city, visiting the castle, and my favourite part is when we see a man making giant bubbles.

Mum and Dad even organise for me to be in the middle, and I see all the bubbles go around me.

Mum goes to work for a couple of days, and then we prepare everything to fly back to Australia.

Chapter thirteen

Ready to take on the world
(August–September 2016)

Eliott

I'm trying to get back into my normal routine but am having trouble with sleep. I'm tired early, but then I wake up after a few hours and want to play, and Mum and Dad keep telling me it's night-time. They even take me to the window so I can see that it is dark outside. I don't know what's happening, but they explain that it's something called 'jet lag', and my body needs to adjust. Within a few days, I start sleeping more normally.

Mum is going back to work, but Dad still has another two weeks with me. Then I will have to go to day care three days a week instead of just the one. And someone else is also going to join our little family: a nanny.

The day Mum goes back to work, Dad and I have a visitor.

'Eliott, my love, this is Jennifer!' Dad says.

A very smiley lady comes to the door. 'Well, hello! You must be Eliott. I'm Jen, and I've heard so much about you. How are you today?' the lady asks me.

Jen looks a bit like Mum — same height, same age, but different eye colour, and her hair is different. She also has drawings on her arm. She sits next to me, and we start playing together. She's very gentle, smiles a lot and sounds enthusiastic about everything we're going to do.

Dad and Jen talk, but she stays close to me and asks me what I think a lot. When I need a nappy change, we go together, and she sings a lovely song. Jen is going to be my nanny, and I'm looking forward to tomorrow already!

Maman

Jen will be looking after Eliott two days a week. We thought it would give Eliott a good balance between being at home and being in day care. This gives him time to explore and make friends, but also rest at home a bit. It's also likely that he'll have at least one weekly appointment: occupational therapy (OT) one week, speech therapy the next, and then physiotherapy.

Eliott is now fourteen months and starting to pull to standing and bear weight on his legs. He sits independently and has built a lot of confidence with his commando crawl. Thanks to the report sent through by the developmental clinic, and the referrals they made, we're going to start physio and occupational therapy at the hospital. It's a bit overwhelming to organise everything, and to make sure he has enough therapy but also have time to — quite simply — be a baby.

After two months off with family and loved ones, I am feeling a lot stronger. I'm also coming back pregnant and with the uncertainty of not knowing whether the baby has the same condition as Eliott. If we don't find out what Eliott has, then this will be a stressful pregnancy. But somehow, and against all odds, I feel hopeful.

I've started bonding with this baby, this new life growing inside of me, and against every recommendation ever given in a similar situation, we've even given the baby a nickname. We've been calling it 'crevette'. It's a common nickname for a baby in France, meaning 'prawn'.

On Tuesday, we see Henry for Eliott's appointment, and while we're with him, Jen spends time with Elody, the epilepsy nurse, who has offered to give her some training on how to react if Eliott were to have a seizure.

I arrive at the hospital directly from work and find Ced, Jen and Eliott in the waiting area. I haven't met Jen in person yet, and I desperately want her to like us, so I'm feeling a little anxious.

To everyone I have met since having Eliott, I am 'that mum'. I am the mum with a child who's a bit different. He's one, and only well-trained eyes could see the difference between him and a fourteen-month-old with a more typical development. But regardless, I'm that mum who spent too much time in hospital, who knows far too much about a complex condition like epilepsy, who knows what seeing death about to take her baby feels like, and who is scared about what the future might hold because it's so uncertain.

I want Jen to see us as a normal family trying to do what's best for their baby. I want her to love him. I desperately need her to be part of Team Eliott. I want to do everything in my power to give him everything he needs, and I need everyone on the team to have his back.

She and I have exchanged emails and text messages, and last night after her first day with him, she sent a text saying: *I had an amazing day. Even while having a short nap, Eliott is such a charmer. Looking forward to finally meeting you tomorrow.*

I fell in love with her immediately!

After the appointment with Henry, Jen looks after Eliott while Ced and I go to get a dating scan for the baby. The doctors also want to check that Crevette is growing well. It's quite emotional seeing this little baby on the screen. We have no idea what will happen — if he or she is healthy or not, if we're ever going to be able to hold this baby in our arms — but for a few seconds, we pretend it's all okay, and we allow ourselves to feel truly happy to see our little Crevette on that hospital monitor.

The first weekend after I started back at work, I run the City2Surf, an annual running event. Ced and I love it, and we've run it four times already. My work has a marquee on the beach, and we usually head there after racing the iconic fourteen-kilometre run from the city to Bondi. Last year, Ced considered running it but didn't find the time or the motivation to train, and I'd barely recovered from Eliott's birth.

This year is special, not just because we're going back to the starting line, it's that we're running it as a family with Eliott (in his pram) and Crevette (in my belly)!

We've packed his medication, a change of clothes, nappies, and have attached some toys to the pram to keep him entertained. Previously, it's taken us one hour twenty minutes to run it, but I'm not as fit as I used to be, and we don't know how much we're going to have to stop for Eliott if he gets hungry, thirsty, needs a nappy change, or simply is bored and needs to be carried for a bit. We're planning on two hours to finish the race.

We head to the starting line and position ourselves at the 'back of the pack' with all the prams and the walkers. We alternate between running and walking, and Ced pushes Eliott in his pram all the way through. Eliott is super excited to see the runners — many of them have dressed up, and there are even people playing music along the course. We don't need to stop at all for him.

Crossing the finish line feels like such an accomplishment. We've made it! We're starting to get back into being able to do things we did before having Eliott. Running is one of them, and running the City2Surf used to be the thing that would motivate us and make us feel lucky to live here.

It's extra special because as I take Eliott in my arms to give him a cuddle and stretch my arm to grab the medal that's being handed to me by one of the volunteers, I realise that I'm carrying my two babies!

Eliott starts occupational therapy at the hospital and speech therapy privately at home. In all the new requirements, everyone trying to get used to the routine, Jen is amazing.

It's only her second week, but it feels like she's been with us forever. She's really bonded with Eliott, who already adores her. We trust her completely, and she's shown so much empathy and care that we know we've found someone we can trust.

The speech therapist calls me at work and gives Eliott a glowing report; he's very social, has great eye contact, and babbles a lot. I know there's a 'but' coming, and that 'but' is the reason why we're paying so much money for her to come.

So, I take a deep breath and, even though I don't want to hear the bad things, I say, 'It's great to hear he had such a good session. Thank you so much for that. But tell me, what did you think of his delay? How can we help him?'

'Oh ...'

I can sense she wasn't ready for that.

'Well,' she continues, 'yes, he has some delays, but it's hard to assess at this age. His receptive language, how much he understands, should be better. He couldn't follow instructions or repeat gestures from a song, nor point to something if I asked him. These are things we'll have to work on.'

There it is: the things I didn't want to hear. I knew it was coming, but it's still so hard to hear.

'How can we help him?' I ask.

'Well, there are some strategies, and I'll send you exercises. One thing that might help — given you speak French to him at home — would be to pick one language and stick to it. Either you only speak French to him, but that would be hard, given he goes to day care and his nanny speaks English, or you only speak English to him.'

I'm processing this and finally respond, 'We can't really ask our families and friends to speak English to him. And is it not better for his brain development to learn the two languages?'

Later, when I tell Ced, he too is amazed at her suggestion.

We're a bit lost.

We've been complaining that we haven't been able to get much professional support for therapy, so should we follow her advice? But this is so impractical and doesn't consider our family dynamic. It doesn't make sense to us.

I'm still pondering this, when Ced laughs and says, 'Anyway, you'll never guess what else that new speech therapist did. Jen was just telling me that she tried to poach her!'

How could she? What a joke.

We have wasted precious time not having the right support in place that first year, when Eliott's neurons where connecting, and his brain was maturing, developing, and now I'm done. If someone isn't going to support him as much as they possibly can, then we must move on and make the hard calls — especially if they're going to take away our support and poach our nanny!

That night, Eliott starts crawling properly. I have such a strong feeling of hope, pride, and accomplishment whenever we reach a milestone. This is a big one! I send messages to everyone in the family with a little video showing Eliott on all fours in his little white pyjamas — he's looking at the camera and grunting as he lifts himself up on his hands and knees and starts moving forward.

The following day, I get a call from Brooke. She has the results from the lab and wants us to come in for a consult. The results weren't due for another eight weeks at least. I'm so shocked that I accept without asking any questions.

I make an appointment for tomorrow, but when I tell Ced, he suggests that I call Brooke back and ask if they can just tell me the results over the phone.

When I call her, I sense that she is not that keen on telling me over the phone, but she knows that if I ask, it's because we need to know. I can hear my heartbeat thumping. I don't know what to expect, but there is a small sense of hope crawling in my mind.

'I can tell you that you don't need to do any more research on it, as you know this condition well already. It's a mutation of his KCNQ2 gene, and it's a de-novo mutation, so Cedric and you are not carriers. We'll run through everything in detail tomorrow.'

How can it be?

I didn't know what to expect, but I certainly didn't expect that. He was tested for KCNQ2, and they used two methods to test and retest, but we were told it may be risky to try for another baby because KCNQ2 came back negative. And de-novo? A mutation only occurring in Eliott, not inherited ...

During the meeting the next day, they say they're investigating why the first results were negative, and they'll let us know as soon as they find out. We organise to have the baby tested as soon as possible. The fact that it's de-novo is good news for the baby though, because Eliott hasn't inherited the condition from us.

We tell our family and friends, and everyone is happy and relieved to hear that it's de-novo, because to everyone, it means that if we are to have another baby, the risks are low.

'You must be relieved to know it's not coming from you,' they say.

For me, however, it's the opposite, and no one gets that.

How horrible to think that he's the only carrier in our family. It's the inception of one of my biggest fears, as I'm afraid that one day, he'll ask, 'why me?' and 'why am I so different?' and 'why don't you, Dad, or Crevette have it?' I'm afraid that he'll feel alone and different. That he will feel misunderstood and battle demons only he knows about.

Eliott

Last week, Mum bought a bike, and she and I have been going to day care on the bike. I have my own little seat at the back. I wear a blue helmet with little trains on it, and when we start cycling, I feel the wind on my face. We don't go fast, and the day care is only two kilometres away, so it's a short ride, but I love it.

Mum occasionally stretches her arm to the side, and I can feel her hand pressing my knee or my feet and hear her say, 'Eliott, my baby, how are you? Can you see the red car? Look, I'm putting my arm out, we're turning.'

Dad has explained to me that it's his turn to go back to work. But I love day care, and now I have Jen to look after me too.

Today, Mum tells me I have to do another test where they put the things on my head. Henry wants to check that I'm okay after going to hospital in France. Jen is with us and holds my hand while she sings the sausage song to me: 'One fat sausage sizzling in the pan, sizzle sizzle sizzle, and it went bang!' I love this song, and I've stopped listening to Mum, who's showing something to Jen.

I then hear Mum and Jen laugh, and Mum says, 'I promise, you'll see. Just play the song when I ask.'

We enter the familiar room, and I recognise the chair in the middle and can see all the toys on the shelves, all the drawings that other kids have done. I smile at the man who's seen me quite a few times already.

I then feel the cold wax on my head; I don't like the feeling.

But the man is gentle ... and I do like all the colourful strings!

'Oh no, buddy, don't pull those!' the man says.

I hear Mum apologising when I pull on the different colours. We start the test, and I have a bottle of milk.

'Now would be a good time for him to sleep,' says the man.

'If only it were that easy ...' Mum laughs.

I'm already tired because we woke early to come here, and now that my belly is full of warm milk and Mum is rocking me, I do feel like I could take a nap. My eyes are closing, but I resist because there is so much happening, and I don't really want to miss anything. This seems like an important test.

'Jen, you can play the song now.'

My lullaby starts to play. I hear the first few notes of 'Uptown Funk'. I yawn, and I'm out.

Maman

We've been back for less than a month, and I already feel so tired! We've all had to get used to the new routine. Ced and I are going back to work full-time, and there's a lot to think about in terms of Eliott's diagnosis.

We've been warned by all our friends that once kids start day care, they get every illness going around, especially in winter, but thankfully, Eliott hasn't been sick yet. I'm hoping he's managed to build his immunity by going once a week before our trip home, but my gut tells me it's only a matter of time.

The molars are still causing him grief, and he's been coughing ever since we got back from France, a light cough, but we've come back from the European summer to the thick of an Australian winter, so he's bound to catch a cold or something.

On Friday, I get a call from day care to say that Eliott has a fever, and they're calling to check what I would like to do. Within five minutes of getting the call, I'm in a cab rushing over from the office, and I've called Ced, who is meeting me there with the car. We agree that if Eliott is hot when I get to day care then we'll give him his medication.

When I arrive, it's just after 12pm, and it's nap time. The shutters are all closed, and the room smells like lavender oil — if Eliott wasn't at risk of having a seizure then I would probably appreciate the relaxing atmosphere. The educators have stripped Eliott out of his clothes, and I give his chubby cheeks a kiss; he's hot. Boiling hot.

204

I grab his bag, which always has the Phenytoin, along with his emergency medication, and I give it to him, as I have done too many times over the last fifteen months.

The educators ask what they can do to help, and they're amazed at how calmly Eliott takes his medication. They're used to kids screaming and kicking to avoid taking paracetamol.

By the time we're ready to go, Ced has arrived. He looks at me anxiously, and I tell him that I've given Eliott his medication. He takes Eliott is his arms and gives him a cuddle. With a reassuring voice, he says it will all be okay. We're going home to rest.

Overnight, Eliott's cough gets worse, and he wakes up with a sore throat. He's miserable all weekend, and swallowing seems painful. We ask the home doctor to come, as we want to make sure there isn't anything worse going on which could be causing the fever. It could go to his chest or evolve into an ear infection — the ghost of his status epilepticus back in November, triggered by the fever from his chest infection, is haunting me.

Thankfully, his throat is red but everything else is good. The nights are horrendous, as we must wake him to take his Phenytoin at 12am and give him paracetamol and water to drink.

In the early hours of Sunday, we hear a bad bout of coughing in the baby monitor, and Eliott wakes up screaming. He cries in our arms for an hour. He's exhausted but doesn't want to go back to bed, and at 4am we give in and take him into our bed. We usually avoid it, but we need the sleep, and we all end up dozing until 7.30am.

I stay home on Monday, and it feels like stolen time when he ends up napping on my lap for two hours. I just enjoy being able to spend the time with Eliott and take it easy.

When Jen arrives on Tuesday, Eliott is almost back to normal, but I'm afraid that he is going to be difficult after another bad night. I apologise to Jen in advance, but in the evening when we arrive home, she assures us he's been sweet all day. He's starting to eat again and has napped well in his cot. I'm now convinced she has some kind of magical powers that soothe Eliott!

Before we know it, it's early September and we're celebrating Father's Day. Eliott has created some drawings at day care, and Ced loves receiving his first official craft from Eliott.

He's fifteen months on 9 September, and it's another day off work for me, as we have our appointment to test Crevette.

I've researched information on the doctor who's doing the procedure, to reassure myself, but it still takes all my strength to stay calm and not move while the doctor puts a twenty-centimetre-long needle into my belly and gets some placenta to test. I pray that everything goes well and that we've made the right choice by going ahead with it.

I can feel that this baby is special, and I already want to meet my Crevette badly. The risk of miscarriage with this test is about two per cent. It's considered quite low, but we've been so unlucky that I don't want to take any risks, and so I stay in bed for most of the weekend. The riskiest period after the procedure is the following forty-eight hours, but they say anything can happen up to ten days.

The risk of Crevette having the same condition as Eliott is low and means the highest risk we might be facing is that the invasive procedure leads to a miscarriage. Every time I think about this, I cry, but the thought of having another child with the same condition is scarier, and I know we couldn't survive that. We may barely survive miscarrying a healthy baby, but we wouldn't survive having another child with the same condition, knowing we had the means to find out and avoid it.

The following week, we have a follow-up appointment with Henry, who's happy with Eliott's overall progress but is also starting to worry that Eliott isn't communicating or understanding simple instructions. A fifteen-month-old should understand a lot more. This is challenging to hear.

Henry listens to our concerns and our adventures with the first speech therapist. He laughs when I recount how she was trying to poach Jen — our Mary Poppins — and suggests a new speech therapy centre next to the hospital.

One afternoon while I'm at work, I get a call to say that we're going to have a healthy baby.

Oh, Crevette! I love you so much already.

'Do you want to know the sex?'

It's a baby boy! We're going to have two boys! I call Ced straightaway, and I feel this huge relief. Crevette is safe.

Brooke calls me one day to explain that the reason Eliott's initial tests for KCNQ2 came back negative was because the sample they thought was Eliott's was someone else's.

Silence.

My stomach drops.

I don't want to imagine what could have happened. We could've changed Eliott's treatment based on those results; we could've started more medication that might have hindered his physical, mental, and emotional development; we could've stopped Phenytoin, which is known to work well with KCNQ2.

The worst is that we could've decided not to risk it and not have another baby. We could've waited a few years before doing more genetic testing, and then realised five years down the track that our opportunity to have a healthy child and a chance at a normal life had come and gone. And we could've terminated a pregnancy for no reason.

Eliott

One Friday in mid-September, I have a sleepover at Chiara's. It's a treat to have someone to play with. Chiara is a year older than I am, so she shows me her toys and how to play with them, and she reads me books.

In the morning, Ethan takes Chiara to her gym class, and I stay home with Sophie. We play with one of Chiara's little ponies. It's got long pink hair and sings when you press a button. I ask Sophie to press the button again, and again, and again. It's so much fun.

When Mum and Dad arrive to pick me up, they give me a kiss, and we all sit in the living room to have a chat.

'We have some news,' Mum says with a huge smile.

Sophie looks happy; maybe she already knows what it is? 'And ...'

Mum laughs. 'We're pregnant! Eliott is going to have a baby brother. We got some test results earlier this week, and the baby is fine.'

Both Mum and Sophie have tears in their eyes when they hug. It's wonderful to see them so jolly.

Unfortunately, on Sunday, I have another fever. I take my medication again. I have lots of trouble sleeping, and I don't feel like myself. I'm irritated and not happy about things. I feel hungry then not, and I often wake in the middle of the night but can't go back to sleep.

I usually call for Mum and Dad, but I can't say 'Mum' or 'Dad', so I cry and yell. They always come and give me big cuddles, but I know they're tired and not happy.

They gently tell me not to worry, and that it's the medication doing this. We just need to be patient and take it easy for a few days. But I still don't like it. It's hard for me.

They're right though, as the fever drops that night, and the next day I feel better.

I have a great couple of days with Jen, but on the following Sunday, I don't feel good again. My molars are hurting, and I can't sleep much. I can't even eat my dinner. I don't know how to tell them how I feel, so I cry a lot and am grumpy.

After my bath, some friends arrive. They're coming over to have dinner with Mum and Dad. I see them just to say goodnight. But I don't want to go to sleep. I usually go to sleep easily after our bedtime routine, so surely if I try to change that, Mum will understand. But she doesn't.

My teeth are hurting so much that I keep waking up and crying. Mum comes back to the room and rocks me and sings to me so I can go to sleep. By the third time, I've cried so much that I'm feeling hot, but not enough that Mum thinks I have another fever.

I finally fall sleep.

In the middle of the night, I feel a cool hand on my forehead. Mum must've felt that I still wasn't feeling well. She picks me up from my bed, and Dad puts a syringe in my mouth. I taste the familiar sugary syrup.

Mum whispers, 'It kills me to give it to him again. It's the third time in three weeks, but he shouldn't be hot at this time of night. I think he was trying to tell us something earlier.'

A few minutes later, I'm relaxing in Mum's arms and going back to sleep when suddenly I feel something. And this time, I also see something so frightening that I scream. It's a very deep, almost primal scream; I have never been so scared. And I feel it, once more: my brain and my body give in. My body stiffens so much that I can't do anything anymore. I am having another seizure.

Maman

Not again! Not like this, just after giving him his medication. By the time we get to hospital, it's 4am and we've barely slept. I'm so physically exhausted and emotionally drained that I lie down next to Eliott and sleep with him in my arms.

In the morning, Ced asks me what I want for breakfast. I'm starving and there is only one thing that I feel like. 'Can you get me a bacon and egg roll?'

He looks at me and laughs. 'Sure, is that you or Crevette talking?'

I've never had a bacon and egg roll in my entire life. 'And a muffin for Eliott?'

Ced kisses my forehead and goes on his bacon and egg roll mission.

While he's away, Eliott wakes, and the nurses bring in his breakfast and some toys for him to play with. One of the hospital volunteers has arrived and is blowing bubbles to amuse Eliott. He's a gentle middle-aged man, clearly aiming to do good and craving interaction with kids. And at this stage, poor Eliott is exhausted. He had his second loading dose of Phenytoin in a week, one dose of Midazolam, and he's not interested in the bubbles. The volunteer tries for a few minutes to get his attention and then looks a bit annoyed.

The rational me knows that what I am viewing as an inquisitive or disappointed look is probably more a look of concern. He's looking at Eliott, and I feel like he wants to ask why my child isn't more interested in the bubbles like every other child. This man, a volunteer, is too smart and too empathetic, and probably too kind to ask a question like this, but the rational me isn't here anymore. And I'm not very patient.

I don't want to talk to him and explain the horrible night we just went through, that I'm exhausted and hormonal, and that I just want to go home with a healthy toddler and my bacon and egg roll.

Ced comes back, and I start crying. Somehow Ced gets it straightaway and just gives me a big cuddle and another kiss on the forehead.

The volunteer packs his bubbles away, probably to go and see if another kid may be more responsive and appreciative, but before he does, very gently, he leans down to Eliott's level and says, 'Goodbye, buddy', and he waves at us and says he'll come back later if we want.

I am left feeling even worse.

We see the same neurologist we saw in May, who agreed to try the new plan where we only give Eliott his Phenytoin when he has a fever. I'm afraid he'll say we're not managing well, given Eliott has had two seizures in two months. He's asking us about the plan, and I feel like a student who just failed a test. We missed it. I didn't check on Eliott enough. He was trying to tell me something, and I didn't listen.

What kind of a mother does that?

But the neurologist lives in a world where people can have dozens of seizures every day, and he says we did everything right. So, I feel grateful. He looks at Eliott and turns towards us to tell us that he understands how hard it is for us. We need to remember that the plan is working. If we feel confident about it, we should keep going. Two seizures in two months aren't many compared to the risks of having Eliott on Phenytoin all the time. We'll get better at it, and we did the right thing.

However, the screaming beforehand is interesting, and it sounds like Eliott may have had an aura. Some people with epilepsy can see them coming a few minutes or seconds before they happen, and that's probably what happened last night.

We're discharged around midday and go home to get some rest.

Eliott doesn't have a fever anymore and has a great day with Jen.

For good or bad, we realise that these moments in our life — which have now become far too common — are simultaneously affecting us more when they happen, but we recover from them faster.

Our survival instincts kick in, and the need to go back to normal is so strong that we both go back to work the next day, and Eliott gets back into his normal routine.

Chapter fourteen

The holiday marathon
(October–December 2016)

Maman

Thankfully, beyond all the drama of the last month, there are also many good things happening. Eliott is making so much progress. He's pulling up to standing a lot more, is a super happy baby, and we're grateful that after every seizure, he's been waking up and continuing as he was before. We've heard about kids who regress badly after seizures and must relearn skills that were previously acquired.

We've done a lot of thinking around what we need to do to help us in the next few months. Should we push for more therapy, even if it means taking time off work or going part-time? Should we work as much as we can until the baby is born and then take a sabbatical? Or is there a third option?

The trip to France was so beneficial, and it's easy to identify that a big part of it was just being in the right headspace — we were on holidays, spending quality time with family and friends — so we decide that over the next few months, we'll travel more. It's the right time to do it, while I can easily travel, and Eliott is still little and we don't have to pay for an airfare for him. We are conscious that we're lucky to be able to do it, as epilepsy is a tricky condition, and some people can't travel easily — jetlag and lack of sleep can be triggers for seizures.

We're also lucky to be able to afford it and can make the choice to stop saving and review our long-term saving plans.

We're investing in our mental health. It's all about us as a family, and how we can create positive memories and find our balance.

We're calling the next six weeks: 'The holiday marathon'.

We start with a weekend away with friends in the Royal National Park. Julie has booked a house for two nights. There are three kids going: Eliott, Chiara and Lila. It's wonderful to watch them playing together.

Sophie, Julie and I go for a short walk one of the days, and Sophie says, 'I love these weekends away with you guys.'

'Yes, it's so nice to be able to get away for the weekend,' adds Julie.

'And I love that our kids get along so well together,' Sophie says.

I am so grateful for the way she consistently manages to acknowledge our daily struggles, while at the same time these small remarks show that in her mind, Eliott is just part of the pack.

Sophie is looking at Julie and me when she says, 'I think we should go camping one weekend. The weather is perfect at this time, and I'm sure the kids would love it.'

Julie and I reply at the same time, 'Yes, great idea!'

We laugh, and then I say, 'We can extend the holiday marathon with a camping trip! That will give us a fabulous mix of experiences!'

'Do you remember how Leonore kept talking about Mackerel Beach near Palm Beach? Maybe we could go there, it looks amazing.'

My heart sinks, and it feels like I'm having palpitations. They couldn't possibly realise, but we can't go camping there. 'Is that the one you can only access by ferry?' I ask, as tears well.

Julie has picked up on the fact that something's wrong, but I can tell her mind is still racing to figure out what it might be. 'Yes, it is,' she says, 'but it's very easy to carry everything there, apparently.'

I keep my tears in check long enough to say, 'We can't do that. You guys do it, obviously, but we can't go where there's no road access. If Eliott were to have a seizure in the middle of the night, we need to know that an ambulance can get to us or that there is an emergency plan in place.' I then let the tears fall.

'Oh, wow, you really need to think about it all the time!' Julie says.

Yes, we do.

Unfortunately, the following Thursday, I'm in a meeting when day care calls. I recognise the room leader's voice.

'Claire, I'm sorry to bother you, but Eliott just woke up from his nap. He's not hot, but we feel something's not right.'

My heart skips a beat. I trust the day care completely; they wouldn't call if they didn't think it important, and a scary feeling is slowly creeping in.

When I walk into the centre, everything is dark and silent. It's nap time again. I don't know what to expect, given the room leader couldn't tell me much besides the fact that she had a hunch that something was wrong.

I see Eliott, in his nappy, playing with her on the other side of the room. He looks relaxed and smiles when he sees me. I go to take him in my arms, and he feels hot.

The room leader looks at me and says, 'We took his temperature when he woke from his nap, and he was at 37.2, so not a fever, and he's happy playing, but he looked off. We took it again after we called you, and it was 37.5.'

'Can we take it again, please?' I ask.

She grabs the thermometer and puts it under his arm. When it beeps, she shows it me. '38.2'.

'Oh, gosh,' I say. 'I don't know how you figured out that he was off, but thank you so much.' I draw the loading dose of Phenytoin, with all the educators watching anxiously.

We take his temperature again at home, and he's at 39.3 degrees. He went from 37.2 to 39.3 in less than two hours. I'm amazed and grateful to the day care staff, so I call them to thank them again. It's now been well over thirty minutes since he's had his loading dose, so he should be safe, but we're setting our alarm clocks every two hours to monitor him through the night.

Eliott's gums are bright red and look sore, and we're just praying that the molars pop up soon. It feels like every tooth is giving him so much grief. *When will it stop?*

The fever suddenly drops just before midnight, and when he wakes up in the morning, he's feeling much better. We've had another big scare and have had to give him Phenytoin yet again, but we've avoided the worst.

And miraculously, the molar finally cuts through the gum. *Hooray!*

Eliott

On the days when I'm with Jen, we go to the playground, to the library, and to see the physio and the occupational therapist. The physio has said that I need to practise getting up and down stairs, so Jen and I go to the lobby in our apartment building, and I go up and down the carpeted stairs. I quite like it, and Jen then takes me home to wash my hands once I've done it a few times and had enough.

We're also practising walking, and I'm now starting to stand on my own and can support my weight for a few seconds, which everyone seems really excited about. Jen sings a lot, and I like seeing her hands do the actions and listening to her voice.

Maman

On the Wednesday evening before leaving for a trip to New Zealand, we have dinner with friends down the street from us. We walk there, and Eliott falls asleep in his pram. On our way home, I notice Eliott's face looks a bit flushed. I stretch my hand towards his forehead and can already feel that something's not right. He's boiling hot. *Not again!*

We quickly walk home, and as we arrive, Ced rushes to get everything ready. We can't take any chances, and it feels like we're on autopilot when we give him a loading dose of Phenytoin and set the alarm clocks again.

We barely sleep that night, and I want to cancel the trip. Ced, however, is more practical. In his view, Eliott is now on Phenytoin, so he's protected. We don't know what he has, and it could be another twelve-hour thing, so we should go.

I reluctantly get ready.

The house we've rented in New Zealand is amazing, and we feel blessed that we've made it. On our way there, I check where the closest hospital is and triple check that we have enough Phenytoin and Midazolam.

We've agreed together that we will stay near the house until Eliott feels better.

And Ced's right — in less than twenty-four hours, the fever is gone. We think that it was probably the molars again, as he didn't develop any other symptoms.

We spend Friday exploring the little town and plan a hike for the next day. It's an easy one, given I'm already five months pregnant, but we love to hike, and Eliott has a blast. Quickly, as we start to pick up the pace on our walk and head into the woods, I notice his head slowly falling to the side, and his eyes closing. Within minutes he's asleep. Being surrounded by the wilderness and rocked by our voices must make him feel relaxed.

Ced and I talk about everything and anything: Eliott, therapy, day care, Jen, work, Crevette, our current rental apartment and whether we should move before Crevette arrives, and of course how incredible this experience has been, even with Eliott sick earlier in the trip. I welcome the space to think about other things, and to take deep breaths as we walk up and down mountains. This is why I have always loved hiking so much.

When we return to Sydney, we have a short week. Eliott shows that he's happy to see Jen again after being away, and it is so sweet to witness. In a short amount of time, she's managed to create a deep and trusting relationship with him and is his strongest advocate, after us. But she also has such a great attitude, is so proactive and keen to help us, that we feel like anything is possible.

She teaches us new songs, new games, shows us new places to visit with Eliott, new activities to do, and new recipes to try for him. She is so patient and easy-going, it's inspiring. And without being conscious of it, it allows us to get enough energy to face all the daily challenges.

At the weekend, Eliott has another sleepover at Chiara's. Being able to organise these sleepovers has felt like the life raft we needed. Sophie and Ethan have been so encouraging and are always happy to see Eliott. Chiara welcomes him like a little brother and looks out for him beautifully.

Every time we leave him, I show Sophie the medication, and we go through the emergency procedure again. They're the only friends who have taken Eliott overnight, to give us some respite, and we are ever so grateful, especially when we're always so tired.

Eliott always sleeps well when he's with them, and they love the opportunity to teach Chiara about having guests and playing with friends. It's great all around, as we also love having her over. Eliott has had about one sleepover a month, and it has meant the world to Ced and me to have these evenings together and lie-ins in the morning!

A camping trip concludes our holiday marathon. We are thankful to our friends for listening to our concerns about going to Mackerel Beach, and instead go to the Hawkesbury region, north of Sydney.

When we get there, Sophie, Ethan, Julie and Anthony have already set up camp in a great spot with lots of shade by the river. We have lunch, and the three kids love having a picnic outside. They nap in their prams, and in the afternoon we organise a dance party for them. The stars twinkle, the wheels on the bus go 'round, and the little bunnies hop all afternoon.

After an exciting picnic dinner, everyone goes to sleep, and Eliott falls asleep easily for once! I look at his cute, chubby face asleep on the mattress — he looks so peaceful and content. I touch his forehead and it's cool. I like that he's going to sleep next to us tonight. I give him a gentle kiss on the forehead and leave the tent as gracefully as I can — while crawling out on all fours!

I look at Ced and notice the tiredness from all the recent sleepless nights, the worry with Eliott being sick, the packing, the unpacking, but I also see a glimpse of what we had in France: the strength to keep going. We have proven to ourselves that we can do this.

I know our lives will always be different and more challenging, but we *can* go camping for the weekend if we feel like it. It's a bigger battle to keep up with everyone and not get left behind, and it will continue to require some adjustments, but we can keep going.

With only a few weeks left before the Christmas holidays, we have a meeting with a community-based organisation that provides at-home support services. Not only will the home visits ensure that it's easier for Jen and Eliott to manage, but we'll also get a key worker who centralises all the requests and organises the different therapists based on Eliott's needs. It sounds exactly like what we've been looking for, and we can't wait to start.

Eliott's key worker is called Joe. I meet with him and one of the managers on a Friday afternoon. Joe walks into the room — he's a tall young man with long blond curly hair — and talks slowly as if he's cautiously weighing every word before speaking. He's sweet and looks touched by our story. He's a physio, has recently started working with the organisation, and Eliott would be the first child he supports as a key worker. He's evidently keen to do a good job. Eliott is going to love him, as he's currently obsessed with people's hair. We couldn't manufacture a better fit!

The interview is long, and I realise that despite my optimism and how badly I want Eliott to be fine, I have to answer 'no' every time I get asked a question about his abilities.

I cry a lot, and the manager keeps saying that it sounds worse than it probably is because they're trying to assess what his needs are, and the system is deficit based. They look for weaknesses, not strengths. At one point during the interview, the manager asks how Eliott's feeding is going.

'He loves to eat!'

'Great. Does he show you what he wants? For example, if he wants milk, will he point to the fridge?'

'He doesn't.' I always feel like I'm letting Eliott down, having to admit there's so much he can't do.

'Yet,' the manager says, smiling.

That one word makes me feel better. She's right, and I see Joe glance at her, clearly making a mental note.

Eliott isn't doing it ... *yet*.

It's a good lesson for Joe and me.

Joe starts the following week. He goes to day care on the Friday to meet the staff and to see how Eliott operates in that environment. The director and Eliott's educators have been so helpful and supportive and have made sure they could accommodate Joe's visit. I get positive feedback when I pick Eliott up that day and wait to get the written report, not thinking too much about it. Everyone has been saying that Eliott's been doing amazingly well lately.

On Monday, I'm working from home when I notice Joe's email in my inbox — it's the report.

I continue with what I'm doing for work, and when I have a break, I decide to read the report.

The results are so unexpected!

The report is negative; it's very factual and highlights a lot of things Eliott can't do, which I wasn't even aware of.

I call the day care centre to get a better understanding of what happened and why we haven't been told that he was doing so poorly.

I hear a big sigh on the other end of the line. 'Oh, Claire. What does the report say?' the director asks, softly.

I read her the whole report. 'I thought he was doing so much better. I didn't realise it was that bad.'

The director takes a deep breath. 'Honestly, Claire, I'm really angry with this report.'

Okay, maybe it's not just me!

She continues, 'Why would he write it like that? We know Eliott needs more attention, we all know it, but he is doing well.' She recites one of the sentences: '"Doesn't know how to pack away" — of course he doesn't, he's fifteen months old. Honestly, I'm going to give Joe a call. A lot of what he's written is correct, though.' She recites again: '"Is getting stronger on his feet"— well, that's correct. But he needs to write it differently or give you a call before. It's too hard for you to read this not knowing what's age appropriate and what's not. How are you feeling?'

'Not good,' I admit. 'It's so hard, as we're trying, but it's never enough.'

The conversation lasts well over an hour, and I'm forever grateful to her for having been there for me that day. More than that, she follows through, and the next day Joe calls me during my lunch break.

'Claire, do you have a minute?'

It's 12.30pm, and I'm waiting in line to order at the food court in my office building.

'Yes, sure.' I leave the line and sit in an armchair in the lobby, the weight of Crevette tiring me already.

'I'm really sorry. The day care mentioned you were upset about the report. I have re-read it, and I can see why you'd be upset. I was trying to be factual, but Eliott did good things when I was there too. I was just trying to highlight

220

where he can improve, so we know what to work on.'

'Thanks, Joe. It's nice of you to call and apologise. It was just difficult to read this. During the interview, you said you were going to focus on his strengths, and it really didn't feel like that at all. I know I'm probably a bit more emotional than usual.'

'I get that, and I'll work on the wording next time. I'll also give you a call beforehand if I feel like you need to be aware of anything special.'

I hear the concern in his voice, and it makes me feel more positive about it all.

The last few weeks before the Christmas break are bustling — work is hectic, and Eliott is sick again. He has gastro — thankfully without a fever, so we don't need to give him Phenytoin — but no one gets any sleep.

A week and a half before the break, I must travel for work, and Cedric needs to work late, so Eliott goes to sleep at Sophie and Ethan's but wakes at 4am and can't go back to sleep. We're exhausted, and now we're making our friends tired too!

We're staying in Australia for Christmas this year, and Ced's decided to create a new tradition — he's bought an Advent calendar. It's gorgeous and made of linen with little red and green pockets. The numbers look like they've been handsewn. He puts something in it for every day.

One day it's a little chocolate, one day a little poem, one day a little toy for Eliott, such as a box of crayons, and one day it's one of my Christmas gifts delivered early!

Ced and I are going to the Opera House for the Christmas carols — it's our first 'date night' in a while. Jen is coming to look after Eliott.

As always, it feels magical to have that stolen time together. We're grateful that we can leave Eliott with Jen, knowing that they'll spend a good evening together; he'll have fun, and she's there if he needs anything. Having her in our lives has been such a blessing. Going from a team of three to a team of four has made us a lot stronger.

Just before Christmas, we attend a catch-up with the mothers group. Everyone is meeting for breakfast on the grassy knoll in Bondi. I've decided to take Eliott on my own. Ever since the barbecue last year, Ced's not been able to come to any of the group events. It's been too hard for him to witness how advanced other kids Eliott's age seem compared to Eliott. But I've found it helpful and a supportive group, so I keep going.

We've organised to each bring one gift to share, so everyone leaves with a gift!

The sun is shining, and it's very relaxing. Once all the babies have had food, a few dads decide that they're going to take the babies to the ocean for a swim. It's hot, and it will be pleasant to put them in the water. I would love for Eliott to go, but I'm not overly confident — given I'm now six-month pregnant — to go in the waves carrying Eliott.

However, I ask two of the dads if they can wait for me. 'I'd love to put Eliott in the water,' I say as I'm putting Eliott in his swimming nappy and rash guard. And I point to my pregnant belly. 'But I don't have a great sense of balance at the moment, so I'd rather go with you in case the waves are a bit too strong.'

They smile at me, and one of the dads replies, 'Come on, buddy, let's get you in the water!'

It is the first swim of the season, and Eliott absolutely loves being in the water. He's obviously impressed by the waves at first, but we don't go in too deep, so it's mostly his feet getting wet, and he's having so much fun. I know this is going to be an amazing summer!

Eliott

I loved swimming in the ocean. I was a bit scared at the beginning because the waves were huge, but Mum was laughing and kissing me, and saying what a big boy I was to go in the waves, so I relaxed quickly. She was carrying me and showing me how to jump when the waves arrived.

I heard Mum and Dad say that we should make the most of being so close to the beach this summer, especially if we have to move in a few months. Do we have to move? Why would we move?

On Tuesday, Jen doesn't come to our place in the morning. Mum and I hop in the car. Dad gives me a kiss and says he's sorry, but he has to go to work.

'Are you going to be okay?' he asks Mum.

'Yes, don't worry at all. It's only a routine appointment. I'll call you when we finish, and we'll pick Jen up on our way to the hospital, so all good. I'll say hi to Henry for you!'

After we've driven down the street to Jen's place, she jumps in the car and gives me a kiss, 'How are you, lovely? How did you sleep?'

I think I slept well, but Mum makes a funny face.

'It's been so hot lately, and he's started waking in the middle of the night again to take a bottle.'

Jen looks at me and gives me a kiss on the hand, 'Ooohh, Eliott! That's not good. You must be tired. But I get it, it has been hot lately!'

I like her so much — she gets me.

We arrive at the hospital, and Henry calls us in almost straightaway. He's not wearing his colourful pants today, but he's smiling as always.

'How is Master Eliott today?'

I hear Mum talk about how sick I've been lately, and Henry is pleased to hear that despite all the sickness, I haven't had a seizure since the one in September. 'Okay,' he starts, 'I think it's time to review his medication and the plan. We'll just change the dosage, as he's now getting quite big.'

After the appointment with Henry, we have a session at the feeding clinic because I'm struggling to eat chunks. I choke easily when I drink as well. We've been at the hospital for a long time already, and I'm starving. The therapist says it's good if I can eat and drink in front of her.

But then when I drink out of my sippy cup, I start to choke.

The therapist looks concerned. 'Does he often do that?'

'Yes, quite regularly.'

'I think you might need to try to give him a thickener. It's natural, just a powder you put in his water to thicken it so it's easier to drink. I'll give you some to try at home, and I'll write down the name so you can buy some if it works.'

Mum puts me back in my pram, and we head to the car. As Jen puts me in my seat and Mum puts the pram away, I hear them talking.

Jen turns to Mum. 'Do you want me to drop you into the city on our way home?'

'Yes, please. What did you think of that thickener recommendation?'

'If he needs it, I'm happy to prepare it.'

Jen has put music on in the car, and I'm falling asleep. Just as I close my eyes, I hear Mum say, 'Well, I think that's just too much, as he's doing okay without it. I'd rather we teach him to drink properly.'

Jen immediately replies, 'I was hoping you'd say that. I don't think he needs it either.'

At the weekend, we stay near the house because I'm not feeling well. I can't hold anything down, and I'm tired. I feel hot, and when Mum and Dad take my temperature, they say it's 39 degrees. So, they give me my loading dose of Phenytoin. It's a bigger dose, but then I only have to take two doses every day instead of three. This is much better, as it means Mum and Dad can give it to me before bed and then again when I wake in the morning.

It's Saturday evening, and I'm feeling so bad that I can't go to sleep. Mum and Dad give me a bottle, which I manage to keep down, and I finally go to sleep.

I wake up again while it's still so dark outside. I moan. I don't feel good.

Mum rushes to my room and takes me in her arms. 'Oh, Eliott, my baby, you're burning hot again.' She's kissing my forehead softly. I sense that she's scared. 'Ced, can you come, and don't make too much noise, just in case.'

When Dad comes in, I'm not feeling like myself.

Mum looks at Dad, and suddenly says, 'He's too hot. I'm going to get him an extra dose of Phenytoin and paracetamol.'

'Okay, go get everything ready, and I'll stay here with him.' Dad takes me in his arms, and when Mum comes in, she gives me the medication.

We wait a little bit, and then Dad says, 'We need to get his temperature down.'

'You're right. Can you run a cool bath for him?'

It's weird being in the bath in the middle of the night. But it helps a bit, and after a while I start to feel better. Dad dresses me in a onesie, and I fall asleep quickly.

I feel a cool hand on my forehead a couple of times through the night again, and when I wake up in the morning, I'm much better. Thankfully, the outside temperature has dropped, and it feels cool today.

Maman

We've planned to leave for the Blue Mountains to celebrate Christmas Eve with George, Charlotte and Iggy. I'm looking forward to the break and to spend some time in a cooler place. This is the hottest summer in years, and being six-months pregnant in this heat is no fun.

We love our apartment — it's so conveniently located and so homey — but we can't get any air flowing through it and have had numerous nights where the inside temperature has stayed close to 30 degrees.

Eliott has been getting into a bad habit of waking every night because he's so thirsty, so we give him a bottle of water and put him back to sleep, but it's exhausting.

On Friday, Eliott's grumpy, and sure enough, a couple of hours later, he's febrile. I'm crying while I give him his second loading dose in a week. The night is one of the worst ever. He wakes up restless and hot at 2.30am and screams until 4.30am.

We decide to push our departure back and instead of celebrating the holidays, we set our alarm clocks for the night. We have to unpack clothes, toys, and bottles, and it is a bad reminder of his first Christmas, when we had to unpack only a few days before we were due to fly to France.

No matter how much we wish we could go, we're not taking any chances. Leaving today is just a bad idea.

We end up celebrating Christmas Eve just the two of us, and while we're trying to have dinner, Eliott wakes up screaming twice. It's not even 10pm yet.

Fortunately, on Christmas Day, Eliott is feeling better. We have breakfast and then open our gifts. Somehow, we are managing to turn this into a great Christmas. Despite the fatigue and the stress, we're able to enjoy it. When we saw Ewan before the weekend, he gave Eliott antibiotics, fearing things would get worse over the holiday when everyone is away, and now that they have kicked in, Eliott is back to his usual happy self. He is now old enough to enjoy tearing the wrapping paper apart and has a blast.

We leave for the Blue Mountains later that day. We'll only have two nights there, but we're looking forward to spending that time with our friends.

Being away is good, but also bittersweet. Eliott and Iggy are only six months apart, but the gap between the two is starting to widen. We love watching Iggy grow up, but it's difficult to witness the difference between him and Eliott.

When Charlotte and I were both pregnant, we constantly talked about our kids growing up together and becoming best buds, and it is hard to imagine that it may never happen, because we don't know how Eliott is going to be. The past few weeks have shown us just how different our lives are. Here we are, spending time with our best friends, Eliott's godparents, and yet we've never felt so isolated.

We find we're happy when it's time to go home, and we spend some time at the beach. We also spend time with Ethan and Chiara, as Sophie has to work between Christmas and New Year. We have arranged to celebrate New Year's Eve at their place. It's walking distance from our place, and it will be fun for Chiara and Eliott to be together before us adults celebrate the new year.

In the afternoon, Ced is on the balcony reading while I play with Eliott in the living room. He's been stronger on his legs lately and has been able to walk while holding our hands. We're practising a few exercises and singing action songs when I notice that he's intrigued by Ced's laptop on the couch.

I open the laptop and show Eliott how my fingers can play with the keyboard; the sound of the clicking makes him giggle. While he's still watching the laptop, I take him a metre away from the couch, and then ...

'CED ... COME HERE NOW!'

Ced rushes into the living room, looking anxious and obviously concerned. 'What is it?' he asks.

'Look at this. Are you ready?' I answer with a huge grin, and I can see by his smile that he's understood. I turn to Eliott and show him the laptop again. 'Do you want to have a play with Daddy's laptop?' I ask him, and then I let go of him.

Eliott looks at the laptop and puts one foot in front of the other, then another, then another, and just like that, he is walking!

I look at Ced, who's crying too, and we both start laughing.

'This is amazing!' He picks Eliott up, who clearly doesn't understand what the big fuss is about. 'I'm so proud of you! You're walking! And you did that to reach the laptop; what a geek! And to think the doctors said he may never walk!'

Chapter fifteen
The next stage of grief
(January-April 2017)

Eliott

I am almost nineteen months old, and I've finally figured out this walking business. I just love it. I can be like Mum and Dad and walk to go wherever I want. I'm still a bit unsteady, but I try to do more and more.

The day after I take my first steps, we're all at home still on holidays, but we run into Jen on the street. I haven't seen her for over a week, so I'm excited to see her.

'Hi Eliott, hi Claire. Happy New Year to you all!' she says. 'I got the video yesterday!' Jen turns to me. 'Eliott, I saw you taking your first steps! I'm so proud of you!' She looks at Mum again. 'He must be so proud of himself! Such a big boy!'

'Yes, you should have seen his face! And both of us were crying, of course!'

Jen lowers her voice and looks like she's about to share a secret, but she's smiling, and I hear her say to Mum, 'Ron and I were both crying too. We are so happy for him, and for you both. It's amazing. And I hope you don't mind, but I shared it with my mum too. She was ecstatic.'

'Oh, that is so sweet, and it means a lot. We're lucky to have you, Jen.'

While I'm at day care this week, Mum has two days at home.

She's been cooking a lot — today she's cooked pies, and I get to try the sauce. It's a creamy sauce with chicken, garlic, onion, bacon, and leeks. I open my mouth and eat it all. Mum mixes it with a sweet potato puree.

When I finish, Mum laughs and says, 'Well, it looks like you can start eating like us, baby! I'm glad you liked it. It's such a pleasure to cook for you.'

Maman

Eliott being able to walk is such a game changer. Some kids with KCNQ2 are more impacted than Eliott is, some unable to walk.

I'm a bit concerned that he hasn't learnt how to stand independently. It's taken him so long to learn to walk that it could take months again before he masters this skill, but we'll just have to be patient.

I've picked him up from day care early on my way home from work. I'm standing next to the French window that leads onto the balcony, watching Eliott crawl towards the balcony. About a metre away from the window, he stops, goes from his knees to his feet, shifts his weight back, and slowly brings his hands towards his feet. He stands and starts walking towards the window. He holds onto the window frame, lifts one little foot up over the frame, and ventures onto the balcony. *What has just happened?*

I'm so amazed at what unfolded in front of my eyes that I can barely speak. I ask Eliott to do it again so I can record it on my phone and send it to our family and friends.

It's 10 January; he only started walking ten days ago, and now he's managed this! If this is the progress he's capable of, maybe the sky is the limit.

As we're settling back into our routine after the Christmas break, Eliott comes down with gastro again, and with the outside temperature over thirty degrees throughout the night, he's thirsty but can't hold anything down. We monitor his fluid intake and give him 50ml of water at a time. He's unhappy and screams for more; he probably thinks we're preventing him from drinking. But on the odd times we let him have more, he throws it all up, so we have to be careful. We're up every couple of hours.

Thankfully, it only lasts twenty-four hours before he starts to feel better, and at the same time, the outside temperature also drops. I'm physically struggling with it all and find everything uncomfortable and tiring.

Ced is making sure he comes home early from work and helps as much as possible, and I've slowed down a bit at work. I only have one business trip left planned in January, and I'm rather looking forward to it. An air-conditioned hotel room and uninterrupted sleep. In these circumstances, I don't mind flying when I'm seven months pregnant!

I'm due to start maternity leave early March. Crevette is due mid-March, so that will leave me a couple of weeks to rest before the birth.

In February, Jen starts taking him to swimming lessons. I go along for the first one. He clearly loves it and doesn't seem to mind that the pool isn't heated and is a bit chilly. He's wearing a new wetsuit, so he seems comfortable. He's not really following any of the instructions but is having a lot of fun. It's another big milestone. No one knows if the seizures will stop and if he'll ever be able to swim unsupervised, but we want to make sure he gets that exposure. He loves being in the water, and it's good for his muscle tone.

We finally feel like we have a bit of stability, which is all going to get completely disrupted in a couple of months when Crevette arrives.

We're trying to make the most of these easier weeks and spend as much time with Eliott as possible before we go from a family of three to a family of four.

On a Tuesday in mid-February, I'm looking after Eliott, who

has been sick again and has had to be on Phenytoin for a couple of days. We experienced the usual pinch to the heart when we had to give it to him, but we know we can't take any risks. We've gone through the same cycle of seeing him struggling with mood swings, and the insomnia, and this time we're noticing a lack of coordination.

This is a new twist.

We'd never really noticed, but it's easier to see the difference now that he's walking. It's the second time he's had Phenytoin since he started walking, and he's clumsy and falls a lot more when he's on it.

That Tuesday, Jen has had to take the day off, and Eliott and I are at the playground when I get a call from Suzy from a charity called KCNQ2 Cure Alliance. Their primary objective is funding research to find a cure.

I find that appealing, and I want to get involved and help. I also want to make a difference for Eliott and for other families who may be going through a similar experience. I'm not sure how it's going to work, given they're based in the United States, but I am keen to know more about it.

Being honest with myself, I know why I haven't reached out to this group earlier. Doctors, psychologists, family and friends have all suggested finding a community to discuss the challenges faced when having a child with a medical condition and complex needs. It seems obvious — support groups are an effective way of connecting people who are going through challenging times.

I often reflect that before having Eliott, I would have suggested the same thing to anyone in our situation. However, experiencing it firsthand is vastly different. Reaching out to others who are in a similar situation can be helpful, but it also requires acceptance.

I hadn't accepted Eliott's condition.

Every day I just keep fighting and pushing back because I want Eliott to be a miracle. I wanted our story to say, 'He had a rough start to life, but he miraculously caught up and has been fine ever since'.

So far, the thought of reaching out to join a supportive community has felt like giving up on that dream, and on Eliott.

The first thing I must accept and recognise is that getting additional support from people who are living through the same challenges doesn't mean giving up on him. Just like it doesn't mean I have to give up on my dream that Eliott will be the miracle he already is. It doesn't mean I have to adjust how much I fight for him. It's not accepting that we've lost the battle.

I've also come to terms with the fact that even if Eliott does win this battle, our lives will never be the same; our lives have been different to our friends' since the minute Eliott was born. Even if he catches up and leads a 'normal' life, no one will ever take away the pain, the stress, and the fear we've had to live through.

'Hello Claire, it's Suzy from KCNQ2. How are you?' She has a strong American accent, sounds a little older than me, and there is something in her voice that I immediately like. She asks me about Eliott, our journey, and I tell her everything in what now feels like a well-rehearsed speech.

'Tell me again how the doctors found out that Eliott had KCNQ2?' she asks, and I tell her how Henry didn't know why Eliott was seizing so much and called in one of his colleagues who remembered attending a conference and being told about mutations of the KCNQ2 gene.

When she hears this, Suzy sounds quite enthusiastic. 'Oh, this is just wonderful, as that means the awareness we are trying to raise is working. It probably was a conference where one of our medical sponsors spoke; she's this wonderful neurologist down in Melbourne.'

It clicks in my mind, so I say, 'Would it be the professor working on KCNQ2?'

'Yes, that's her. Do you know who she is?'

'Our neurologist mentioned she was one of the world experts, and she discovered the gene. He sent her the video of Eliott when he was only a few days old, and she confirmed it looked like KCNQ2.' I remember that day so painfully. We were happy that Eliott was finally seizure-free, but so concerned about the future. He was still on six or seven medications then and was so little and vulnerable.

Suzy goes on to tell me about her journey with KCNQ2; her youngest daughter, who has just turned eleven, has it. They used to live in the States, but her husband is Australian, and they decided to move back here a couple of years after their daughter was born. Suzy's been heavily involved in KCNQ2 Cure Alliance and shares with me a lot of stories about other kids.

I'm desperate to hear more, and hopeful to hear tips and tricks. Suzy mentions that a couple of things work well with 'our' kids: swimming (as it helps with their core) and horseriding. She talks about some of the kids who are doing well, her daughter included. And I feel hopeful to hear such positive stories; one child has even learnt how to read.

Wait. Do I feel hopeful if there is only one child that can read?

I've never thought about the possibility that learning to read would ever be a concern for my children — you just don't think about things like this when you're picking nursery themes and baby names.

Eliott has a cheeky little look and stops holding onto the swing; he does that sometimes, and we're teaching him to hold the ropes to get a better balance.

'Eliott, my love, hold on — sorry, Suzy.'

'No, that's all good,' she says. 'Are you with Eliott now? Do you look after him full-time?'

'Oh no, I don't, but his nanny was sick today, so I'm looking after him. We're at the playground, and he's just on the swing, so I'm making sure he's holding on.'

'How is his head control?' Suzy asks.

I suddenly feel gratitude. When I was doing my online research and reading the medical literature, I read that some kids with KCNQ2 can be severely affected by the condition.

Yes, Eliott had poor head control when he was a baby, but he also had a big head, and we did a lot of tummy time, and he did physio exercises. This isn't an issue for him anymore.

The tone of her voice when she asks makes me realise that she's prepared to hear whatever the answer is. Be it that he has good head control to very poor. We're probably some of the very few lucky ones.

We keep talking for a while longer, and before hanging up, she mentions another charity that she and other parents have started. It's called Genetic Epilepsy Team Australia (GETA), and the vision is to find a cure for genetic epilepsy. Not just KCNQ2, but others too.

Some parents have kids with other conditions — SYNGAP; SCN2A — and they're organising a conference down in Melbourne at the end of May, with researchers and clinicians talking about their research. There will also be therapists talking about the challenges of raising kids with complex needs and how to best support them and the rest of the family.

'Would you and Cedric like to join?'

'We would love to. My mother-in-law will be here. She's coming to help us after the baby is born.'

That afternoon, Suzy sends me the contact details of a man who lives in Sydney with his wife and their two daughters. One has KCNQ2.

He and I meet the following week. His office is close to mine, and he's keen to chat about our kids. He's very intrigued to hear that Eliott isn't on medication, other than when he needs it. And he tells me about his daughter; she's a year older than Eliott, but sadly appears to be more severely impacted by the condition. It is so hard. He's such a lovely person, and our stories are a sad reminder that it doesn't only happen to others. It is confronting realising that our life is harder than it should be, but easier than it could have been.

I call Ced on my way back to work and can't stop crying

as I tell him about the chat.

I've been so tired lately, and I feel more emotional than usual, but I realise that our chubby little baby, our happy boy, is lucky to have a milder version of the condition.

A few days later, I go to my regular doctors appointment for Crevette. I've had a couple more than usual because I've been so tired. I have low blood pressure, probably brought on by a mixture of exhaustion and the heat. It's far from being uncommon in pregnancy, but it means I must be extra careful, rest more and try not to stress. *Ha!*

He's already asked me if I could stop work earlier, which work is fine with; he wants me to stop one week before my planned leave, which means I'll have three weeks to rest before Crevette is born. I'm looking forward to it.

We have another big change before that; we must move! We love our current flat, but it's small and gets too hot in the summer, so we've been inspecting properties every week, sometimes a few times a week, without success. It's a nightmare.

We get to inspections and realise that the pictures aren't reflective of the properties, or there are another fifteen to twenty other people visiting, or the agents are telling us it will go for more than the asking price. Sydney's eastern suburbs rental market is challenging. We don't want to move too far because we want Eliott to stay in the same day care, and we can't risk losing Jen.

A week before I start maternity leave, and just as we're about to give up on finding a new place to move into before Crevette is born, I visit a house that is exactly what we're after.

The inspection is on Thursday morning, and I'm waiting outside the little house when the agent comes out. There are three other people visiting at the same time, and it looks like they are looking for a flat share. *Maybe we've got a chance with this one, if they're looking for a family?*

I walk into the house, and it looks fresh and clean — bonus points! I video call Ced so he can see it as well. It's a long house, with all the rooms one after the other. The floorboards are amazing. I love the master bedroom with the sunroom. And the second bedroom while small is still big enough to have two little beds once Crevette is old enough to share the room with Eliott. The living room leads onto a spacious kitchen, which opens onto a deck. And down a few stairs is the small backyard. I feel relaxed just standing on the deck.

Later that day, we submit an application and get a call the following Tuesday to say that we've got the house and we're moving ... on Friday! Just what the doctor (didn't) order!

In less than forty-eight hours, our whole apartment is packed up and we're ready to move. It's a rainy day, but we declare it to be a good omen.

The move takes the whole day, and by 5pm, we have to pick up Eliott from day care. However, the new house is still such a mess, and we have heaps more to do, so I send a message to Sophie and Julie: *Help! The move is taking forever, and the house is a mess. Could anyone take Eliott overnight?*

Julie says they'd be happy to have him. So, I pack an overnight bag for him, pick him up from day care and drive him to Anthony and Julie's.

Lila is playing with playdoh and seems happy to see her friend. I thank them again and show them how to administer the medication, should Eliott have a seizure. Julie is listening carefully.

I notice Anthony getting stressed.

'What's the risk of it happening?' he asks.

They're such good friends. They want to help and provide as much support as possible, but it's obviously a concern for them.

'He's not been sick, so it's low,' I reply. 'But if you have any doubt or if he gets hot, call us right away. Even if it's 2am, just call if you're not sure.'

The next day, I message Julie and ask how the night went. We've planned to pick him up and drop him with Jen for the morning to give us a bit more time to unpack.

Julie messages back: *All good, come whenever you're ready. Eliott is still asleep.*

It's 7am — that never happens at home! Lila is a very good sleeper, so I naively think that maybe Eliott saw Lila asleep and went back to sleep. But when we get to theirs to pick up Eliott, Anthony looks exhausted. Julie is smiling but looks tired too.

What happened?

'It's great that he managed to sleep until 7am. You're amazing! How did you do it?'

'Well ...' Anthony starts. 'He woke up at 4am and cried and wouldn't go back to sleep until 5:30am.'

Oh no! I feel so bad.

'We're so sorry. Are you okay? He didn't wake Lila up, did he?'

'No, it was okay. We just didn't know what to do. He wasn't upset at first, just didn't want to go back to sleep. We tried singing, rocking, but nothing worked. He was crying when he was in his bed, so we took him with us. And he fell back to sleep around 5.30am.'

We leave shortly after.

Ced then goes to the old apartment to finish emptying the place, and I go get a few groceries for Eliott's morning with Jen.

When we meet Jen later, she is joyful. 'Hey gorgeous, hey Claire! How's the new place?'

I look at her and start crying.

She gives me a hug, and I tell her what happened.

'I'm sure it was fine. Everyone knows that little kids sometimes sleep terribly. I'm sure they're not upset at you or Eliott,' Jen tries to reassure me.

'Being able to organise sleepovers with Chiara has been so helpful for us to get some respite. This was the first one with Lila. Eliott did the same with Sophie and Ethan last time. If he starts doing that every time, no one will want to take him ever again. How are we going to manage if that's the case?'

Jen is empathetic and understands my concern. She's seen how our little group operates and how important our friends are, especially when none of us have family support. When she drops Eliott at the new house later in the morning, she brings a little drawing made by Eliott. She and Eliott have been busy doing arts and crafts and have prepared something for Anthony and Julie.

'Eliott has prepared this to say sorry!' She smiles. 'I'm sure if you bring them the drawing, it will all be fine.'

I message Anthony and Julie the next day: *We hope you had a better night. Can we bring you a Sunday breakfast? We are on our way to get some croissants. We won't bother you and shall leave them downstairs.*

We drop the croissants and the drawing at the bottom of their building and receive a photo of the three of them eating the pastries, along with a message: *Yum, so good. Thanks. Lila loved the drawing.*

They were exhausted the previous day, but they are such good friends that it's already water under the bridge. I still feel bad, but friendships are stronger than one bad night.

It doesn't take Eliott long to start exploring his new environment. We prioritise getting his bedroom ready, and as soon as he recognises his stuff there, he looks happy. It's like he's understood that we've moved, and it's not a holiday or a weekend away this time.

The baby is due in less than three weeks, and given Eliott was ten days early, I want to make sure we're out of boxes by the time I give birth. I also want to prepare our hospital bags. Ideally, I'd get a little bit of rest as well!

The house is a winner, and it's cool. Miraculously, Eliott starts sleeping well again, and he quickly goes back to sleeping through the night. I love the house already!

Before we know it, Crevette's due date arrives. Everything is packed and ready for us to go to the hospital, and we've organised for Eliott to stay with Jen if I go into labour during the night.

But nothing happens.

I am now over term and don't feel any indication that the baby is coming anytime soon. I finally get the rest I was craving, catch-up with friends, and swim a lot.

I'm induced on a Saturday evening. After running a few errands to get the place ready for Mum's arrival, I wasn't feeling well and went to the hospital for a check-up where they decided to induce me. I'm ten days late now, and they don't want to take any chances.

Eliott goes to Sophie and Ethan's for a sleepover, as Jen is away today.

Leaving him is very emotional. He's so little still, and we have barely found our balance together. We're going to have our world disrupted again. It also brings to mind so many memories of what his birth was like. I've had to go back to hospital a few times, and every time it's been tough to be confronted with these memories.

A few midwife check-ups have not gone well because I kept having these flashbacks of walking in almost two years earlier to have Eliott, thinking our lives were going to change for the better. I still experience the pain of leaving lost and scared a few weeks later.

I warned Ced that it would be challenging to be back in the delivery room, as he hasn't been back to the hospital, and he has prepared himself mentally.

But when we walk in that afternoon, he cringes. We explain everything to the staff, and they're very understanding.

After an uneventful first night in hospital, the contractions start around 8am. Sophie and Ethan contact us and inform us that Eliott had a great night.

Phew!

I can now focus on Crevette.

We move to the delivery suite around 12pm, and the contractions are in full swing. As we walk through the doors, I notice Ced isn't doing well. He's doing his best to be supportive, but I recognise the signs that he's struggling. We explain everything to the midwife again. I have the feeling it helps Ced to be able to talk about it, especially as the midwife shows great compassion.

To take my mind off the contractions, Ced gives me another update. 'Your mum has landed in Sydney, so she took a cab to the new place. Sophie will bring Eliott to her soon, and Jen is coming back to help look after Eliott, given your mum will be tired from the flight.'

All is well. Everyone is ready. It really does take a village.

At 4.04pm on Sunday, 2 April 2017, a very healthy little boy takes his first breath. Baby Oscar is born.

Eliott is a big brother.

Chapter Sixteen

New challenges and higher stakes
(April–June 2017)

Eliott

I've had a sleepover at Chiara's house, and now Sophie is driving me home. She tells me that there's a surprise.

I expect to see Mum and Dad waiting for me, but Mamie Vero is there! She looks so excited to see me.

I show her the new house. She says she's going to stay for a while, and she's sleeping in my room at night.

Jen arrives later, and we go for a walk. Jen stays until dinner and bath time. Mamie Vero is asking me lots of questions and saying I've grown so much.

Just before I go to bed, Dad arrives, and Jen goes home. Dad looks tired. He chats with Mamie and shows us a few pictures of a baby. I wonder who it is …

The next day, Dad takes me to day care, and when he picks me up he's with Mamie. I haven't seen Mum since Saturday, and I really miss her. Dad tells me that she may be coming home tonight and shows me more pictures of a baby with Mum. He says, 'That's baby Oscar.'

Apparently, he's my baby brother — whatever that is!

Maman

The twenty-four hours following Oscar's birth are draining. When I arrive on the maternity ward after delivering him, the midwives have been briefed on our situation. They're especially caring and patient. They even offer to take him for a couple of hours so I can get some rest.

I panic. 'No, please don't. Don't take him. I don't want him to leave my side.' I know he doesn't have the same condition as Eliott and he's healthy, but I can't imagine being in the room all alone without my baby like I had to do when Eliott was taken to the NICU.

I ask to be discharged as early as possible. The midwives suggest staying an extra day, but I want to go home. I don't want to stay in the hospital if I don't need to, and I want to see Eliott.

Ced picks me up late on Monday evening, and it feels so good to take our baby home.

I'm delighted and nervous to introduce Eliott to Oscar. Oscar is a super calm newborn so far.

On Tuesday morning, we show Eliott the new baby asleep in his cot, but when Oscar wakes up, it's the first time Eliott sees Oscar in my arms. Ced is carrying Eliott to make sure he can anticipate any reaction, but to our greatest surprise, there is none. Eliott simply ignores him. He wants to show Mum his books and toys, and he ignores both me and the baby.

Oh well ...

Oscar feeds well from the start. I've decided to breastfeed him, hoping it will be easier than with Eliott, and it is. As with every newborn, he's feeding every couple of hours or so. Mum is sleeping in Eliott's room so she can look after him in the morning when he wakes at 5am, and I can sleep in when Oscar sleeps.

Slowly, we all get into our new routine.

Eliott

On Sunday, Sophie, Ethan and Chiara come to visit. I'm happy to see them and play with Chiara. There are three other friends, including one who is carrying a camera. I've seen her a couple of times, and I like her. They ask me if they can take pictures of me with my brother. They put him on Mamie's bed in my room and tell me they're going to lay me down next to him. Just one picture.

We're a bit close, and Oscar is touching my hair. I try not to move, but I don't like it.

Mum's friend is taking a couple of pictures with her big camera. 'This is beautiful,' she says. 'Eliott, look at me. Give me a smile.'

I try to smile, but I don't want to. I don't really understand what's happening and why the baby is touching me. I start crying and move away.

Mum strokes my cheek. 'Are you okay, my love? Baby Oscar was touching your hair.'

I look at Oscar, who's on the bed and I wonder why he is here.

Maman

Eliott is still ignoring Oscar. We've read that it's very common for kids who welcome a sibling to either ignore the new addition or sometimes become aggressive with the baby. At least he's been gentle so far.

Ced and I can see that Eliott's not sure how to react to Oscar whenever they are close. It's heartbreaking to witness that he doesn't know how to handle it. We're very concerned about managing the transition in the right way, if there is one.

We're lucky that Mum arrived just when Oscar was born. Again, we had initially planned to have ten days to ourselves to get familiar with being a family of four. But Oscar being late has been a blessing. Mum has been able to spend a lot of time with Eliott, and he's so happy with her. We're confident he doesn't feel left out. Ced spends a lot of time with them, and I try to spend some quality time with Eliott when Oscar naps.

Mum teaches him simple things such as covering his eyes to protect them from the lights when she turns them on in the morning, and we can sometimes hear them giggling together through the baby monitor.

For Easter, Jen takes him to the petting zoo at the Entertainment Quarter to see the chicks and the sheep, and the pictures are so telling. He's surprised to see the sheep drink from a milk bottle and shows enthusiasm on the fun rides. He has a blast, and it's a pleasure to see him having so much fun.

Later that week, Eliott brings back an Easter hat he made at day care. He's very attached to this silver, glittery hat. He loves the little plastic chicks glued on top and the colourful feathers.

The day before celebrating Easter at the end of April, Ced goes out to buy a few things for the house and comes back with a swing for the garden. Eliott really loves it, maybe a bit too much. We have a few tantrums trying to get him out! All these experiences may seem insignificant, but they are huge milestones; he is becoming his own little person, with strong likes and dislikes, and interests.

Even the tantrums are a positive sign of his emotional development, and more importantly, they're age appropriate. He's not having them later in life as so many kids with developmental delays do. He's having them just before he turns two. We're welcoming the terrible twos with open arms.

He loved the petting zoo so much that we feel it would be a treat to take him to the Sydney Zoo.

Unfortunately, it's a disaster.

That day, Eliott is grumpy and isn't interested in the animals at all. We wonder if he's a bit too young and decide we should go to the playground in the middle of the zoo. But it's packed, and when Eliott sees all the kids running and jumping, he freezes. Oscar gets hungry, and we end up retreating to the parent's room where we stay for a while.

I'm feeding Oscar while Mum and Ced are trying to calm Eliott, as he's so upset. It's heartbreaking. Even Mum, who's Eliott's biggest advocate and always so positive, doesn't have the strength to say anything for the rest of the day.

Eliott

I love having Mamie here. We've been doing so many fun things. It's starting to get cold, so Mum and Dad bought me a fluffy robe. I wear it in the morning when Mamie gets me out of bed, and in the evening after bath time. I love it! It's bright blue with little red horns like I'm a monster. I enjoy the feel of the soft fabric on my skin.

Mum and Dad said they've given Mamie a challenge. In the four weeks she's here, she will help me to eat independently. I'm twenty-two months old, but I like to be fed. I love having this time with Mum, Dad, or Mamie when they feed me.

Unfortunately, Mum and Dad have said that I need to know how to feed myself. Mamie is showing me by holding my hand, giving me a spoon or fork with food, and guiding it to my mouth. She's very patient, and I'm progressing well.

This month, Joe has come for one of our sessions with a new person, Joana, as he's leaving. Joana says hello to me and then tells Mum that she's going to be my new key worker who will help with my speech.

Later that day, I see Oscar playing on the baby mat and lying in his bouncy chair. He does that a lot, but the rest of the time he seems to be in Mum's arms. I wish I could spend more time with Mum, but I do love having Dad and Mamie to myself.

Maman

It's been really tiring with the two boys, but Oscar's an easy baby, and Eliott's making a lot of progress with Mamie Vero, who continues to teach him how to feed himself.

On 12 April, Oscar is ten days old, and I've made an appointment with Donna, my psychologist. I haven't seen her much lately, but I feel like I need to chat with her. It's been such an emotional journey of late.

It's amazing to have a baby that only needs the normal newborn attention, but it brings back so many memories. We remember what it was like to have Eliott — the appointments, the medication, the struggle with breastfeeding, and the seizures. And just as it's wonderful to avoid all this with Oscar, it's incredibly difficult to realise what a 'typical' parenting experience is like. It just feels so easy, and at times we're resentful of other parents who complain that having a baby is challenging. We know deep down though that we find it easy because our benchmark is Eliott, but we can't help feeling this way.

It also hurts to realise that we can now appreciate what these other parents were talking about when they said that having a child is the most wonderful experience. We love Eliott so much, but everything about being a parent to him has been hard. Now we get it.

When I sit down in the comfy sofa in Donna's room, I let it all out: the fear for the future, the guilt that comes with having these kind of thoughts, the gratitude for having this experience, the joy in having Mum here to focus on Eliott and once more see what a wonderful little boy he is. I dig deep, cry a lot, and try to accept that I still haven't been able to let go of my longing for a 'normal' life as a parent.

Having Oscar is bringing me straight back to the beginning, showing me what it could've been, and in my mind what it *should* have been.

Donna can't fix it for me, but I've known her for years, and she always manages to get through to me. I leave feeling like I have a better understanding of my emotions, and she's given me a few practical tricks to try at home, mostly breathing techniques. She also says something that sticks with me: 'Make sure to do something for yourself. It could be a walk, or a swim, or buy yourself a new pillowcase.'

This is so simple, so small.

At a time when I feel too tired, physically exhausted, and on an emotional rollercoaster, I can accept that a short walk is enough. I can go for a swim when my body is ready, and just take time to enjoy having one single new pillowcase. I don't need the extravagance of a whole new set of bedsheets.

Jen is such an amazing support. She's still looking after Eliott, as we all decided it would be better for him to stick with the same routine. They're going back to GymbaROO this term. And with the weather being more unpredictable, they start going to the library more, which Eliott loves. It's great to get all the pictures of him being so active and happy.

On day care days, Mum and I walk to day care with the pram and Oscar in the carrier. We then grab takeaway coffees and go for a long walk.

On 2 May, we celebrate our third wedding anniversary. The fact that we haven't had to go to hospital this year feels special. How our standards have changed! Mum babysits, and Ced and I go to a restaurant close by to have dinner.

These last few weeks have gone by so quickly, and before we know it, it's time for Mum to leave. Baby Oscar and I drive her to the airport on the Sunday evening, and it's sad to have to say goodbye. I know Eliott is going to wake up the next day and feel sad not to have Mamie Vero next to him. She's slept in his room on the sofa bed for the four weeks she was here, and they had their own little morning routine. But Mamie Francette is arriving soon, and I hope that we'll be able to take our time and just enjoy having her here, now that we're back into a bit of a routine.

Eliott

I woke up on Monday, and Mamie Vero wasn't in the room with me — she's gone home. Dad came to pick me up and said that he was going to take me to day care. We'll have a week just the four of us before Mamie Francette arrives.

On Sunday, we celebrate Mother's Day. I give her the gift I made at day care, and she looks happy. Dad gives me a couple of other gifts to hand to Mum. There are some books, which are a gift from Oscar: *The Very Cranky Bear* series. Dad says Oscar is a serious baby, so it suits him! I give Mum a book too, it's called: *My Mum is the Best.*

Dad has organised a weekend away for Mum; we'll go in a couple of months. He says it's a cabin in the middle of the forest, with kangaroos everywhere! I can't wait, and it looks like Mum can't wait either. She gives us all big kisses and hugs, and it's a wonderful day all together.

The next day, Mamie Francette arrives, and she's so excited to see us.

Maman

It's a relief to have Francette here with us. Our two mums are very different. Francette needs to always be active and likes being busy around the house, so if the boys are napping, she'll clean, tidy, cook dinner, or rearrange the whole kitchen! At this stage, it's exactly what we need. She's keen to make sure she's supporting us as much as possible.

Lately, Oscar has been sleeping on me during the day. He sleeps well at night, only wakes to feed two or three times and then goes back to sleep on his own, so I don't mind that he sleeps on me during the day.

Ced says that we probably both need it — me more than Oscar. And he's right, I'm craving that simple contact with him, knowing I don't have to plan a hospital trip or a doctor appointment, or wake him to give him medication. I like watching him sleep so peacefully, and I enjoy that quiet time to read a book or listen to podcasts. When he naps on me, it's often for hours on end, and Francette brings me a cup of tea, a snack, and hustles around the house.

When Oscar is six weeks old, it's time to get his first immunisations. I'm really scared, but he and Eliott are different babies. Unfortunately, Oscar does get a bad fever and is out of sorts all day. There is no risk of a hospital trip, but it's heartbreaking to see him so unwell. I somehow understand the distress of the mums who were complaining about seeing their perfectly healthy child have their immunisations. Oscar is usually so healthy and chilled. He seems to be suffering more from not understanding what is happening to his little body.

Eliott now sleeps through most nights but wakes up early. Francette looks after him in the morning, like Mum did, but she's getting tired. A week after she arrives though, Eliott wakes up screaming in the middle of the night. It's 3am, and I'm about to go back to sleep after feeding Oscar.

Eliott is inconsolable. We give him a bottle, which he drinks quickly but dribbles a lot of it out, so I have to change him. He's extremely distressed, and we end up cuddling him but saying a firm 'no' every time he starts screaming again.

Francette is looking at Eliott, and she's looking at Ced, then me, obviously wondering what might be happening.

We're all so tired, and at one point I lose it and raise my voice at Eliott. 'Stop it, you're going to wake Oscar up. STOP! STOP! STOP!'

But he doesn't.

Ced takes over while I go to the bathroom and calm down a bit. When I manage to recover enough, Ced is about to lose his temper too, and I take over. Eliott is now calmer and sobbing gently. I cuddle him and shush him to sleep.

Francette looks like she's about to pack her suitcase and go home. I give her a half-smile and tell her she can go back to bed, and she lies down on the sofa bed next to Eliott's cot. We turn the lights off, and I gently put Eliott in his bed once he's calmer.

'You're okay, baby, just go to sleep. No, don't cry, you're okay.' It takes a good five minutes of shushing and patting, and he falls asleep. I leave the room as quietly as I can, saying, 'I'm sorry, Francette. Hope you have a good night.'

Francette is clearly trying her best to make do with the new pattern of Eliott's poor sleep. Thankfully, there are no other episodes like that one, but he keeps waking early, so early that I decide to keep track of it, as well as his night wake ups.

The following week, he wakes up screaming again at 1am. It could be night terrors, as he's inconsolable and yet completely fine in the morning, but it doesn't fit the description that well, as he's awake when it happens.

I talk to Joana about it, and she suggests writing down all the details to see if there's a pattern. Just as I did when he was a newborn, I start tracking sleep, food intake, and other noticeable events. I remember that last year we had noticed his sleep wasn't as good when he had sugar in the evening, so maybe it's something similar this time around?

Thankfully, we have a good support network now, with Francette being here, Eliott in day care three days a week, and Jen with us the other two days. Having full-time care for Eliott means that his routine isn't too disrupted, and I can get enough time with Oscar. It also means that when they're both a bit older, I can plan to have some time to myself before I go back to work. This is something we couldn't manage when Eliott was a baby.

But one morning towards the end of May, Jen doesn't look like she's doing well. And when I ask her if anything is wrong, she's almost in tears when she says, 'Claire, I'm so sorry, I don't know how to say this, but my fiancé has been transferred with work. We're moving to Queensland.'

Eliott

On the weekend, Dad goes to Melbourne, and I'm not happy about it. Baby Oscar has been at home with us for almost two months, and he spends a lot of time with Mum. He's always in her arms, and they seem to spend most of their time in the

250

bedroom. Every time I walk in, he's sleeping in her arms.

I love Mamie Francette, but I want Mum, and I don't want Oscar to spend so much time with her. So, I scream and throw a lot of tantrums to express how I feel. I just don't understand why he is staying with us.

Maman

I can't get over the fact that Jen is leaving. I've been crying so much over the past few days. We had it all planned, and now we must find a way to make it work. She's pleased about the move, so I'm trying to be happy for her but can't think of how we're going to make it work at home.

She's kindly offered to help us find a replacement, but I don't think I want a replacement. We'd planned to keep her as Eliott's nanny for the duration of my maternity leave. This was a difficult financial decision, but it made sense for Eliott's benefit. Plus, that meant we didn't have to go through the recruitment process again when I go back to work.

On the weekend, when Ced is away at a conference, Eliott is difficult. Francette and I are having a hard time. I don't know if it's because he needs more attention, is starting to realise that Oscar is here to stay, or just that he's picking up on how upset I am and how stressed Ced is.

Initially, we were all meant to go to the conference organised by Genetic Epilepsy Team Australia, but the logistics are too much. We know that it will most likely be an emotionally challenging day, and so we decide that it's easier for Ced to go on his own. He flies there and back on the Saturday.

It's 9pm, Francette and I are in the kitchen trying to unwind after a harrowing day with Eliott, when we hear Ced's footsteps on the balcony. He's gone around the house to come through the kitchen door to avoid the risk of waking the kids. He looks shattered. I'm eager for a full debrief though, especially as we haven't had a chance to talk at all today.

However, when I ask him about it, Ced just looks at us and says, 'I'm sorry, I don't want to talk about it tonight. It was informative but confronting. I'm exhausted. The only thing I can tell you is that our little warrior is a miracle. After a while, I stopped showing pictures of Eliott, as I felt bad. Some of the kids can't walk, and they're much older. It's clear though that we're not getting the support he needs, so we need to adjust some things.'

The next day, we decide to break things up and take a long walk to Watsons Bay. It's just what we need. Eliott is eager to go out, and we've managed to get a second-hand double pram, so Oscar is in his bassinet and Eliott is in the seat next to him.

Ced takes his camera and is keen to take pictures to capture these moments with his mum. The walk also gives us time to talk.

We start by discussing Eliott's challenging behaviour, and we conclude that it's good that he's showing frustration. Sure, it's hard to manage, but we must make sure he gets enough attention, and that Oscar gets what he needs. We feel the pressure of doing right by both boys.

Neither of them asked to be born. We decided we wanted to have children, and our world was turned upside down when Eliott was born. However, this isn't happening to *us*. This is happening to *him*. Our role as parents is to support him and to give him all the tools to be the best he can.

Having Oscar is saving our life by allowing us to have a chance at experiencing what it feels like to be a normal family, but we have to manage everything carefully to allow them both to have the space to grow, as members of our own unique family, and as individuals.

While we're discussing everything, Oscar is napping and Eliott is clearly enjoying being outside. He's so calm and happy, it's hard to believe that he was so difficult yesterday.

'Are you feeling better today?' I ask Ced softly.

'Yes, thanks,' Ced replies, with a smile. He knows me too well and has guessed where I'm going with this question. 'It was tiring, but I'm glad I went. It was great to meet other families.'

'Did you meet Suzy and her husband Alex?'

'Yes, she was the master of ceremony. She's extremely talented at what she does. I also met the professor working on KCNQ2. She gave a speech explaining the basics of genetics and genetic epilepsy. You probably know all this already.' I can see pride in his eyes.

I've done a lot of research to get up to speed and keep myself abreast of developments in the genetic epilepsy field. I've been reading medical journals and doing online classes to understand it more. I still feel lost, but I'm trying.

'It must've been amazing to meet her.' I'm acting as if she was a famous rock star. And, to us, she is.

'She was lovely. She was amazed to hear that Eliott started walking at eighteen months.'

Ced explains that one of the sessions was around specific therapies that work for 'our' kids. One of the speakers was a speech therapist, who highlighted key things that work, such as working on receptive language, and the importance of getting speech therapy as early as possible.

I feel exhausted just listening. We've tried. We've seen four speech therapists, and we've found them all terrible.

'I think we should try to find someone new. I agree with you that the ones we've seen weren't good, but they just didn't know about these conditions. I talked to the speech therapist after the session, she's in Melbourne, but she may know someone here. I'll email her.' Ced seems determined and reinvigorated.

The following week, we all go to the library. Jen's been taking Eliott there and he loves it, so I'm keen to see where everything is and for Jen to show me all her tricks! I want to make sure that we can keep doing the activities he loves. I know all about doctors' appointments, but not the pleasant things.

At the weekend, we're off to Noosa! Francette is eager to visit somewhere outside Sydney, and we're excited that Oscar's first trip is to Noosa, just like Eliott's. We have a fond memory of that trip with Eliott, and it's nice to think that their first plane trip is the same.

We walk through the little town, go to the pool in the complex, and Ced goes for a run in the national park.

On the second last day, we decide to go for a swim in the ocean with Eliott. Even though it's winter, the water is quite warm.

After a good twenty minutes of splashing about in the waves, Eliott's getting cold, so we decide to go home. As soon as we reach the street, and Eliott understands the fun is over, he starts screaming. To calm him down, Ced tries to take him in his arms. But he's fighting so hard and hitting Ced.

'Just put him back in the pram,' I say. 'I can push him, and hopefully as soon as he recognises that we're going back to the apartment, he'll feel better.'

The tantrum came on so suddenly and was worse than what we've ever seen before. Thankfully, we realise that it's just a tantrum, so we try to stay calm. We sing, make funny noises ... but it's a big tantrum; he's obviously desperate.

We've walked the entire town with Eliott screaming, arching in an attempt to get out of the pram, and I've caught his arm twice as he was about to unintentionally hit Oscar, who is sleeping in the bassinet next to him.

Finally, we reach the sidewalk that begins the uphill leg back to the apartment. I take a few deep breaths, readying myself to push the heavy double pram up the hill, complete with a sleeping newborn and a screaming toddler.

When he tries to launch himself out of the pram one more time, I lose it. Completely!

I stop the pram, put the brakes on and go around to face him. 'Eliott. That's it. I've had enough.' I can hear my own voice. It's calm but completely detached. There's no love in it; it's an authoritative tone. 'You want to get out of the pram and walk ... be my guest.' I then unstrap him and put him on the sidewalk. 'Look at this hill, Eliott. You're going up!' I point to the hill, and he starts walking, sobbing.

I catch Ced looking at me, and feel bad, but I can't calm down.

Francette walks up to Eliott. 'Come on baby, Mamie will carry you,' she says.

'No, Francette. Please don't. He wanted to get out of the pram. He's been screaming at us for ten minutes. He was about to hit Oscar. He's going to walk up,' I say as calmly as possible.

She starts walking up, and I tell Eliott again, who's stopped screaming but looks so lost. 'Eliott, up. You're walking up.'

He starts walking, very slowly, and after 100 metres, my heart breaks. I feel so bad. I look down at Oscar and see his sweet little face.

Who am I? What did I just do? What kind of mother am I?

Yes, Eliott has been very difficult lately, and it would be so much easier to have a normal life. But there's nothing that can excuse my reaction. I'm the adult.

Ced is holding Eliott's hand, who's now actually quite happy to be walking, and when he gets tired halfway up, Ced carries him.

I'm just left behind puffing as I push the pram up. No one is talking.

When we arrive at the apartment, Francette takes Eliott and goes to get dinner ready. I give Oscar to Ced and head to our bedroom. I go to the shower and switch on the taps. Still fully clothed, I step in and let the warm water pour over me. I let myself fall to the floor and sob.

It feels like the water is just washing away all the stress and the only thing left is the guilt.

255

After twenty minutes, Ced walks in.

'Oh gosh, what are you doing? I thought you were just taking a quick shower to rinse from the ocean swim. Come here, let's get you out.'

'I'm such a bad mother, Ced, what have I done?'

'What do you mean? Yes, you lost your temper, after he screamed for ten minutes.'

'But he's so little, why did I do this? His little face ... He looked so lost. I don't want to be that mum.'

'Don't worry. Yes, it was a bit too much, but he was fine. And you calmed down quickly.' Ced is putting a towel over my shoulders. 'Where are your dry clothes? Can I get you anything?'

I just can't stop crying, 'But your mum ... she must think I'm a horrible human being.'

He laughs. 'No, don't worry. She's seen worse. She just thinks you're tired and trying to do your best. Next time, we'll all do it differently. Okay?'

I kiss him and try to get over it.

When I finally get dressed and walk out of the room, Francette is feeding Eliott his dinner, and Oscar is doing his tummy time on the rug.

'I'm so sorry, Francette.'

'Don't worry about it, honey, I get it. It's all good.'

I don't feel like it's all good, but I'm determined to do better. Maybe I should read more about positive parenting.

Eliott

Today we see Henry, and Dad tells him that we're on the lookout for a new speech therapist. Henry asks about my speech — am I saying words yet? Am I using sentences? Can I follow simple instructions?

Mum and Dad look sad when they reply that I don't. Henry says I'm doing well, but speech is important, and at my age I should start forming sentences, or at least show that I have a good understanding of what is being said. He suggests we reach out to someone called Danielle. Mum sighs and promises to give her a call.

I haven't had a seizure since September, so Dad is keen to understand when they can stop giving me medication in prevention.

'Not before he's three,' replies Henry.

They all agree that it's better to err on the side of caution for an extra year.

Mum, who is holding Oscar, gives Dad a look and then asks, 'Henry, have you received Oscar's birth announcement?'

'Yes, thank you very much. It was lovely.'

'The reason I ask,' Mum carries on, 'is to see if you've noticed his middle name. It's Henry.'

'Yes, it's a great name! Good choice.'

'We wanted to tell you that we gave him the middle name of Henry in honour of you. You've done so much for Eliott and us, always believing in him and telling us to treat him like a normal child, and we wouldn't be here without you.'

Later that day, Jen is trying to encourage me to use words. She keeps asking me to say 'more' before I can get any food! At afternoon tea, I want an extra piece of apple, so I give 'more' a go to see what happens. Jen laughs and hugs me.

When Mum comes home that evening, Jen says, 'Eliott said "more".'

Everyone is excited, and Mum cries — with joy, she tells me.

A few days later I turn two! At day care, we have cake (with candles on it!) and everyone sings 'happy birthday'. Now I remember what a birthday is! I love it!

The next day, we go to the playground next to our house and Mum decorates the little house there. She explains to Mamie that she's rented it for the morning so we can have my birthday here. They finish getting everything ready just as everyone arrives. There are friends from day care, Mum's mothers group, and other friends. It's great. Even Jen and her fiancé come along.

It's a terrific day!

Maman

Francette leaves a few days after Eliott's birthday. And that same week, day care asks us if they can put Eliott on a little stretcher bed for his nap — it's time for him to leave the cot room and get used to sleeping on a stretcher so he is ready to transition to the other room next year.

On his first day sleeping on a stretcher, day care sends us pictures with a short note: *We're so proud of Eliott! He's done so well sleeping on his big boy's bed.*

Ced and I are overjoyed and forward the pictures to our families. Over the past week, we've had many changes, and many happy moments.

I haven't been able to contact the new speech therapist Henry recommended, and I don't have much hope that she will be any better than the other four we've already seen, but I promise Ced that I will at least call and arrange to go to one session before making a judgment.

It's been a month since Jen announced that she was going to be leaving us, and suddenly her last day is here. We organise a dinner to say thank you and have organised a few gifts. We give her a book with pictures of everything she and Eliott did this year, and a little pouch with Eliott's drawing and her name engraved on it. In her card, I tell her how much she's meant to us and to Eliott, and how having her has allowed us to go back to having what has felt like a normal life. She came into our lives when we needed it the most, and she's leaving before we feel ready to continue life without her.

Chapter Seventeen

The four of us
(July 2017)

Eliott

A few weekends after my birthday, I wake with a fever. Mum and Dad decide to give me Phenytoin to avoid taking any chances.

Thankfully, the fever breaks and I can go to day care on Monday. Mum and Dad give me my dose in the morning just in case, but they say that I look better and that it will be fun to be with my friends. But I don't like it. I'm not feeling well. I cry a lot to make the day care ladies understand that I'm not enjoying myself, and I don't eat anything. They call Mum before lunch, and Mum comes to pick me up.

I'm happy to see her and give her a big cuddle.

When we arrive home, Mum asks if I want lunch. I don't. She gives me a milk bottle instead, and when I open my mouth to take it, Mum gently puts her finger in my mouth.

'Oh, Eliott, my love, it's your teeth again. Take your milk and let's put you to bed, you look exhausted.'

I sleep most of the afternoon, and shortly after I wake up, there is a knock at the door.

'Oh, that must be Sally.' Mum sounds enthusiastic.

We open the front door, and a tall lady walks in. She has long blonde hair and is smiling brightly.

'Hi Claire, I'm Sally. It's lovely to meet you,' she says in French.

'Thanks a lot for coming to help us. We're glad the

timing worked out. My husband is working late for the next few weeks, and it's challenging managing them both at dinner and bath time.'

I'm not sure where Jen is.

Mum shows Sally around the house and how the medication works. I hear her explain that I don't have seizures often; in fact, I haven't had one in almost ten months, but we need to be careful. I'm feeling better after sleeping this afternoon, and now I'm bored.

Sally takes my hand. 'Would you like to show me your toys, Eliott? Or read a book?' she asks me.

I like her already.

'I'm going to feed Oscar, so can you give Eliott his dinner in twenty minutes, and I'll come and help you at bath time once Oscar is in bed?' Mum asks her.

I haven't eaten all day, so I'm starving, and I eat a lot.

When Mum comes back, she sits down and smiles. 'One down! How is it going here?'

'Very well,' replies Sally. 'He's eaten well. We've had a play, and he's shown me all his books.'

'Great. Eliott, should we get you changed in your room, and you can have a bath?'

When we get to the bedroom, I don't know if it's because I've eaten so much, but something feels wrong again. Not a fever this time, but something is bothering me. I start crying.

Sally and Mum try to reassure me, but I just keep crying.

We hear footsteps, and Dad walks in with a huge smile. 'I've managed to get home early!'

'Oh, thank you! Ced, this is Sally. Eliott was better after a big nap earlier, but he's now out of sorts.'

I'm a bit frustrated that they're not getting it, so I cry some more.

Mum is talking to Sally, explaining I've been on medication, so I'm not myself. I might just be tired.

They're not getting it, so I cry louder. I cry so much that I'm having trouble breathing.

'What is it? Is he okay?' Mum says, clearly concerned.

'I don't know. I think he's just very upset,' replies Dad while rubbing my back.

'I'm going to get his water. Sally, you can feel free to go home. I'll send you a message to let you know how he goes, but I'm sure he's fine. Thank you so much for today, we'll see you tomorrow.'

When Mum comes with my water bottle, I'm breathing normally.

'Where's Sally?' asks Dad.

'It's past 7pm, so I told her she could go home. She's good, very gentle and patient. I think Eliott likes her. She sounded so concerned about him tonight though. I hope we haven't scared her.' Mum strokes my hair. 'He looks a bit better.'

I move to look at her, and I feel pain again, so I start to cry, and my breathing becomes shallow. It feels like something is blocking my airways.

'Let's call the home doctors and see if they can come tonight. He's now been like this on and off for over an hour. I'm afraid it's the Phenytoin, as it can impair your breathing.' Mum is looking at me anxiously.

'Yes, I think you're right. Let's not take any chances.'

Maman

I get my phone and call the home doctors and explain everything. When they hear Eliott's breathing over the phone, they advise me to call an ambulance.

When the ambulance arrives, they decide to take Eliott to the hospital. Ced goes with him and updates me throughout the evening.

Upon arriving at the hospital, Eliott's temperature peaks at forty degrees, so they give him more paracetamol, as well as a dose of Phenytoin and admit him on the ward.

Oscar and I both sleep well at home that night, and in the morning, I feel ready to go back to the hospital and help Ced, who probably didn't get any sleep. I take a few minutes to reflect on how different my children are. Oscar isn't even three months old and has already dropped the number of night wake ups to one or two and even slept through for the first time!

When we arrive at the hospital, Eliott's feeling much better. It's been about ten hours since the last dose of paracetamol. They've given him his Phenytoin this morning, but we should get discharged quickly.

Sally messages me to check that we're okay. She offers to come a little early and take Eliott to the playground if he feels up to it, so we can rest. We gladly accept the offer, and when she arrives, she has a huge smile on her face. They have a great afternoon, and Eliott is slowly returning to normal.

It feels like his body was trying to shake something off. We thought he was better, but he must've been fighting something that needed to come out with a fever.

We finally stop the Phenytoin a few days later and try to get back into our routine. I go to GymbaROO with both boys in the morning; however, Eliott is struggling, and it's a battle with the two of them. I'm glad that this is the last class of the term.

On the weekend, we go to the second birthday party for my colleague's daughter who is on the autism spectrum. She is very active and was walking well before one. Her main issue is communication, and just like Eliott, she's not talking yet. She has different challenges, but it's been helpful to have someone at work who understands what our day-to-day challenges and struggles are.

She organised the birthday at a local indoor playground because her daughter loves it, and I can see why! Eliott has a blast, and it's nice to be able to message the mums in my mothers group and tell them that we've finally tried the new place everyone recommended.

We're having normal weekends, even if I still feel so very different from all the other mums I run into daily.

The following week, it's my second consecutive day of looking after the two boys on my own. The boys are on their best behaviour, but it's tiring. We go to the Bondi Winter festival in the morning, and Eliott really enjoys watching the ice skaters and the ferris wheel.

Back at home, when it's time to feed Oscar, I ask Eliott to stay with me, but he's being mischievous. He goes to the bathroom and unrolls all the toilet paper, then tears it into little pieces, then comes to the bedroom and takes all the nappies and everything out of the changing table ...

Finding a balance between letting Oscar take his time to feed, while also giving Eliott enough attention is hard. I end up having to take them both with me in the bathroom when I have a shower — any privacy is long gone!

Eliott has been difficult, but with all the recent changes and his last illness, it's no wonder.

Finally, we get pictures from day care that demonstrate how much more engaged he is becoming.

At the weekend, while Ced is training for a running event, I go to the playground with a friend. We've brought a ball, and my friend is playing with Eliott while I push Oscar in his pram ... and Eliott starts to kick!

It feels like all the hard work may be paying off. After weeks without much change and lots of tantrums, he's making progress. We have his annual review at the assessment clinic coming up in a couple of weeks, and I'm actually looking forward to it. It's been a tough but good year. We've done so much. Eliott has done so much. I can't wait to see how much he's moved up the scale.

Before I know it, it's my birthday, and I've got both boys all day. So, we go to the park in the morning to make sure that Eliott has an opportunity to burn off a bit of energy. I'm also starting to manage getting both boys down for their afternoon naps at the same time. More often than not, I put Eliott down, and Oscar ends up sleeping on me, but he's been doing one nap a day in his cot, and I've decided that I have more important battles to fight than this one. It's not ideal to let him sleep on me still, especially on the days I have to look after them both, but I enjoy it, and so does he.

Today, we have our first appointment with the new speech therapist, but I can't be bothered, as I know it's going to be another painful appointment where I'll have to explain the whole medical history again. Then she'll give me tips and tricks without looking at Eliott, and we'll have wasted time. Plus, her practice rooms are so far away from where we live.

When we arrive at the speech therapist rooms, I put Oscar in the pram so he can stay with Sally in the waiting room, but he doesn't like it, so I put him in the carrier.

Just after 4.30pm, one of the doors opens and a little kid comes out. He's followed by a tall lady with a heavy frame.

Danielle has short hair and is wearing a funny pair of glasses and a long colourful necklace with large beads. 'Well done today. Give me a high five. You be good this week!' she says in a deep voice.

It looks like she's known that kid for years and acts halfway between a cool aunt and a concerned teacher.

Danielle then turns to face us. 'Okay, Eliott! You're up, sausage!'

We all walk into the room, and I introduce everyone. 'Thanks for seeing us. Like I said on the phone, our neurologist has recommended we see you.'

'I've worked a bit with Henry. Can you remind me a little more about Eliott's condition?'

I start from the beginning, but she quickly interrupts. 'How is his communication now? What is your biggest concern?'

'He's communicating a bit more, but he's only saying a few words. He's starting to repeat sounds, but not much. He's our first, so I don't know what he's meant to do, or where he should be at.'

Danielle sits Eliott in front of her on a little chair and

starts playing with him, making him repeat sounds, and for the next twenty-five minutes, she just looks at Eliott and how he's responding to her prompts. Every time I try to comment on something, she subtly and politely ignores me to focus on Eliott.

'Look, I think there's a lot of good things. He's smart. But there's also a bit of work. I can see he's trying to communicate, but I think he's struggling with motor planning. Have you heard this before?' She explains that it's his ability to plan how he's going to move. It is valid for gross motor skills, such as walking and running, but also for communicating and forming sentences. You can't speak if you can't plan what you're going to say. 'Does he fall or hit furniture a lot?'

He does. Not as much as he used to, but he still often runs into furniture.

She suggests weekly sessions to start, and we can reassess. After fighting to get him more regular therapy sessions, this is music to my ears.

The four of us leave shortly after, and I look at Sally and say, 'How amazing was she? She actually didn't want to listen to me, she just wanted to work with Eliott!'

Later that same night, after telling Ced all about the session with Danielle, I'm mindlessly on my phone scrolling through social media, when I see an arts and crafts class that happens to be on a Wednesday morning. I text the class teacher, Kate, and book for the next day.

'I'm glad you're finding activities to do with the kids, and so happy it went well with the new speech therapist. The conference really gave me hope that there was so much we could do. We need to find our people,' says Ced.

When we arrive at the craft class the next day, Kate walks towards us, her hand stretched towards me. 'You must be Claire. And you must be Eliott. Your mummy said you might like to do arts and crafts with us this morning.'

Three more kids arrive, all looking like they've been

coming for weeks and having fun here.

Kate gathers everyone around her, and we all sing the welcome song. She has such a lovely singing voice, and Eliott is hooked. Thankfully, Oscar is asleep in his pram, and I can focus on Eliott. Today's theme is ice-cream! She shows the kids the three different activities, and then the session finishes with a sensory activity; she's dyed dry rice with food colouring, and the kids will drop them onto shaving foam — to practise their pinch grip — and see how it looks when the colourful rice hits the foam.

Eliott loves everything about the class and has the biggest smile.

Just when I think it's over, Kate asks the kids if they're ready for story time. She reads a book with all the children sitting around her. Then she gets up, opens a box next to her and takes a few musical instruments out. 'Let's have a party!' she says, joyfully.

How much energy can one person have?

I'm exhausted just looking at her. But the kids are loving it. It's clear they adore Kate, and I haven't seen Eliott so focused, engaged, and happy in a long time. We finally sing the goodbye song and head home.

It feels like it could be overstimulation and a recipe for a challenging day, but it's quite the opposite. Eliott is super sweet for the rest of the day and even naps for three hours!

When Cedric comes home that night, Eliott proudly shows his artwork off.

'Who did this? This is amazing, Eliott,' enthuses Ced; he's almost crying.

I couldn't have imagined a better couple of days, and I'm confident that looking after them both for two days a week is going to be challenging but so rewarding.

Maman

Our weekend away to the Hunter Valley, about three hours north of Sydney, is the special Mother's Day treat from Ced.

It's located in the middle of nowhere and surrounded by kangaroos. Eliott is curious about them, but we keep him in our arms because kangaroos can be quite dangerous — they have long claws, so we don't want to take any chances.

It's such a special weekend, and on the way back home, we reflect on how lucky we are to be able to do this. Eliott hasn't had a seizure in almost ten months, and he's making great progress — the review at the clinic next week will tell us just how much progress and what we need to focus on for the coming year.

I'm secretly hoping he's caught up, even though I know he's probably not yet at the 50th percentile, but I'm positive he's getting closer. I don't need him to be above average. If there's one thing I've learnt through all this, it's that average is good. He doesn't have to be the smartest kid on the block, just smart enough to become whoever he wants to be.

On Thursday, Ced has taken the morning off work to come with us to the clinic. The social worker and the paediatric psychologist are both lovely, and we spend the first hour talking about Eliott's development. Eliott is playing nicely with a few toys. They start the assessment, and Eliott does a great job.

I can barely hide how proud I am, and Eliott looks elated and is clearly doing his best. I'm always humbled by his resilience. He's such a good baby, always trying his hardest. He seems to do his best for every appointment. Maybe he can sense how important it is.

He does better on all the tests; he's now walking and running and kicking a ball. They present him with a small ball, and he only manages to kick it backwards, but who cares? I cheer him on.

We're back in the room for the final test, the one that he had completely failed last year, where they ask him to recognise and pick familiar objects. I'm dreading it. To be fair, we haven't really focused on that. The speech therapists have been helping us with tips on how to help him communicate and focus on getting words out. However, we haven't focused on receptive language — how much he understands — Danielle has, but we've only seen her twice.

The psychologist lays the objects on the floor, and I can feel my breathing get shallower. I realise I'm stressing more than I should.

She looks at Eliott, who is looking curiously at the different objects. 'Okay Eliott, do you want to give me the spoon?' she asks.

He looks at the objects and picks the spoon.

Hurray!

'Eliott, do you want to give me the car?'

He picks the teddy bear.

'That's okay. We'll try another one. Do you want to give me the sock?'

Eliott looks at her, picks up the sock and gives it to her.

'Ock,' he says.

What? How amazing!

'Eliott, do you want to give me the doll?'

He looks at her again, then picks up the doll.

'Olly,' he tries.

I'm crying. It must be day care; they've been playing with dolls to encourage pretend play.

She tries a couple more — 'train', 'bear' — but either he's no longer focused, or he doesn't know, and he doesn't get any others right.

But three out of five or six ... surely that's impressive! And he's tried repeating the sounds.

We're invited to go to the waiting room again, and thirty minutes later, they call us back in.

'Okay, we have the results. But remember, these are only numbers, they don't mean anything just yet, as he's so small,' says the social worker.

My mind is racing.

'Eliott has obviously made a lot of progress, and it's lovely to see this. But as you know, between one and two years of age, all kids develop at an exponential rate. Eliott

268

has made huge developmental gains, but the gap is widening. He's fallen below the first percentile overall.'

How is this possible?

After everything we've done this year?

After everything he's done this year?

How could he be under the 1st percentile now? There is nothing below that.

'His strengths are now gross motor skills and his social skills. Did you notice how he would ask you for help when he couldn't do something? It's great that he's communicating and getting you to support him, but he won't be able to make as much progress if he continues to do that. His language and fine motor skills are the weakest at this stage. He has what we call a significant "global developmental delay". Don't get too upset by the label, it's just going to give him access to further support. We'll make sure his file is transferred to the National Disability Insurance Agency, so he can get on the scheme, and you can have more support when it gets implemented in the next few months.'

To get him on National Disability Insurance Scheme (NDIS)? Surely this isn't a good thing?

I shut down, and Ced manages to get us all back to the car and safely home. Neither of us speak about this for three days. I cry a lot and look after the boys however I can. Ced has also completely shut down.

On Sunday, we've been invited to Ced's boss's house for lunch. It's been planned for weeks, and we can't reschedule. Life must go on.

In the morning, we pack everything, ready for the day. I've grown concerned about Ced not talking at all about Eliott's review. I've managed to talk a bit to Mum, and somehow, I've gathered enough strength to realise that the little boy I was so proud of on Wednesday is still the same after the review on Thursday. I know that he can still improve before the next review, and we must focus on helping him. But I was so convinced he had already improved this year, and the realisation that we're literally the furthest away from our goal of catching up has taken everything I had left.

The truth is that I'm scared about what it means, as well as heartbroken — although that word isn't strong enough to describe what I feel — and I'm even more scared for Ced. He hasn't talked in days, and he looks like a shadow of himself. I'm worried about all the dark thoughts he must be experiencing. He's always here for me, and I need to be here for him. Neither of us can do it alone; there must be a way to bring him back.

It's the worst timing because I know he'll get a bit angry at me for not respecting his wishes to be left alone, but the car trip is probably the most tactical time. We're stuck for at least the hour-and-a-half drive to his boss's house, and he'll have to stay composed for the lunch. As a sign of fate, both boys fall asleep within minutes of leaving the house. It's early for Eliott; he must've been exhausted.

'Ced, I know you don't want to talk to me.'

'It's not that I don't want to speak to you, I just can't.'

I'm treading lightly here. 'Have you managed to talk to someone about it? Even if it's not me? Maybe call your friend in France?'

'I don't want to call him, as he doesn't get it.'

'Okay, what can I do to help?'

'Nothing. I just have to accept it, but I can't right now.'

Okay. That's fair enough, and I get that.

We've been able to get over everything, but this has been a huge blow after feeling better over the past few weeks. I decide to try another angle.

'I'm with you, but I'm afraid you're shutting down. You always force me to talk when you see me doing the same, so please talk to me. We must find a way, together.'

Ced looks at me, and I know I've struck a chord. 'I'm just so angry at them for delivering the message this way. Eliott was in the room with us, hearing everything. How can they drop a bomb like this and not offer any kind of support for us? And look at him.' Ced looks at Eliott in the rear-view mirror, so I turn around — he's fast asleep, but his sleep seems quite agitated. 'Even when he sleeps, he does weird stuff. Why is this so hard?'

I think Eliott is probably dreaming; the agitated sleep surely isn't anything to be concerned about, so we should focus on one issue at a time.

'He's probably having a bad dream. I agree with you on the clinic though. It was poor delivery. But they had good points. We'll get Eliott more frequent sessions with Danielle. I'll find him a new occupational therapist, and we'll ask day care to get a support worker,' I say.

Ced seems better, and he's still looking at Eliott from time to time.

We're trying to find our way back one more time, and we're a team. We'll fight it together, all four of us.

We're only twenty minutes away from arriving at our destination, and I'm looking outside the window while we're driving on the freeway. I've met Ced's boss and his family, and I'm looking forward to seeing them. They've been incredibly supportive of Ced at work, and maybe that is just what we need today — a delicious, relaxing lunch to take our minds off things.

I'm holding Ced's hand when I hear it.

Three distinctive screams.

It takes me half a second to turn around, but even before I look at Eliott, I know. Deep in my bones, I know.

'CED, STOP THE CAR! HE'S HAVING A SEIZURE!'

Ced stops the car on the side of the road, and we both jump out.

'Where is his bag?' Ced yells.

'I've got it.' I'm already by Eliott's side, and thankfully his bag is on the floor under him. I try to unstrap him out of his car seat, but he's so stiff there's nothing I can do. Ced takes over watching Eliott, and I rip apart the protective foil of the Midazolam. I draw the liquid, and Ced takes a few steps away to let me back in.

'Eliott, I'm going to give you your medication, my love. It's all going to be fine, baby,' I say, and open his mouth to squirt it in between the cheek and the gum like we've been taught.

Oscar has woken up and has started screaming, so Ced goes around the car to pick him up. I see him take his mobile and dial '000'. Within seconds, Eliott's body is relaxing. I quickly take him out of his car seat.

Ced has parked on the footpath, and a few metres behind is what looks like a community hall. Hopefully someone is there. I carry Eliott, who's no longer stiff but unconscious, and I kiss his forehead. He's cool. *No fever?* I want to knock on the door but can't use my hands, so I start banging on the door with my foot. No response. I go around the house, but it looks empty.

When I go back to Ced, a passer-by has stopped and is next to Ced, helping him give directions to 000. Eliott is slowly coming back to himself, and I'm focused on how I'm going to give him the Phenytoin while he's in my arms. I then register that the passer-by is holding Oscar, so Ced can help me.

I pass Eliott to Ced so he can hold him while I give Eliott the Phenytoin, and once it's done, Ced passes me the phone so I can talk to 000.

The passer-by is next to us, shushing Oscar and rocking him. He looks concerned but can obviously see that it's out of his control and the best he can do is what he's already doing — making sure we can focus on Eliott.

I'm talking to 000 and asking them again where the ambulance is, when I hear despair in Ced's voice, 'He's clustering!'

Eliott's little body is twitching. Not full-blown seizures, but little clusters. We finally see a first responder vehicle arrive. It's just a vehicle, not an ambulance.

'The ambulance is right behind me. I was the closest,' says the lady who gets out of the vehicle. 'Lay him on the back seat, and I can check his vital signs.'

But just as Ced hands Eliott to me, and I lay him in the back of the car on the seat, his whole body stiffens again.

'Ced, he's having another one, get me the Midazolam.'

Ced runs to the car and back, and I look at the first responder.

She says, 'You do that, as I can see you know what to do. I'll assist you, so what do you need?'

I draw the liquid again and give it to Eliott. I ask her for the time. It's only been thirty minutes since it's started, and probably about twenty-five minutes since we've given him his loading dose of Phenytoin. It must be finally kicking in because this time his whole body relaxes and he falls asleep.

The ambulance arrives shortly after. We thank the passer-by profusely, and I hop into the ambulance. They want to take Eliott to the closest hospital, but Eliott is stable, so I ask them to take him to the hospital where he's been treated in the past.

On the way there, I can't stop crying, and I can hear myself repeating out loud, 'Ten months ... we thought he had outgrown them.'

Chapter eighteen

A little time capsule outside of this world
(July–November 2017)

Maman

When we get to hospital, we feel so lost. Ced arrives with Oscar and looks shattered. He tells me Oscar screamed the whole trip, which lasted forty-five minutes. I take him in my arms to give him a big cuddle.

'How is he?' Ced asks, looking at Eliott.

'He was fine during the trip and has been sleeping since. I think I might call our friends and see if they can come. I don't feel like doing this alone.'

Ced nods, 'Yes, that's a good idea. You go and I'll look after them here.'

I call Jasper, with whom we had spent New Year's Eve with last year, and he's here in less than twenty minutes. He's always been deeply concerned about Eliott and is happy to just wait there with us. We all know that one of the concerns is whether he'll be okay when he wakes up. I just keep repeating that he was fine and didn't have a fever, and everyone can see this is quickly becoming my main concern.

It's a whole new ball game if seizures start coming suddenly and without warning.

I'm starting to spiral.

How are we going to manage and keep on living that semi-normal life we've worked so hard to create if seizures can now come without warning?

I know that it does for most people who suffer from

epilepsy; however, being able to make some plans over the last few months gave us so much hope. *Do we have to give it up so soon?*

I don't want to admit it, but I feel let down — by myself, by the universe, by the situation. I let my guard down and allowed myself to feel hopeful and trust that we could do more, only to end up in hospital again. I can't help but picture a whole series of worst-case scenarios.

I'm lost in dark thoughts when the nurse comes to see us and check Eliott's vital signs. His temperature is rising. An hour later, he still feels hot, and they check again — it's over 39 degrees.

We eventually learn that Eliott caught the severe strand of influenza that's been going around. The seizure was the first symptom. Eliott is sick for a week. He's extremely weak, sleeps a lot, but he doesn't have another seizure. We keep him on Phenytoin for a solid week while he recovers.

One morning, as I'm feeding Oscar on the sofa, Eliott waddles towards me for a cuddle. He lays his head on my knees, and as I rub his back, he falls asleep, still standing. I've never seen anything like it.

A few days later, on Tuesday, I also wake with a fever. I haven't had one in twenty years, and I can't even get out of bed. The home doctor comes and leaves me with a script: one week of antibiotics. I have strep throat. Ced takes the week off work, and we call in Sally to help. But managing a sick toddler, a sick wife, and a newborn is too much, even with Sally's help, and Ced also catches something.

By Thursday, Eliott and I are feeling much better, far from back to normal, but at least we can start to get out and about, just in time for Ced to feel at his worst.

Even baby Oscar gets sick. In comparison, he is lucky. He develops a low-grade fever and a bad cough. Thankfully, he hasn't caught my strep throat or Eliott and Ced's flu, but it's still enough to make him wake three or four times a night, and one night he doesn't want to leave my side and sleeps with me. I'm so tired that I feed him back to sleep every time.

On Friday, not even a week after the seizure, and after having gone through a horrific week, Suzy and Alex, the couple from Melbourne we met through the KCNQ2 Cure Alliance charity, come for afternoon tea. We wanted to make sure we could feel well enough to welcome them and have a chat. I've been looking forward to seeing them, and Ced was keen to continue the discussion from the conference he attended in May.

We talk about everything: our journey, what works and what doesn't with our kids. They're further along on the journey than we are, given their daughter is older, but there are a lot of similarities. And it's good to see how they've managed over the years, and how they're now trying so hard to make a difference.

I'm inspired by all the work they're doing with KCNQ2 Cure and GETA.

After a three-hour nap, Eliott wakes and gets to meet them. It's an emotional moment. Poor Eliott is still so tired and weak from the flu, but he has finally recovered and is proud to show off all that he can do! Suzy and Alex are so excited to see how well he is doing.

The following week, we go back to our routine. We need to go back to normal. Desperately. Well, as close to normal as we can, which isn't easy. After the last assessment, after the last seizure, it feels like something has permanently been damaged. Not one single seizure in ten months, and he has one without a fever. *What does that mean?*

I vividly remember an appointment with Ewan shortly after Eliott had his status epilectics. It was such a difficult time, and I was struggling to make sense of everything. I had once again shared with him how I couldn't understand why it was happening to us, that I felt like I was being punished, and that I needed to feel hopeful again. I longed to feel grateful for my life, and I wasn't. I was feeling nothing but sadness, despair, disappointment, and I was feeling like a total failure.

'Claire, I think you're doing an amazing job, but you've lost your sense of security. It will take a very long time to recover from this. But you'll get through it; you and Ced are strong,' he had said at the time.

These were kind words about our strength and ability to survive. But what stuck with me was: we had lost our sense of security. It helped me understand why I was feeling so vulnerable. I wasn't feeling safe in my own life anymore. I needed to find a way to build back up.

One of the ways was to identify actions that we could take to improve things, such as helping Eliott with therapy, fighting to get him more support earlier on, and spending time travelling as a family. It was also to seek and grow a stronger support network.

Today, eighteen months later, I'm left with those feelings again. I'm thinking about the support we've had from friends, and amazing people such as Jen and Sally, but there's nothing better than family support. After these horrific couple of weeks, there's nothing I want more than to have my family around.

My brother Jean-Mi arrives on Monday, two weeks after the seizure. He made the decision to come for three weeks shortly after hearing that Jen was leaving us, and the timing couldn't have been better. He's coming when our tanks are empty.

When he arrives, Eliott is in day care, so Oscar and I pick him up from the airport. We have a relaxing day together, and Jean-Mi is jubilant to see the boys. He's thrilled to meet Oscar. And in the evening, he can't stop commenting on how grown-up Eliott is.

Jean-Mi is my baby brother, and his opinion means

everything to me. He's managed to grow into such a fine man. He simultaneously acknowledges the seriousness of the situation while saying that the review means nothing (using slightly stronger words), and he keeps saying that Eliott is amazing. He's proud of his nephew. Isn't that more important?

To show Jean-Mi around Australia, we've booked to go to Hobart, Tasmania, for a few days. It's a wonderful trip, and I'm grateful for this chance to just take time out to be together.

Eliott is surprising us every day. He no longer needs to have a highchair, can eat like us, and is showing us how happy he is to discover a new city.

The following week, we spend Tuesday and Wednesday together with Jean-Mi while Ced is at work. Our days are organised around activities for the boys. We've started GymbaROO for Oscar, and we continue going to arts and crafts and speech therapy for Eliott. We're even seeing a new occupational therapist who works with Danielle, as she thinks it will be beneficial for Eliott to focus on both.

Mid-August, Eliott has an EEG. He's now twenty-six months, and Henry has asked that we start a routine annual EEG to check that his brain activity is normal. Because he had the seizure at the back end of July, this first one has been organised quickly. And just to be sure that there's nothing going on when the risk of missing something is at its highest, Henry asks that Eliott have a 'sleep deprived' EEG.

The night before the 8am appointment, they want us to put him to bed at 9pm and to wake him at 3am.

Now that's an impossible task!

Against all odds, and with help from Jean-Mi, we manage to get him up at 3am, play and give him breakfast, and thanks to my brother's singing skills in the car, we get him to his appointment without him falling back to sleep. We even manage to get him to sleep shortly after the electrodes have been placed on his head.

Soon enough, I'm asked to wake Eliott up again, and we make him watch the flashing lights to check his photosensitivity. His bag with the medication is within reach as always, and I'm mentally reciting my checklist of what to do if he were to have a seizure, but thankfully nothing happens.

The results come in later that week, and they're the same as last year: minimal activity, more than the average person, but not enough to warrant the need to put him back on medication. The next EEG is due in twelve months!

While Jean-Mi is staying with us, we're starting to get ready for the two big moments of the next few months. One is our upcoming trip back to France. We've decided that I should make the most of being on maternity leave and go back for six weeks. Eliott is bigger now, so going back in winter should be more manageable, and I really want to go home and introduce Oscar to everyone.

Mum has also offered to come to Australia at the end of October and fly to France with us mid-November, so I don't have to handle the trip with the two boys on my own, and we're looking forward to having her back.

The other big event is the Oxfam Trailwalker. Ced is running it and has been training hard. It's a 100-kilometre team event to raise awareness and funds to fight poverty.

It's an important event for us both.

My friend Jasper got me into it and helped me train when I ran my first one back in 2011, then another one in 2012. Ced and I ran one together in New Zealand just three weeks before we got married in 2014.

In my speech at the wedding, I commented on how the experience had made us stronger as a couple. Running has become a big part of who we are, and ultra-running has become a part of who we aspire to be. It's allowed us to test ourselves and go beyond our own limits.

I couldn't be prouder of Ced for running the Sydney event this year.

Eliott is at day care that day, and Oscar, Jean-Mi, and I go to the second checkpoint at the thirty-kilometre mark. Their support crew is there, and we help them fill up the water and cheer them on. Jasper has also come to cheer them on.

In the evening, Jean-Mi helps me with the boys, and then stays home to babysit while I go to the sixty-kilometre checkpoint. Ced and his team are going strong, and I'm so pleased for them all!

When they cross the finish line the next day just before 12pm, we're all there to cheer. Eliott loves the finish line atmosphere. We've seen a few teams finish, and Eliott has understood that everyone is clapping and cheering for the people who run under the banner. So, at some point without notice, I see him run a good fifty metres out from the finish line, turn around, and run back! How amazing! He's just so proud of himself, and it's cute to see. When he sees Ced in the background running towards us, he's so excited! Ced and his team finish, and Eliott runs towards him.

I promise myself that I'll be back on the trails next year!

Jean-Mi heads to the airport that afternoon after three amazing weeks. We know it's not going to be long until we see him again, but it's still emotional to watch him leave.

Eliott

The weekend after Jean-Mi leaves, Mum says that she's going to start a new challenge for us. We're going to copy Kate's ideas from arts and crafts. During class, we've been looking at one letter every week. We did P for plane, S for star, and Y for yellow. So, Mum and I bought some craft supplies; crayons, paper, glue, paint and paintbrushes, and Mum found little wooden letters that she said we are going to use every week to learn the letters.

On Tuesday, we start with the letter A. We eat an apple for morning tea, an avocado for lunch, and we go to see the aeroplanes in the afternoon.

I like how Mum seems happy with the idea and is more relaxed. I really like doing crafts with her. It's not just about crafts, as she also gets me to help hang the clothes out to dry and I water the plants with Dad — both activities start with the letter A in French.

I've been trying to make her understand that I think she is spending too much time with Oscar, by crying and throwing tantrums. And I think she now understands me because when Oscar has his morning sleep, Mum and I spend time doing these activities. This makes me content, and I think we have a good time.

Maman

With Jean-Mi gone, I have eight weeks on my own with the boys on Tuesdays and Wednesdays before Mum arrives. And with some suggestions from my family, I fill much of the time with entertaining things for the three of us to do.

We're feeling a lot better. Everything feels manageable. Eliott is doing new things every week, and he's starting to surprise us. It's the first time in his life he's doing things without us having to show him and teach him multiple times. Oscar is a wonderful little baby that makes us feel normal, and there is a sense of hope.

After everything we've experienced, a big lesson has been to surround ourselves with people who help us.

Danielle, the new speech therapist, and Kate, the arts and craft teacher, have quickly become strong members of our support network.

We're learning that sometimes it's more important to have a tribe that can give us the strength to keep fighting than someone or some review telling us he's delayed, and not even giving us constructive ways of helping Eliott.

Mum has even been telling me to call one of her friends

in France who is a therapist. She supports kids with developmental delays. I've been pushing back because I've never felt like I had the time or the mental space to talk to yet another person. I also didn't want to burden someone I had never met with our issues. But in time, she has become one of our most trusted advisors.

We spoke shortly after the assessment/seizure episode. She said that Eliot was still so young and full of potential. The combination of that conversation, the arrival of Jean-Mi for a few weeks, and seeing Eliott make so much progress during the two days he's at home with me has given us some strength back.

Unfortunately, one Tuesday in early September, Eliott is extremely difficult. He wakes up crying, screams every time Oscar is feeding or is in my arms, and keeps making weird movements. Not seizure-like movements, but after what happened in July, when I told Ced not to worry and he had a seizure, I don't trust myself. We're in the car driving home from a session with the occupational therapist when I grow more concerned.

We're only five minutes away from home, and I'm stressing out. I pull the car over to the side of the road, grab Eliott's bag, and draw the loading dose of Phenytoin.

I look at Eliott, who looks desperate and simply unwell. 'Eliott, you don't look well, my love. I'm going to give you your medication, so you feel better.'

He looks at me, then the syringe and pushes it away.

'Eliott, I think you need it. Does your head hurt?' I'm almost crying. Something is telling me he's off, and I'm scared it's too late. Or am I scared that I'm giving it to him, and he doesn't need it? I don't know anymore. I feel so bad that once again I'm lost and out of place. 'Eliott, I think you're unwell. Can Mummy please give you your medication? It's for your head.' And while saying this, I touch my head, and then I touch his chest, to try to make him understand that it's for him, for his head.

He looks at me and opens his mouth.

'Thank you, my love. We'll drive home slowly and take it easy for a while. I think you'll feel better now.'

The rest of the day, Eliott seems to be better. I think he knew he was off and was trying to tell me. I'm feeling equally good for having been able to listen, but also bad for not listening earlier. Poor bubba was trying to communicate, and I just thought he was having a bad day and throwing tantrums.

When Ced comes home that night, he gently takes my hand and gives it a soft kiss. 'You did really well today. But you can't keep beating yourself up. We'll all get better at understanding what's happening. It's amazing that you saw what Eliott was trying to tell you. He'll get better at communicating, and we'll get better at listening.'

Eliott

Mamie Vero is back! Mum told me that I will be spending more time with her and Mamie Vero until we go to France. We go to a dance lesson with my friend Chiara, go to the beach, to the pool, and finish packing.

At day care, I spend time in a new room. It's the class above and is called the 'Explorers'. This is a big transition — it's a bigger class, has less teachers, and a larger playground. I'm afraid, but I can tell that Mum and Dad are proud of me. I need more help to go up and down the stairs to the play area, in and out of the sandpit, and to sit on the higher chairs, but I love discovering the new class, and the new teachers.

I've seen Joana, who comes to help me speak, a lot more at day care than home; she's talking to my teachers to help them with the transition.

At home, I love having Mamie Vero here, and I want to be able to use her name, but I can't form many words yet. I manage to say 'Ninnie', and she seems to like it.

We see Henry for one last routine appointment before leaving for France, and he's pleased when Mum tells him about my progress, and about everything we've been doing. He's glad it's all going well with Danielle.

It's mid-November, and we're ready to face the twenty-four-hour flight to take us home for Christmas. The four of us: Eliott, Oscar, Mum and Ninnie all leave in the afternoon and will be there four weeks before Dad arrives.

Chapter nineteen

Our French Christmas
(November-December 2017)

Maman

Arriving in the middle of winter, we're confronted by a ten-hour time difference (when it's only eight in summer) and extremely cold weather. The boys are struggling to sleep. Thankfully, one of my friends comes to help and does three nights of baby-sitting so Mum and I can sleep. The boys wake at different times throughout the night.

We spend three weeks in Caen with my family and see Mum's friend, the therapist, so Eliott can get therapy while we're here. She's very encouraging, and every time I ask what she thinks of his development, she gently responds that he has a lot of potential, but that she can't predict what it will be like in the future.

I feel a bit disappointed by that response, but at the end of each session, she says something like: 'He's showing us that he's interested in body parts, and he likes the bath. Why don't you ask him to wash himself tonight in the bath?' Or: 'He's showing an interest in understanding sequencing. You said he likes to bake with you, so why don't you get him to crack the eggs and mix them in next time?' All these tips are help me progress as a parent too.

We then head to Paris, where we've rented an apartment for the weekend. Mum comes along, and we have such an enjoyable time. We visit some of my friends, and it feels good to reconnect with everyone.

On Monday, together with the two boys, a heavy suitcase, a double pram, and a full picnic basket, we take a two-hour train trip to Bordeaux, where Ced's family lives. When we reach the station in Bordeaux, Mamie Francette and Tatie Karine are there to welcome us.

Spending these four weeks in France on my own with the boys has been wonderful, but also more emotionally tiring than I thought it would be.

Travelling with an eight-month-old and a toddler in the thick of winter is hard. I'm grateful for the family support, and thankfully, Eliott enjoys discovering new places and meeting new people. That's one of the things I'm always amazed about with him. He has such a curious nature and just loves to be surrounded by new people, with new things to see.

But because it's winter and there isn't much to do outside, both boys are quickly bored, and Eliott needs to burn off energy. He's not active enough and doesn't nap much during the day, so the days are long, and the evenings are difficult with an overtired toddler. At least he's so tired that when he finally goes to sleep in the evening, he falls asleep within seconds and sleeps more in the morning. We often have to be careful about how much noise we make at 8am!

When Cedric arrives mid-December, I'm desperate to see him, and so are the boys. With Ced here, we go to see his brother for a couple of days and take long walks in the nearby forest, and we even find a little café where we have a delicious breakfast as a family, something which is a bit unusual in France but is so familiar in Australia.

A few days before Christmas Day, we celebrate by having a Christmas dinner with Ced's family, and the boys are spoilt with books, toys and clothes. Eliott receives the cutest cooking utensils, and Oscar gets a bag for when he starts day care in the new year. They're both so thrilled, and we're very sad when we have to leave the next day.

We're going back to Caen for Christmas Day. We take the train all the way back, three hours to Paris, change over between stations, and another two hours to Caen. We arrive exhausted just after lunch.

Ced stays home in the afternoon to mind Eliott while he naps, and Mum and I go out with Oscar for some last-minute Christmas shopping for my grandmother.

While we're out, Ced calls. 'Where are you? I might join you. Eliott woke early from his nap and is screaming. I think he just needs to get some fresh air.'

They join us and we get a hot chocolate. Eliott seems okay and isn't upset anymore, but he doesn't look like himself either. Ced thinks that it may have been too hot in the bedroom and he has woken up with a headache; he was holding his head a bit.

We all go to sleep early that evening and hope that he'll be better the next day.

Ced and I haven't had one minute to ourselves, so Mum offers to take the boys to the park to see some farm animals. One of her friends is coming to help, so she doesn't have to manage the boys on her own. We're hoping to go for a run, enjoy a tranquil lunch, and finish our Christmas shopping together.

In the morning, Eliott is better but isn't very hungry. It's usually a telling sign that something is off, but he's as interactive and playful as usual, so we don't think too much of it. He's not upset like he was yesterday, so we head off for a quick run and come back home just as Mum and her friend are about to leave for the park.

We give them both a big kiss, and I thank Mum and her friend for 'giving us the day off'.

A few hours later, we're buying a toy for Eliott in a cute little toy shop when my phone rings. It's Mum. I look at Ced and give him a sign that I'll just be a minute and walk out of the shop to take the call. It's cold outside, but not as much as it's been the past few days.

Mum knows how much we need this time, just a few

hours to ourselves to do things at our own rhythm. But more importantly, she knows that we have this rule between ourselves, 'only call if there's an emergency'. She would not call for something benign. I answer and hear Mum crying. 'Mum, is everything okay?'

'Oh Claire, darling, Eliott just had a seizure.'

How did this happen?

I swallow with difficulty. 'Is he hot? Where are you? Did you call an ambulance?'

'I don't know what happened. I was pushing Oscar in his pram, and Eliott was running when he fell. He started crying, so I stopped the pram and took him in my arms, and then suddenly he started screaming. It was the screams like you said, and then he became stiff and had a seizure. I asked my friend to give me the medication, and the park wardens came to see if we needed help. We're waiting for the ambulance now. He's recovered.'

I can hear that she's doing everything she can to hold herself together. She's just had to do one of the bravest things not many grandmothers would be able to do.

And being a mum, she still finds the strength to reassure me. 'He's doing fine, my darling. He hasn't clustered, and I've given him his Phenytoin. But there is some syrup on his scarf. Oscar is safe and in my friend's arms now, and I'm holding Eliott's hand while we wait for help to arrive.'

'Mum, you did exactly what you should do. You did really well. Take him to the hospital, and we'll meet you there. Did he get hurt? Is he hot?' I feel my body is about to shut down, but I'm on autopilot.

'No, darling, I don't know what happened, maybe it's the fall. He's not hot at all.' I can hear despair; she knows why I ask. She carries on, 'The wardens are asking me a question, and I can see the ambulance coming. Can I call you if they have a question?'

'Of course, Mum, I'll get Ced, and we'll meet you there. Don't worry about us, just get him there and make sure they know you've given him one dose of Midazolam already.'

We hang up, and I walk back into the tiny store. Cedric is still holding the toy we were looking at getting for Eliott, and he's holding another one, debating which one to get. What felt like innocence two minutes ago is going to be shattered. He looks up and sees my face.

'Eliott had a seizure; we have to go,' I say.

'What?'

'Eliott had a seizure. Mum just called; they're taking him to the hospital.'

Other shoppers are looking at us, but we don't really pay attention. Ced drops both toys at once, and we rush outside.

'What do you mean he had a seizure? How do we get to your mum's house from here? I'll run home.'

He doesn't get it.

'No, we must go to hospital. They're on their way.'

But Ced's desperate to act, and I don't blame him for that. In fact, I probably love him even more — his fight or flight response is to run towards Eliott as fast as he can. Literally.

I continue, 'Ced, listen to me, they're not at home. They were at the park. Eliott fell and had a seizure. The ambulance is taking them to hospital. We must meet them there. It's too far to walk.'

But there are no cabs, no uber, no way to get to hospital quickly.

Ced is looking at me anxiously. 'What do we do?'

I do the only thing I can think of and call one of my closest friends.

'Hey, what's up?' he asks joyfully when he answers.

It's 23 December, and he's at home with his family, no doubt getting ready for the holiday.

'Ted, Eliott had a seizure, and we need to get to hospital. I don't know what to do.'

'Where are you? I'll be there in ten minutes.'

In the car, I call Mum again, and she reassures me that they're on their way to the hospital. Her friend is driving

Oscar back in her car to feed him his lunch and put him down for his nap.

Life must go on.

When we get to the hospital, we look like mad people. We rush through the emergency room, but Eliott and Mum haven't arrived yet.

When Eliott finally comes in, he's on a stretcher bed. The first responders are pushing him, and they say he's fine.

He's stable and just needs to be monitored.

Ced and I rush to his side and give him lots of kisses on his forehead and on his little hands. I give Mum a big kiss, and Eliott is taken to a treatment room. Ced goes with him, and I manage to thank Ted quickly.

The hospital staff then let me into the restricted area and point me to Eliott's room. When I walk in, Eliott is still asleep on the bed, and Ced is holding his hand. A couple of metres away, leaning against the back wall, is Mum.

They all look up as I walk in, and Ced says, 'This is my wife Claire, Eliott's mum.'

The young doctor smiles at me and holds up a piece of paper that I immediately recognise. It's the seizure management plan I typed and printed, which is always with Eliott in his medication bag. 'Did you do this?'

'Yes,' I respond, walking towards the bed and around Ced to reach Eliott. I start to gently stroke his hair.

'This is brilliant. I'm sorry you had to do it, but it's so useful for us. Your mum here did a great job, and at this stage, there's nothing additional we need to do. Do they happen often? Do you know what caused it?'

I look at Mum, who looks to be in shock, and at Ced, who seems as puzzled and sad as I am.

'No,' Ced responds. 'The last one he had was in July. They've all been caused by fever or sickness. I don't know what could have caused this one.'

I then say, 'Me neither. Could he be on the verge of getting sick? That's what happened in July before he had the flu.'

290

The doctor suggests a similar process to the last time we were here. They'll put a numbing patch on his hand in case he needs a cannula later, and if a fever breaks, we can run more tests. In the meantime, they'll keep us under observation today, and we can reassess when he wakes up.

The doctor leaves the room, and while the nurse is fussing around Eliott and talking to Cedric, I check on Mum, who is still leaning against the wall.

'Mum, I'm so sorry you had to do this,' I say and start crying. 'Thank you so much for what you did for him. You did an amazing job. Thank you for giving him his medication quickly and being there with him. Thank you for keeping him safe.'

We train everyone who must look after Eliott because we need them to be able to respond in an emergency. But I know how confronting it is to witness a seizure, especially when it's someone you love. And I know being able to react quickly and calmly takes a lot of strength.

'Oh my darling, it's quite normal that I gave him his medication and stayed with him. I'm just so sorry it happened.'

'Ted is waiting for you, to take you home. Why don't you go and have a rest?' I help Mum with her bags, and we're walking back through the corridor towards the closed doors that separate the restricted area where we still are from the waiting area where the real world starts again.

I'm about to press the button that will unlock the door when she crashes into my arms. I feel her legs give in, and I must hold her before she falls to the ground. She's crying uncontrollably, like I've never seen her cry before, not even when Dad died.

I hold her as close as I can and softly shush in her ear, 'That's okay, Mum, he's fine, thanks to you. Ced and I can't thank you enough for what you did.'

'I don't know what happened. I should have seen it. I'm so sorry. He was fine, he was a bit tired, but he was happy to be outside and watching the animals.'

291

She manages to calm down and starts to breathe normally after five minutes, and when I get her to Ted, he puts his arm around her shoulders and gives me an enquiring look. I nod back: she's fine, but she's in shock. I thank him again and promise to call later with an update.

They leave and I go back to the room where Ced and the nurse are packing Eliott's belongings to move to a day room.

When he wakes up later that day, he's fine. He's groggy, but once again we see our smiley, happy baby come back to himself. By that time, Mum and Jean-Mi are here, and they've brought toys and snacks. Eliott is hungry and is clearly pleased to see that the French hospital food is of good quality. He eats all his mash and ham, followed by the yoghurt. Shortly after, we're discharged and can go home.

Eliott

It's Christmas Eve. Mum and Dad are cooking, so Ninnie doesn't have to do it, as she's hosting at her apartment. There's a lot to do, and usually we take a walk with Ninnie in the afternoon, but today we all stay home.

In the evening, Jean-Mi arrives with my great-grandfather and Mum's friend.

It's wonderful to have people here, but I'm still tired, so I go to bed early.

It's Christmas Day, and everyone is well dressed. Just as we leave Ninnie's apartment to go to my great-grandparent's place, I hear Mum tell Dad, 'Thank you. I know you don't feel like going anymore, so we won't stay late. Let's ask them if we can finish lunch a bit earlier so we can come and put Eliott to bed sooner.'

When we get there, my great-grandparents are in the lobby and welcome us with open arms.

'Merry Christmas! How is little Eliott? What happened? Is he getting sick?' they ask.

They all hug and give Oscar and me big kisses, and as

Dad takes us into the other room, I hear Mum thanking them.

'Thank you, Merry Christmas to you too. We don't know. We've been monitoring him very closely, but he's not getting sick. Maybe it is from the exhaustion. We're going to be careful over the next few days.'

When we get to the living room, there are presents under the Christmas tree, and my great-grandmother has set up a festive table with lots of plates, glasses and decorations. We open our presents, and it's fun to tear up the gift wrapping.

However, Mum and Dad keep touching my forehead, and they're not smiling as much as usual. Oscar and I play with our new toys and books, and then we have our lunch in the kitchen.

Once Oscar is in bed for his nap, Mum and Dad tell me it's time for my nap too. We go up to the spare bedroom where I've slept a few times with them, but I don't want to sleep. I missed a few naps when we were down at Mamie Francette and Papi Jean-Claude's house, and I quite enjoy spending the whole day with everyone.

Mum is saying I really should sleep, but Dad says it's okay. I'm allowed to stay with the adults and skip my nap for today. I'm tired though, and a bit grumpy, so Dad takes me outside and we play while everyone is having their Christmas lunch.

We go home early in the evening, and Mum and Dad tell me how proud they are of me.

When we leave a few days later, Mum and Dad tell me that we have a long trip ahead of us. 'Do you remember last month? We took the plane with Ninnie to come here? Today we're going home, the four of us. We'll be home soon,' Mum tells me.

It's a long trip again, and Mum is constantly checking my forehead and looking at me. I sleep a lot on Dad, and Oscar sleeps on Mum.

After such a long trip, we finally arrive home.

I'm so happy when I recognise our house, and Mum and Dad look happy too!

Dad had baked and prepared a few things that he froze before he left to meet us in France, so we just reheat a quick dinner, and sit down to eat.

It's dark outside, and Mum and Dad are laughing and saying this is a weird dinner. 'It's past 11pm!' But they tell us how proud they are of us, how we've been good on the flight and during the holiday, and how they're overjoyed to be home with us to see the new year in.

We're about to finish dinner when we hear loud bangs outside.

Mum's face lights up, and she gets up. 'Oh, Happy New Year! The fireworks have started!'

We all walk out on the deck and try to see the fireworks. Mum and Dad kiss and give us both big kisses too.

'Happy New Year, babies. This year is going to be a big year!'

Epilogue

This is a book about Eliott, about redefining what 'normal' is, moving past our darkest moments, and finding a way to our 'new normal'.

Our new mantra has been: adapt, adjust, pivot.

It's been one hell of a road, a bumpy one, which too often has felt like a no-through road. But we have all fought as hard as we could to survive, and to create a balance for ourselves.

This is also a book about hope, and as I write this, I know that the fight is far from over. We keep on fighting the disease, for Eliott to get the right support, and for us all as a family.

I know we've found a better balance and new coping strategies, but we are far from having won the war, and are still deep in the trenches. As I write these words, Eliott is only six and a half years old. So young.

And yet, in his short lifetime, we've already experienced big wins, and so much loss. We have witnessed individuals and organisations going out of their way to make sure Eliott is cared for and included in activities. And we've also heard the harshest comments directed at his differences and our family, and therefore felt excluded many times.

As he grows up and evolves, so do his needs.

A few years have passed since I wrote the final lines of this book, and as the years have flown, we've been so proud of Eliott for everything he does.

We continue to face so much uncertainty from the COVID-19 pandemic that shook the whole world. The last

295

few years have been challenging for our family. In addition to the fear of catching the disease, the risks for Eliott, and coping with all the new rules put in place around the world, our family has moved back to France.

Eliott doesn't cope well with change. He remains a very curious little boy but needs routine to feel safe.

The move was positive overall, as we've been blessed with more family support, a more coordinated approach to Eliott's care, and an education system that promises to offer more options than what we had access to in Australia.

But that also meant giving up the life we had created for ourselves and the balance we had somehow managed to achieve on the other side of the world.

About a year after we moved back, it was clear Eliott was missing his life 'down under' and the familiar faces and places. Over the summer, he started displaying anxious behaviours. It began with small screams of frustration over an activity he wasn't keen on. And it quickly escalated, within a month, into full-blown episodes that left everyone physically and emotionally drained.

One day, I took him grocery shopping, and he started showing signs of frustration in the toothpaste aisle because I wouldn't let him brush his teeth there. He started vocalising and complaining as we walked by the cereal boxes. By the time we got to the cash register, and it was too late to leave the shop, he completely lost it.

He started screaming and kicking, tried to bite me, and threw a few yoghurts across the floor. Everyone watched as I tried to calm him down, shushing, reassuring him as best I could without losing it myself.

And suddenly, it stopped — the anger, the frustration, the anxiety evaporated. He sat down by my side and quietly started playing while I packed the groceries away, like it never happened. As I packed the strawberry yoghurts and the toothpaste into plastic bags, I started crying under my face mask.

I'm grateful to the cashier who offered me a tissue. And

with the most genuine look on her face, she asked if I was okay.

I didn't know how to respond.

The lady behind me smiled kindly too, and said, 'You did very well. You can't anticipate when this is going to happen; it just springs on you at the worst time.'

These episodes became more common, and we stopped going out for a little while.

When it started impacting his attitude and behaviour at school, our French neurologist suggested medication to help him — antipsychotic medication.

Every bone in my body was screaming no, but Eliott wasn't doing well. He was clearly suffering, and these episodes were impacting his ability to participate in school activities and our family life. So, we tried.

He's been on medication for a few months, and things have improved. It may not work forever, and we will keep revisiting the need for medication, but it has helped him in the past few months. Sometimes it feels like we are never on solid ground for too long, as there is always a major decision to be made, always new challenges to face.

I often think back to that outing to the grocery store. It was traumatic for us both; Eliott was so clearly lost. That wasn't just my little boy having a hard time, it was the disease rearing its ugly head.

And what did that lady mean: you can't anticipate when *this* is going to happen?

What was *this*?

It looked like an autistic crisis.

Could he be autistic?

He'd never done anything of that degree before. He looked beyond himself; this wasn't my child. He looked as if he was having a bad trip, like when he was given a high dose of Phenytoin just before his first birthday. Except this time, he hadn't had Phenytoin for a few months.

Someone later suggested it might be autism spectrum disorder (ASD), another acronym for us to learn, another world to explore, another diagnosis we don't want to hear. A lot of children with genetic epilepsy are 'on the spectrum'.

This wasn't the first time we had concerns, but it was the first time it felt so real. And over the past few months, we noticed new behaviours. Eliott has developed an aversion for loud noises and has more sensory issues than he ever did before. He used to love messy play but now can't stand to have anything on his hands. He can't tell us what's going on, and we can't figure it out. He's made tremendous progress again this year but is still far behind and has significant issues with communication. So, the neurologist has referred us to get an assessment for ASD.

No one knows what the future holds. Maybe the symptoms will keep evolving, and we'll have to keep adapting. Maybe these episodes are just his way of expressing his frustration — maybe my gorgeous six-year-old is just trying to tell me that he's too tired and can't manage anymore. Maybe he feels trapped in a body and a mind that won't do what he would like them to do.

If that's the case, then that's okay. I can take that. There is nothing worse than the fear of seizures coming back, of another disease taking over my precious child.

If he's trying to tell me that growing up is hard, I agree — it is.

Often, I cup my hands around his face and tell him I'm proud of him and I love him. When I look deep into his eyes, all I see is my baby boy. My sweet, smart, funny, curious, strong, loving baby boy — I can see all of him.

These moments are precious.

He's started saying 'I owve you' and putting his hands together to mirror the heart shape I create with mine to show him I love him. This fills my heart with joy, every time.

Each evening when we say goodnight, we say I love you. And if it's one of those evenings when he's upset, I lie next to him and talk to him, my hand stroking his hair. I whisper, 'Eliott, I'm here, my love. I've got your back. Just listen to my voice. Shhhh, baby. I love you no matter what. Eliott, when you wake up, a new day will start, but for now, my love, it's just you and me. Listen to my voice. I love you more than anything.'

He ends up falling asleep a bit calmer — resting and gathering strength to live and fight another day.

Hope is your middle name.

Acknowledgements

I would like to specifically thank my beautiful ELIOTT. You are everything. You have rocked my world, turned it upside down, then back up again. I love you more than you will ever know, and there is nothing I want more than to continue to support you and watch you achieve all the wonderful things I know you will accomplish in your life.

OSCAR, you saved my life. I tell you every day and will keep telling you for the rest of my life: you are my perfect baby. You allowed me to become the mum I have always aspired to become. You have made me a stronger and better person for you and your brother.

CED, you are the sunshine of my life. You are my rock, you make me laugh every day, and you are my better half. You are the yin to my yang, and the yang to my yin, the same way I seem to be yours.

MUM, thank you for being my safety net, my role model, for having the strength and the grace to hear it all — the good, the bad, and the ugly. But most importantly, thank you for loving us unconditionally, and thank you for letting us see how gorgeous Eliott is through your eyes when we are in our darkest place.

JEAN-MI, thank you for loving your nephews so much, and for being by our side, no matter what. I am so proud to be your sister.

THE AUDIBERT FAMILY, thank you for welcoming me into your family, thank you for raising such a wonderful man, and thank you for always jumping on board and supporting my crazy ideas!

The incredible team at NIGHTSTAND PRESS. Particularly

KIT for believing in me from day one. I am forever grateful for the guidance and support. Thank you for trusting me and for helping me put our story into words. *The Letter E* would not have been possible without you.

JAMES and DEM for indirectly introducing me to KIT, and for your family friendship over the years. You have always been here, celebrating all the wins and victories, and helping us get back up when things were tough. Thank you for encouraging us to go further (sometimes literally!) and for welcoming us with open arms when we needed it. We are forever grateful.

CAMY and GUILLAUME — Eliott's godparents. You are family to us. I miss our crazy trips, dinner parties, long chats and yoga practice. But I have loved watching our kids grow up together.

HUGO, ERIN, ANTONIA, BEC, DAVID, ERCEL and SUSAN, thank you for saving Eliott's life, and ours. For always having his back, working tirelessly to find answers while looking after us too. Thank you for believing us and trusting us from the day he was admitted in the NICU, and for reminding us to have faith when we couldn't. Thank you for the ongoing love and support for our family, even if we moved away for a little while.

Everyone from the KCNQ2 Cure Alliance, thank you for being our tribe. SARA and ANDREW, thank you for listening, and for being here. SARA, thank you for giving me strength when I had none left. Thank you for holding my hand so many times, and for being an inspiration to me. I admire you so much. No one wants to be part of this exclusive club, but if we had to fight a war alongside other warriors, we're lucky to be in your camp — KCNQ2 has nowhere to hide. We will find a cure for all our kids.

The two DEBBIEs. DEBBIE M, you have been such an amazing support. Eliott adores you, and we thank you for bringing the most beautiful smile to his face every time he saw you. DEBBIE T, you have magic in you — pure magic. You are incredible, and I'm forever grateful to have found you. Thank you for your pragmatic approach, the love and empathy for us all, and the pizza night!

JADE, KIRSTIE and CLEMENCE — our wonderful nannies. You have had such a positive and long-lasting impact on the boys and on us. I've learnt so much from you all, and I've felt incredibly lucky to have you in our lives. Thank you for the dance parties, the celebratory hugs, the shoulder to cry on, and for looking after our children and loving them like they were your own.

PRISC, PAQ and REGINE, for reading early versions of The Letter E and helping me make it the best version it could be.

PAQ, again, for the beautiful cover photo. And more generally for capturing so many of our family memories, for babysitting the boys, for flying back with us in the middle of the pandemic, and everything in between.

AL, for showing me what it means to be a leader. For advocating for diversity and inclusion a decade before everyone else did, and for showing me that authenticity, empathy and flexibility can live in a high-performing culture when it's modelled from the top.

And to LOX STOCK AND BARREL, thank you for feeding me smashed avocado toasts and quinoa bowls, for having the best soy flat whites in Bondi, and for letting me write surrounded by your friendly staff and patrons!

About the Author

Claire Audibert is passionate about diversity and inclusion, and raising awareness for KCNQ2 to help shed light on this rare disease and how it can affect families. She believes that sharing her story can help others understand what it feels like to welcome a child with special needs and give parents strength and hope in knowing they're not alone.

After living in Australia for many years, Claire now lives in France with her husband and two sons. *The Letter E* is Claire's first book.

Find out more about Claire:
www.alltheletters.com

Made in United States
North Haven, CT
22 August 2022

23091454R00186